The Ripper Reports

Jack the Ripper & the Whitechapel Murders
as reported by the Victorian Press

TM THORNE

Copyright © 2021 TM Thorne

All rights reserved.

ISBN: 9798705905379

THE RIPPER REPORTS

ABOUT THE AUTHOR

TM Thorne lived in London for many years before giving in to property prices and the demands of raising a family, and now lives messily in the English countryside with her motorsport-mad husband and son and three demanding cats.

When not writing about her much-missed city, spending time with her family or tripping over engines and spanners littered around the house she likes to eat, drink and feel guilty about not doing enough exercise.

You can find out more about the author and sign up to her mailing list through social media or on her very own website:

Instagram: Instagram.com/tmthorneauthor
Facebook: facebook.com/tmthorneauthor
Twitter: @tmthorneauthor
Website: www.tmthorne.com

OTHER TITLES BY TM THORNE

FRANKIE FINCH BOOKS

Notorious:
Danger, Deception, Desire

Accused:
Stardom, Scandal, Survival

Caged:
Rock, Ransom, Retribution

Driven:
Racing, Rivalry Revenge

THE LONDON VAMPIRE SERIES

Spooked

Jinxed

NON-FICTION

The Ripper Files:
Jack the Ripper and the Whitechapel Murders
as reported by the Victorian Press

Launched Into Eternity:
Accounts of 19th Century Executions
as reported by the Press

Unsinkable:
The Titanic Disaster as Sensationally Reported
(and Mis-Reported) by the Press

THE RIPPER REPORTS

INTRODUCTION

My aim in compiling this book was to share the research I've done in Victorian press archives on the Jack the Ripper murders, saving you the trouble of searching and poring over century-old, blurred newsprint. As someone who has been fascinated by the Whitechapel murders for many years, I was amazed how much new information I was able to discover. The press reports of the time are currently one of the main sources of information available since so much of the original case information has been mislaid, pilfered or was lost during the Blitz.

If you already know the Ripper crimes well, you will be astonished by the fallacies and misinformation initially reported as events unfolded, and if you are new to the crimes of Jack the Ripper you can experience the rollercoaster of press reports as the Victorian public would have done at the time.

I don't pretend to know who the Ripper was, and neither do I put forward any theories in this book, I just lay out the information for you to use as you wish.

Reading the Victorian press reports, it is clear there was an underlying current in Victorian society of victim-blaming, anti-Semitism and a general fear of foreigners, as well as an unbridled enjoyment in the discussing the shocking details of these crimes (and, hard as it may be to believe, even exaggerating them).

There were tens of thousands of news publications in Victorian Britain, so these articles are just a small sample of the coverage these crimes attracted, and by no means comprehensive.

I have tried to show the variety of different attitudes towards the Whitechapel murderers, the victims, and to Jack the Ripper himself, as well as the appetite the public had for every tiny piece of information about the murders, inquests, arrests and wild theories. It is also interesting to note the amount the coverage across the country, which increased with each new murder and shows the mounting hysteria which spread throughout Victorian society, with letters, sightings and confessions reported throughout the UK.

In a book of this type a certain degree of repetition is unavoidable, but I have attempted to minimize this wherever possible.

Jack the Ripper still makes newspaper headlines today, so it is difficult to know when to stop reporting. With this in mind the reports contained are confined to the year 1888 covering all of the canonical five victims, and ending shortly after Mary Jane Kelly was killed in her rooms in Miller's Court.

The traditionally accepted Ripper victims (the canonical five of Mary Ann Nichols, Annie Chapman, Elizabeth Stride, Catherine Eddowes and Mary Jane Kelly) are all covered here, with the addition of two earlier murders: Emma Elizabeth Smith and Martha Tabram. There is great debate as to whether these were in fact early Ripper victims, but I have included them as the press of the time very much regarded them as linked cases.

The articles are in chronological order, and the chapters simply mark the date of each new murder. Because of this not all information about a particular victim is included in 'their' chapter. Later information, for example the result of an inquest, is included when it was reported.

NOTE

The newspaper articles compiled here have been transcribed by hand from old newspapers and press reports, some of which were blurred and torn and which themselves contained variations and inconsistencies in names, place names, spelling and grammar. Wherever possible I have kept the text as it was in the original articles, even if it may appear as incorrect when read today.

The news articles were published in columns so I have sometimes added line breaks to make the text less unwieldy and easier to read.

CONTENTS

	Acknowledgments	i
1	Emma Elizabeth Smith & Martha Tabram	1
2	Mary Ann Nichols	24
3	Annie Chapman	53
4	The Double Event: Elizabeth Stride & Catherine Eddowes	100
5	Mary Jane Kelly	250
6	Index of Names	330
7	Index of Street Names	342

With thanks to The British Newspaper Archive

EMMA ELIZABETH SMITH

Died: 3 April 1888

MARTHA TABRAM

Died: 7 August 1888

THE RIPPER REPORTS

FRIDAY 6 APRIL 1888

SPIRIT OF THE NEWS

Yesterday the authorities of the London Hospital informed the coroner of the death in that institution of Emma Elizabeth Smith, aged 45, a widow, lately living at 18, George-street, Spitalfields. The deceased was out on Bank Holiday, and when returning home along the Whitechapel-road, early on Tuesday morning, she was, it was alleged, set upon and severely maltreated by some men, who afterwards made off, leaving her on the ground in a semi-conscious condition. She was subsequently conveyed to the hospital, where she died.

Source: *Lloyd's List*

SATURDAY 14 APRIL 1888

THE WHITECHAPEL OUTRAGE INQUEST AND VERDICT

London, Saturday.

This afternoon Mr. Wynne E. Baxter, the East Middlesex coroner, held an inquiry at the London Hospital, Whitechapel, touching the death of Emma Elizabeth Smith, aged 45 years, a widow, lately living at 18,

George Street, Spitalfields, who is alleged to have died from injuries received at the hands of some persons unknown, who brutally assaulted her when returning home along Whitechapel Road on bank holiday night.

Chief-Inspector West attended on behalf of the commissioners of police. Mary Russell, of 18, George Street, stated that the address was a common lodging house, and the deceased had been a lodger there for some months. Witness acted as deputy. The deceased got her living on the streets, and when she returned home one night she told witness that she had been thrown out of a window. When she had had drink, the deceased acted like a mad woman. On bank holiday the deceased left the house in the evening apparently in good health. She returned home between four and five o'clock the next morning, severely injured, and she said she had been shockingly treated by some men. Her face was bleeding, and she said that she was also injured about the lower part of the body. The witness took her at once to the hospital.

Deceased further said that she was coming along Osborne Street, Whitechapel, when she was set upon and her money taken from her. On the way to hospital the deceased pointed out the spot, and said she did not know the men nor could she describe them. Witness believed that the statements made by the deceased were to be relied upon.

By the Coroner - Deceased had often come home with black eyes that men had given her. She was not so drunk as not to know what she did. Mr. George Haslip, house surgeon, deposed that deceased was admitted suffering from severe injuries. She had been drinking, but was not intoxicated. She had a very serious rupture of a recent date and also some bruises on her head. The right ear was torn and bleeding. She told witness that at 1.30 that morning she was going by Whitechapel Church when she saw some men coming, and she crossed the road to get out of their way, but they followed her. They assaulted her, robbed her of all the money she had, and then commenced to outrage her. She could not say if they used a knife. She could not describe them, except that one looked about nineteen. After her admission she slowly sank, and died at nine o'clock on Wednesday morning.

Witness had made a post-mortem examination, and found that the injuries had been caused by some blunt instrument which had been used with great force. Deceased stated that she had not seen any of her friends for ten years.

The coroner said that from the medical evidence it was clear the woman had been barbarously murdered. Such a dastardly assault he had never heard of, and it was impossible to imagine a more brutal case. The jury returned a verdict of wilful murder against some person unknown.

Source: *Belfast Weekly News*

TUESDAY 7 AUGUST 1888

MYSTERIOUS TRAGEDY IN WHITECHAPEL
SUPPOSED MURDER OF A WOMAN

About 10 minutes to five o'clock this morning, John Reeves, who lives at 37, George Yard-buildings, Whitechapel, was coming down stairs to go to work, when he discovered the body of a woman lying in a pool of blood on the first floor landing. Reeves at once called in Constable 26 H Barrett, who was on beat in the vicinity of George-yard, and Dr. Keeling, of Brick-lane, was communicated with and promptly arrived. He immediately made an examination of the woman, and pronounced life extinct, and gave it as his opinion that she had been brutally murdered, there being knife wounds on her breast and abdomen.

The body, which was that of a woman apparently between 35 and 40 years of age, about 5ft. 3in. in height, complexion and hair dark, wore a dark green skirt, and brown petticoat, a long black jacket, and a black bonnet. The woman is unknown to any of the occupants of the tenements on the landing on which the deceased was found, and no disturbance of any kind was heard during the night. The circumstances of the tragedy are, therefore, mysterious, and the body, which up to the time of writing had not been identified, has been removed to Whitechapel mortuary. Inspector Ellison, of the Commercial-street Police-station, has placed the case in the hands of Inspector Reid, of the Criminal Investigation Department, and that officer is now instituting inquiries.

Up to this afternoon no clue of any kind had come to the knowledge of the Commercial-street Police authorities.

Source: *The Globe*

SATURDAY 11 AUGUST 1888

A WHITECHAPEL MYSTERY
HORRIBLE OUTRAGE ON A WOMAN IN GEORGE YARD
FOUND STABBED IN 39 PLACES

THE RIPPER REPORTS

FULL DETAILS

At about ten minutes to five on Tuesday morning, a shocking discovery was made by John Reeves, waterside labourer, on his descending the stairs of 37, George-yard-buildings - a block of model dwellings, inhabited by people of the poorest description, and situated just off the Whitechapel-road. On reaching a landing of the stone stairs, he discovered the body of a woman lying in a pool of blood. Reeves at once called Constable T. Barrett, 226H who was on his beat in the vicinity of George-yard, and Dr. Keeling, of Brick-lane, was communicated with, and promptly arrived. He made an examination of the woman, and pronounced life extinct, giving it as his opinion that she had been brutally murdered, there being knife wounds on her breast, stomach, and abdomen.

The body was that of a woman apparently between 33 and 40 years of age. The deceased wore a dark green jacket, and a black bonnet. The woman was stated to be unknown to any of the occupants of the tenements on the landing on which the deceased was found, and no disturbance of any kind was heard during the night. The body was at once removed to the Whitechapel Mortuary, and Inspector Ellesdon, of the Commercial-street Police station, placed the matter in the hands Inspector Reid, of the Criminal Investigation Department. The murder - for little doubt could be entertained but what the deceased had met her death by foul means - has been the subject of considerable speculation on the part of the residents of Whitechapel, so unique and mysterious are the circumstances surrounding the case.

The murderer, whoever he was - and there is every reason to suppose that it was a man - had evidently done his work well, for no vestige and no clue of any kind was given to the police to work upon. The mystery was further enhanced by the fact that the woman was utterly unknown to any of the neighbours. The inquest, which took place on Thursday before Mr. Collier, the deputy-coroner for the South-Eastern Middlesex Division, in the Library of the Working Lad's Institute at Whitechapel, was looked forward to with the keenest interest, as being a probably means for eliciting the identity of the murdered woman. As a matter of fact, no less than three persons attended and swore to the identity of the woman in as many different names. The identification, however, of all three was more or less doubted, the greatest credence being attached to a woman who appeared early in the Library with a baby in her arms. She wore a blue dress with a black hat, and a white checked blue handkerchief round her neck. She had been taken by Banks, the coroner's officer, to view the body at the mortuary, and was positive in asserting that she recognised it as that of a woman of her acquaintance named Martha Turner, a married woman.

But although the inquest was ostensibly carried out upon the body of "Martha Turner," the proofs of identity were so vague that the deputy coroner, towards the end of the inquest, expressed the opinion that it was scarcely worth while calling the woman who professed to identify the deceased, as a witness - at all events, not until further proof has been forthcoming of the accuracy of the identification.

The interest evinced in the case was proved by the unprecedentedly large number of summoned jurymen who put in an appearance - twenty of them in all who appointed a Mr. Geary as their foreman. They sat to the left of the coroner, who had on his right Dr. Keeling and Inspector Reid - a smart-looking man, dressed in blue serge, who, without taking so much as a note, seemed to be absorbing all the material points. Before the coroner sat the woman who had identified the deceased as Martha Turner, with a baby in her arms, and accompanied by another woman - evidently her mother - dressed in an old, brown figured pompadour.

THE RIPPER REPORTS

Above the coroner hung a magnificent portrait by Herr Louis Fleischmann, of the Princess of Wales, while other portraits of the Royal Family and landscape pictures were in profusion around the walls of the room. It was in this library, so well and prettily furnished, that the details of the Whitechapel mystery were unravelled. The first witness called was a Mrs. Elizabeth Mahoney - a young woman of some 25 or 26 years, plainly clad in a rusty-black dress, with a black wollen shawl pinned round her shoulders. Her evidence was neither very much to the point or distinctly uttered - indeed, so low was her voice as to elicit a complaint from the jurymen which was remedied by the witness being made to stand immediately next to the jury.

She deposed thus: I live at 37, George-yard-buildings - a block of model dwellings - and am a married woman, my husband, Joseph, being a carman, while I work at a match factory at Stratford, where I work from nine in the morning, usually, till about seven o'clock at night. So far as I can remember, I have occupied rooms in the present house for about eight months. Monday was Bank Holiday, and my husband and I were out all day, and did not return until twenty minutes to two on Tuesday morning. We went straight up to our room, and after taking off my hat and cloak, I came down again and went to a chandler's shop in Thrawl-street to buy some provisions for supper. I came back, having been gone about five minutes; and after having supper we went to bed.

On no occasion, either in coming up or going down the stairs, did I see the body of a woman lying there. It is quite possible that a body might have been there, and that I did not notice it, because the stairs are very wide, and were completely dark, all the lights having, as usual, been turned out at eleven o'clock. I did not get up till half-past eight in the morning, and during the night my attention was not attracted by a noise or disturbance of any kind. I did not know of the body of the deceased having been found on the stairs till about ten o'clock on Tuesday morning. Questioned, at the instigation of Inspector Reid, she reiterated that at the place where the body was subsequently found, it was quite possible - so wide was the staircase - for her, to have passed it without noticing it.

Alfred George Crow was the next witness. In appearance, he was a young man of about twenty-three or four, with closely cropped hair, and a beardless, but intelligent face, and wore a shabby green overcoat. Said he: I live at 37, George-yard-buildings, and am a cab-driver, my number being 6,609. I came home at half past three on Tuesday morning, which is about my usual time, although I am on day duty. I went straight up to my lodgings. I had no light with me, and went up the same staircase as the last witness. On my way up I noticed that there was somebody lying on the first landing. My eyesight is very good, and I noticed a body lying there just as I turned the landing. I am accustomed, however, to find people lying sleeping there, and took no notice at the time - not even to ascertain whether the body was that of a male or female. I don't know, therefore, whether the deceased was alive or dead at the time I saw her. I went to bed, and did not come out again before half-past nine, and up to that time I heard no noise at all of any kind. When I went down the stairs then, the body was gone, and I did not know what had been done with it. When I first saw the body I took so little notice that I am not prepared to say whether or not it was the body of this female at all.

John Saunders Reeves - a short man, with a slight dark beard and moustache, a pale and a contracted face, dressed in corduroy trousers and black overcoat, and wearing earrings - was next called. He was, he said, a waterside labourer, living at George-yard-buildings. In the course of his work he had to get out very early in the morning, and on Tuesday morning he proceeded to go out to work at a quarter to five in the morning. On reaching the first-floor landing, he proceeded, I found a female there lying on her back, in a pool of blood. I did not stop to examine her further, but gave information to a police-constable whom I met in the street. I went up to my room on Monday night at six o'clock, and remained there all night till I went down at a quarter to five, and during that time I heard no unusual noises. I made no examination whatever of the body when I first saw it, but I did notice that all the clothes were disarranged, being open in front. I did not notice any foot-marks on the staircase, nor did I find a knife or any other instrument lying there. The hands of the deceased were clenched, but contained no hair or anything else; nor was there any blood coming from the mouth.

By a juryman: I believe it is quite possible for anybody coming up the stairs in the dark to have passed the body without noticing it.

Police-constable T. Barrett, 226 H - a young constable who gave his evidence very intelligently said: On Tuesday morning I was on duty at about a quarter to five, when my attention was called to George-yard-buildings by Reeves, the last witness. I followed him up the stairs, and found the deceased lying on her back. She was dead, but I at once sent for a doctor. The body was not moved by me or Reeves before the doctor came. I noticed that the hands were clenched, but that there was nothing in them. The clothes were turned up as far as the centre of the body, leaving the lower part of the body exposed: the legs were open, and altogether her position as such as to at once suggest in my mind that recent intimacy had taken place. The deceased was not known on the streets.

Dr. T. R. Keeling gave his evidence as follows: - I am a fully qualified doctor practising at Brick-lane, and was called to the deceased on the morning of the 7th of August at about half-past five. I found her dead. On examining the body externally I found no less than thirty-nine punctured wounds. From my examination of the body it seemed to be that of a woman about 36 years of age, and was well nourished. I have since made a post mortem examination of the body. The brain was healthy; the left lung was penetrated in five places, and the right lung in two places, but the lungs were otherwise perfectly healthy. The heart was rather fatty, and was penetrated in one place, but there was otherwise nothing in the heart to cause death, although there was some blood in the pericardium. The liver was healthy, but was penetrated in five places, the spleen was perfectly healthy, and was penetrated in two places, both the kidneys were perfectly healthy; the stomach was also perfectly healthy, but was penetrated in six places; the intestines were healthy, and so were all the other organs. The lower portion of the body was penetrated in one place, the wound being about three inches in length and one in depth. From appearances there was no reason to suppose that recent intimacy had taken place.

I don't think that all the wounds were inflicted with the same instrument, because there was one wound on the breast bone which did not correspond with the other wounds on the body. The instrument with which the wounds were inflicted, would most probably be an ordinary knife, but a knife would not cause such a wound as that to the breast bone. That wound I should think would have been inflicted with some form of a dagger. I am of opinion that the wounds were inflicted during life, and from the direction which they took it is my opinion, that although some of them could have been self-inflicted, yet, there were others which could not have been so inflicted. The wounds generally would have been inflicted by a right-handed person. There was no sign whatever of any struggle having taken place; and there was a deal of blood between the legs, which were separated. Death was due to hemorrhage and loss of blood.

Mr. Collier having called the attention of the jury to the fact that no perfectly satisfactory identification had yet been made, suggested the advisability of adjourning the inquest till that day fortnight. In the meantime Inspector Reid, who had the case in hand, would do all he could to ascertain the assailant of the woman. "It is one of the most terrible cases," concluded Mr. Collier, with unusual animation, "that anyone can possibly imagine. The man must have been a perfect savage to have attacked the woman in that way."

Source: *East London Observer*

SUNDAY 12 AUGUST 1888

TRAGEDY IN WHITECHAPEL
A WOMAN STABBED IN 39 PLACES

About 10 minutes to 5 o'clock on Tuesday morning a man, who lives at 47, George-yard-buildings, Whitechapel, was coming downstairs to go to work, when he discovered the body of a woman lying in a pool of blood on the first-floor landing. Reeves at once called in Constable Barrett, 26H, who was on his beat in the vicinity of George-yard, and Dr. Keleene, of Brick-lane, was communicated with and promptly arrived. He made an examination of the woman, and pronounced life extinct, giving his opinion that she had been brutally murdered, there being knife wounds in the breast, stomach, and abdomen. There were 39 wounds in various parts of the body, which was that of a woman apparently between 35 and 40 years of age, about 5ft. 3in. in height, complexion and hair dark; with a dark green skirt, a brown petticoat, a long black jacket, and a black bonnet. The woman was not known to any of the occupants of the tenements on the landing on which the deceased was found, and no disturbance of any kind was heard during the night. The body was removed to Whitechapel mortuary.

Mr. George Collier opened an inquest on the body on Thursday at the Working Lad's institute, Whitechapel. She was stated to be Martha Turner, aged 38, a single woman, lately living at 4, Star-place, Commercial-road, but previous to calling the first witness the coroner said that the body had been identified that morning, but he had just been informed that two other persons also identified it as quite a different person, and under these circumstances he thought the question of identity had better be left till the last.

Elizabeth Mahony, of 47, George-yard-buildings, Whitechapel, the wife of a carman, stated that on the night of Bank holiday she was out with some friends. She returned shortly before two in the morning with her husband, and afterwards left the house to try and get some supper at the chandler's shop. The stairs were then perfectly clear of any obstacle, and were the same on her return. She and her husband heard no noise during the night, but at 10 o'clock she was told that a murder had been committed in the building. There was no light on the staircase. The spot where the body was found had been pointed out to her. She was sure it was not there at two o'clock as she went in, as it was in the wide part of the stairs, and quite in the dark.

Alfred George Crow, a cabdriver, of 35, George-yard-buildings, deposed that on Tuesday morning he returned home from work at half-past three. On his way up the stairs he saw somebody lying on the first landing. It was not an unusual thing to see, so he passed on and went to bed. He did not know whether the person was dead or alive when he passed.

John Saunders Reeves, 37, George-yard-buildings, a waterside labourer, deposed that on Tuesday morning he left home at five o'clock to go in search of work. On the first floor landing he saw a female lying in a pool of blood. She lay on her back, and seemed dead. He at once gave notice to the police. The woman was a perfect stranger to the witness. Her clothes were all disarranged, as if she had had a struggle with some one. The witness did not notice any instrument lying about.

Police-constable Barrett, 226 H, deposed to being called by the last witness to view the body of the deceased. She was lying on her back, and before she was moved a doctor was sent for, and on arrival pronounced life extinct. The woman's hands were clenched, but did not contain anything. Her clothes were disarranged.

Dr. Timothy Robert Keleene, 28, Brick-lane, stated that he was called to the deceased and found her dead. He examined the body and found 39 puncture wounds. There were no less than nine in the throat and 17 in the breast. She appeared to have been dead three hours. The body was well nourished. He had since made a post-mortem examination, and found the left lung penetrated in five places, and the right lung in two places. The heart had been penetrated, but only in one place, otherwise it was quite healthy. The liver was healthy, but penetrated in five places, and the spleen was penetrated in two places. The stomach was penetrated in six places. In the witness's opinion the wounds were not inflicted with the same instrument, there being a deep wound in the breast from some long, strong instrument, while most of the others were done apparently with a penknife. The large wound could have been caused by a sword bayonet or dagger. It was impossible for the whole of the wounds to be self-inflicted. Death was due to the loss of blood consequent on the injuries.

At the conclusion of this witness's evidence the inquiry was adjourned.

TWO ARRESTS AT THE TOWER

THE RIPPER REPORTS

The case is in certain respects one of a very puzzling character, owing to the fact that so many stab wounds were inflicted, and that no cries were heard, although the poor woman was on some stone steps, close to the doors of small rooms wherein several separate families resided. It now appears that on the night of Bank holiday there were several soldiers in the neighbourhood, some of whom were seen drinking in the Princess Alice - two minute's walk from George-yard-buildings - and other taverns near. With these soldiers were the deceased and another woman, the latter being known in the district as "Mogg" and "Pearly Poll." One of these men was a private, the other a corporal. It has been ascertained that only corporals and sergeants are allowed to wear side arms while on leave.

This fact, of course, narrows the issue as to the possible identity of the assailant - presuming he was a soldier. Inquiries were at once set on foot by the police and military authorities, with the result that it is stated two soldiers have been placed under military arrest at the Tower. The authorities decline to give their names unless some definite charge is formulated. The two soldiers are said to belong to the Guards.

A perplexing feature in connection with the outrage is the number of injuries on the young woman's body. That the stabs were from a weapon shaped like a bayonet is almost established beyond doubt. The wound over the heart was alone sufficient to kill, and death must have occurred as soon as that was inflicted. Unless the perpetrator was a madman, or suffering to an usual extent from drink delirium, no tangible explanation can be given of the reason for inflicting the other 38 injuries, some of which seem as if they were due to thrusts and cuts from a penknife. On the other hand, if the lesser wounds were given before the one fatal injury the cries of the deceased must have been heard by those who, at the time of the outrage, were sleeping within a few yards of the spot where the deed was committed.

THE RIPPER REPORTS

The difficulty of identification arose out of the brutal treatment to which the deceased was manifestly subjected, she being throttled while held down, and the face and head so swollen and distorted in consequence that her real features are not discernible. There is little doubt, although, she has been variously identified as a Mrs. Withers, and a Mary Bryan, that she is a woman known as Martha Turner.

Mrs. Bousfield, in whose house she lived till three weeks back, states that she had resided in her house for two months with Turner. The deceased had told her that her real name was either Staples or Stapleton, and that she had left her husband 13 years, and had taken up with Turner. Both she and this man got their living by selling trinkets in the streets, such as studs, links, chains, and menthal cones. She used to stand in Cheapside and various places, while Turner occupied other ground. Turner left her some weeks ago, and then the deceased, who paid 2s. per week for her room, got two weeks in arrear, and as she could not pay she suddenly left.

In addition to being identified by Mrs. Bousfield, the deceased has already been identified by one or two other women, who saw her in the company of some soldiers at neighbouring public-houses. There was a dispute, and one of the soldiers struck the companion of the deceased a blow. This was just by George-yard, a long, dark thoroughfare, and it is believed that the deceased was forcibly dragged up to the place where she was found so brutally ill-treated and so fearfully wounded. The police had a description of the two soldiers who, as before stated, are believed to be in the Guards.

Source: *Lloyd's Weekly Newspaper*

THE RIPPER REPORTS

SATURDAY 18 AUGUST 1888

EXTRAORDINARY SCENE AT THE WELLINGTON BARRACKS

At noon on Wednesday there was a parade of Coldstream and Grenadier Guards at the Wellington Barracks, Pimlico. It seems that soon after eleven o'clock two police-officers - Inspector Reid and Detective-Sergeant Caunter - arrived with Mary Ann Conolly (otherwise "Pearly Poll") and requested permission to make certain inquiries in regard to the murder of Martha Turner, at Whitechapel on the night of Bank Holiday.

    The "assembly" call was at once sounded, and the men were drawn up in quarter-column, after which they filed through a passage, where Inspector Reid, Sargent Caunter, and another police-officer were stationed with "Pearly Poll." The woman was asked to scrutinise the faces of the soldiers as they passed for the purpose of seeing if she could pick out either of the men who were with her and the deceased on the night on which the murder was committed. After a small number had filed past, "Pearly Poll" picked out a man wearing stripes, and taken by her to be a corporal, as the one who went away with the deceased woman. "That's him," exclaimed she; "I'm positive."

    The suspect was temporarily detained, and the filing by of the others continued. When a few more had passed, the woman, scanning the features of every one intently, pointed to a private as being the second man. She positively declared that he accompanied her to a house in the district where the murder took place. "Are you positive?" was asked, and "Pearly Poll" nodded, and replied, "Certain."

The military authorities immediately placed all the books, showing the time at which the suspected men left and returned to the barracks on the night mentioned, at the disposal of Inspector Reid and Sergeant Caunter. It was pointed out that the "corporal" was but a private with good-conduct stripes, a man of exemplary character, who was in the barracks by ten o'clock on Bank Holiday night. Other evidence as to his innocence, and also respecting the private's movements on the night of the crime, was also forthcoming.

The former man was at once exonerated while the second, also a man of exceptionally good character, was formally told that further inquiries must be instituted. These inquiries were duly conducted, and he too was told that no stain rested upon him, as it was clearly a case of mistaken identity.

It is asserted that as "Pearly Poll" has "identified" two innocent men, who could not have been in Whitechapel at the time she says, the police will not further seek her aid in elucidating the mystery. Neither of the men wore sidearms when they left the barracks on Bank Holiday, and could not possibly have been in each other's company. The authorities say that they must now look elsewhere for a clue. This clue cannot, they assert, be given by one whom they at first considered the most reliable witness.

Source: *Westminster & Pimlico News*

THE RIPPER REPORTS

SATURDAY 18 AUGUST 1888

THE WHITECHAPEL MYSTERY

The officers engaged in elucidating the mystery of George Yard Buildings, wherein Martha Turner was discovered murdered, have, it is believed, at last obtained a clue, though it is feared it is not of a sufficiently substantial nature to justify the belief that any immediate arrest will take place. Detective-inspector Reid, Inspector Leech, Detective-sergeant Caunter, and other criminal investigation experts, have visited every military depot in London. The names of those soldiers out on leave on the Bank Holiday night were given by the commanding officers, and every assistance rendered to the police in questioning men upon whom the slightest suspicion might be supposed to rest.

The authorities have lost all faith in "Pearly Poll's" assistance, inasmuch as the two men whom she picked out at the Wellington Barracks were proved to have been far away from the scene of the crime when it was committed. One of these soldiers, quartered at Pimlico, was certainly out all night on Bank Holiday, and that circumstance, coupled with the fact of "Pearly Poll's" certainty as to his features, at first placed him in rather an awkward position. However, he was able to prove that he was elsewhere, the truth of his story being placed beyond all doubt.

No weapon with which the murder could have been perpetrated has yet been discovered, though the sewers in the vicinity of George Yard Buildings have been searched. There has, however, been a clue discovered which may be of some service. A woman has, it is stated, come forward and asserted that at midnight a man took a bed in her house, which is situated in the neighbourhood, stating that he had lost his train for the country, and could not return that night. He was dressed in the uniform of a soldier. The story has been inquired into by the police, but the result is not yet known. Some importance, however, is attached to the clue.

A statement was made yesterday afternoon by Louisa Reeves, the wife of a dock labourer who first discovered the body when leaving for her day's work, shortly before five o'clock in the morning. Mrs. Reeves explains that the screams of "Murder!" she heard early in the night must have proceeded from George-street, and could not possibly have been heard by her if they had proceeded from the dying woman. Strange to say, during the night Mr and Mrs Reeves woke up several times under an apprehension that something was going to happen. Not a scream was heard by them when thus aroused from their slumber, for Mr. Reeves went to his door and listened.

"I could not say," remarked Mrs Reeves yesterday, "but I knew something would happen out of the ordinary for me and my old man were never so much disturbed before, though we almost nightly hear cries of "Murder" and "Police." We pay no attention to them whatever." "But that night (Mrs Reeves added) was a dreadful one. My husband thought of what I told him when he left for work - that I knew something was going to happen - for when he discovered the dead body he was afraid to come and tell me, for fear I should go into a fit. We weren't awoke by screams, but there was a something we couldn't understand, that seemed to tell us that trouble was at hand. That dreadful murder has disturbed us all here, and it will be some time before we quiet down and forget last Bank Holiday night."

Source: *Manchester Evening News*

THE RIPPER REPORTS

MONDAY 20 AUGUST 1888

"PEARLY POLL"

"Pearly Poll" is a dangerous person to trust to. She bamboozled the police into the idea that she could give them a clue to the Whitechapel murder. It was done by a corporal and a private in the Grenadier Guards at the Tower on Bank Holiday. Well, the soldiers were paraded. Poll picked out the men. But her "corporal" was a private with two good-conduct stripes on his arm, a spotless character, and an irrefragable alibi. The other man was shown to be equally innocent. So that the police have been fooled all this time following up a false clue. It is always dangerous to trust for identification to the evidence of an ignorant, excitable woman of "Pearly Poll's" class - in fact, her testimony at best is never a "pearl of great price."

Source: *South Wales Echo*

FRIDAY 24 AUGUST 1888

THE WHITECHAPEL MURDER RESUMED INQUEST - VERDICT

Yesterday afternoon Mr. George Collier, the deputy coroner for South-East Middlesex, resumed the inquiry at the working Lad's Institute, Whitechapel, into the circumstances attending the death of a woman supposed to be Martha Turner, aged 35, a hawker, lately living at 4, Star-place, Star-street, Commercial-road, E., who was discovered early on the morning of Tuesday, the 7th inst., lying dead on the first floor landing of some model dwellings know as George-yard-buildings, Commercial-road, Spitalfields, her body being covered with 39 stab wounds. The murder was committed during Bank Holiday night, and is almost identical with another murder which was perpetrated near the same spot on the night of the previous Bank Holiday. Henry Samuel Tabran, of No. 6, River-terrace, East Greenwich, who was the first witness called, stated that he was a foreman packer in a furniture warehouse. He identified the body as that of his wife, 39 years of age. He last saw her alive 18 months ago in the Whitechapel-road. The witness had been separated from her for 13 years on account of her intemperate habits. He at first allowed her 12s. a week, but afterwards, finding how she was living, he only gave her 2s. 6d. a week. The witness identified the body through seeing an account of the murder in The People, where her name was stated. Henry Turner, living at the Working Man's Home, Commercial-street, deposed that he was a carpenter by trade, but latterly he had got his living as a hawker. Up till three weeks previous to this affair he was living with the deceased. They had lived together on and off for nine years. He last saw her alive on the Saturday before her death, when they met accidentally in Leadenhall-street. The deceased was a woman who, when she had the money, would get drunk with it, and was in the habit of staying out late at night. They lived comfortably till she took to drink, when he left her for a time.

Mary Bousfield, 4, Star-place, Commercial-road, deposed that Turner and the deceased lived at her house till three weeks before her death. She was a woman who would rather have a glass of ale than a cup of tea, but she did not get drunk. The deceased was greatly in the witness's debt, and left without giving notice. After that the deceased returned and forced the window, and occupied the room one night without the witness knowing she was there.

Mary Anne Connelly (Pearly Poll), was next examined, but before giving evidence Inspector Reid asked that she might be cautioned previous to being sworn. This the coroner did, and the witness then said she had been living at a lodging-house in Dorset-street. She had known the deceased for four or five months under the name of "Emma." The last time she saw her alive was on Bank Holiday, when they went to a public-house together, and were accompanied by two soldiers, one a private and the other a corporal. She did not know to what regiment they belonged, but they had a white band round their caps. The witness did not know if the corporal had any side arms on. They drank with the soldiers in several public-houses. Then they separated, the deceased walking away with the private up George-yard. Before they parted the witness and the corporal had a quarrel, and he hit her with a stick. She did not see the deceased quarrelling.

By the Coroner: The witness had tried to identify the two men, and at Wellington Barracks, where the men were paraded before her, she picked out two whom she thought were with her and the deceased on the night of the murder.

Inspector Reid: Did you threaten to drown yourself since this occurrence?

The Witness: Yes, but only in a "lark."

Inspector Reid said that the witness had kept out of the way purposely, and it was only by searching that they found her. Many persons had come forward and made statements, but up to the present the police had been unable to secure the guilty party or parties.

THE RIPPER REPORTS

The Coroner, in summing up, said that the crime was one of the most brutal that had occurred for some years. The police would endeavour to bring home the crime to the guilty parties, and he sincerely hoped that they would be captured and brought to justice.

The jury, after short deliberation, returned a verdict of wilful murder against some person or persons unknown.

Source: *The Globe*

THE RIPPER REPORTS

MARY ANN NICHOLS

Died: 31 August 1888

SATURDAY 1 SEPTEMBER 1888

REVOLTING MURDER IN LONDON HORRIBLE MUTILATION

The Central News says: - Scarcely have the horror and sensation caused by the discovery of the murdered woman in Whitechapel some short time ago had time to abate when another victim of crime has been discovered in the same district. The affair up to the present is enveloped in complete mystery and the police have as yet no evidence by which to trace the perpetrators of the deed.

The facts are that as Constable John Neil was walking down Bucks Row, Thomas-street, Whitechapel, about a quarter to four o'clock yesterday morning, he discovered a woman, between 33 and 40 years of age, with her throat cut right open from ear to ear (the instrument with which the deed was done having traced the throat from left to right), and quite dead. The wound was about two inches wide, and blood was flowing profusely; in fact, she was lying in a pool of blood.

The body was immediately conveyed to the Whitechapel Mortuary, when it was found that, besides the wound in the throat, the lower part of the abdomen was completely ripped open, with the bowels protruding. The wound extends nearly to her breast, and must have been effected with a large knife. The hands are bruised and bear evidence of having engaged in a severe struggle; some of the front teeth have been knocked out, and the face is bruised and discoloured. In Whitechapel, naturally, the greatest excitement prevails, and several persons in the neighbourhood state that an affray took place early in the morning, and they think that during this the murder was committed.

Another account states that the deceased, who was from 35 to 40 years of age, wore a rough brown ulster with large buttons, and her clothes were cut and torn in several places. There is at present no trace of the murderer or the name of the deceased. The murdered woman was wearing workhouse clothes, and it is supposed she came from Lambeth.

A night watchman was in the street where the crime was committed. He heard no screams, and saw no signs of the scuffle. The body was quite warm when brought to the mortuary at half-past four in the morning. The brutality of the murder is beyond conception or description. Not only was the unfortunate woman's throat cut in two gashes with a sharp instrument, but the knife was stabbed into the lower part of the abdomen and savagely drawn upwards twice, one cut cutting left of the groin and hip, and the other slitting the abdomen as high as the breast bone. This is the third brutal murder of the kind in the locality, and the police believe the perpetrator must be a ferocious maniac.

Immediately on the affair being reported at the Bethnal Green Police-station two inspectors proceeded to the mortuary and examined the clothes, in the hope of being able to discover something likely to lead to her identification. In this they were not successful, as the only articles found on the body were a broken comb and a piece of looking-glass.

The wounds, of which there are five, could only have been committed by a dagger or a long sharp knife. The officers engaged in the case are pushing their inquiries in the neighbourhood as to the doings of certain gangs known to frequent these parts, and an opinion is gaining ground amongst them that the murderers are the same who committed the two previous murders near the same spot. It is believed that these gangs, who make their appearance during the early hours of the morning, are in the habit of blackmailing these poor creatures, and where their demands are refused violence follows.

Up till noon Mr. Wynne E. Baxter, the coroner for the district, had not received any official intimation of the occurrence, but the inquest will most likely be held on Monday morning. Bucks-row is a narrow passage running out of Thomas-street, and contains about a dozen houses of a very low class. It would appear as if the murder was committed in a house and the body afterwards removed to the place where it was found, the nature of the abdominal wounds being such that it would be hardly possible for them to be inflicted whilst the deceased was dressed. The body was warmly clad.

Source: *Manchester Courier and Lancashire General Advertiser*

SATURDAY 1 SEPTEMBER 1888

HORRIBLE MURDER IN LONDON

Another brutal murder was committed in Whitechapel, London, on Friday morning, when a constable found a woman, lying dead with her throat cut and her body cut open, in Bucks-row, Thomas-st. There were evidences of a desperate struggle. The murderer is unknown. The brutality of the crime leads the police to believe that the perpetrator must be a ferocious maniac. This is the third crime of the kind which has occurred in the neighbourhood recently.

The deceased wore a rough brown ulster, with large buttons in front. Her clothes are torn and cut up in several places, bearing evidence of the ferocity with which the murder was committed. The only way by which the police can prosecute an inquiry at present is by finding someone who can identify the body, and then if possible to trace those in whose company she was last seen. The greatest excitement prevails in the locality, and several persons in the neighbourhood state that an affray occurred shortly after midnight, but no screams were heard, nor anything beyond what might have been considered evidence of an ordinary brawl.

The brutality of the murder is beyond conception or description. Not only was the unfortunate woman's throat cut in two gashes with a sharp instrument, but the knife was stabbed into the lower part of the abdomen and savagely drawn upwards twice, one cut cutting left of the groin and hip, and the other slitting the body as high as the breast bone.

Later details show that the clothing of the woman was not torn and cut as first stated, nor were there indications of a struggle. Part of the underclothing shows that the deceased was recently an inmate of the Lambeth Workhouse. The police, who are making a most careful investigation into the matter, express an opinion that the deceased was killed by a left-handed person, judging from the nature of the injuries. No one has yet come forward to identify the body.

Bucks-row, says another correspondent, is a narrow passage running out of Thomas-st., and contains about a dozen houses of a very low class. It would appear as if the murder were committed in a house and the body afterwards removed to the place where it was found, the nature of the wounds being such that it would be hardly possible for them to be inflicted whilst the deceased was dressed. The body was warmly clad. The workhouse stamp was on one of the undergarments. The body has not yet been identified, though a large number of persons have visited the Whitechapel mortuary. The date of the inquest has not been fixed.

Source: *Widnes Examiner*

SATURDAY 1 SEPTEMBER 1888

THE WHITECHAPEL MURDER

The body of deceased has been identified as that of a married woman named Mary Ann Nichols, who has been living apart from her husband for some years. She was discharged from the workhouse a few months ago, and went into domestic service at Wandsworth, suddenly leaving her situation under suspicious circumstances seven weeks ago. Since that time she has frequented the locality of Whitechapel, and was seen in Whitechapel Road on the night of the murder under the influence of drink.

BODY DRAGGED SOME DISTANCE

It was evident yesterday morning that the murder was committed some distance from the place where the body was found. This was in Buck's Row, about midway down its length. Buck's Row is a short street, occupied half by factories and half by dwellings. Half-way down the street is the house of Mrs Green. Next to it is a large stable yard, whose wide closed gateway is next to the house. In front of this gateway the woman was found by two men, who at first supposed her to be drunk, but closer inspection saw first a pool of blood in the gutter just before her, and then the deathly whiteness of the woman's face stained as it was with blood.

One of them remained by her, while the other found Constable Neil. Constable Neil immediately woke the Green family, and asked them if they had heard any unusual noise. Neither Mrs Green, her son, nor her daughter, all of whom were sleeping within a few feet of where the body lay, had heard any outcry. All agreed that

THE NIGHT WAS UNUSUALLY QUIET.

"I should have heard it had there been any, I think," said Mrs Green; "for I have trouble with my heart, and am a very light sleeper. My son went down as soon as the body was taken away, and washed away the blood-stains on the pavement. There was quite a little pool, though I understood most of it soaked into the woman's dress. I looked out, and saw the body as it lay there. It was lying straight across the gateway, its head towards me. It was not lying in a heap as if it had fallen, but on its back, and straight,

AS IF IT HAD BEEN LAID THERE.

I could not tell at first whether it was a man or a woman, but James, my son, who went downstairs, returned and told me it was a woman. This was four o'clock in the morning." Across the street lives a Mr Perkins, whose wife is not very well. They sleep in the front room, and either Mr Perkins or his wife was awake at short intervals up to four o'clock yesterday morning. Neither heard the slightest sound in the street, and both agreed that it was an unusually quiet night, as there are sometimes brawls and fights or drunken men passing the house which disturb their sleep. They were sure that there was no outcry loud enough to be heard a few feet away.

THE WATCHMAN IN SCHNEIDER'S FACTORY,

just above the Perkin's, heard nothing. The watchman in the wool depot just below made the same statement, and it may be accepted as certain that the poor murdered and mangled victim was taken to the place where she was found after life was extinct. The detectives yesterday searched the stable yard, and every vacant space in the vicinity, in the hope of discovering some clue. None appeared, however.

They kept a sharp look-out for the knife with which the deed was done, but found no trace of it. Everything seemed to indicate that the scene of the murder was some distance away. Meanwhile, the people in Brady Street were in a high state of excitement. Brady Street is a long thoroughfare that runs to the left from the bottom of Buck's Row. Early yesterday morning

FRESH BLOOD STAINS

were observed for quite a distance along the side walks. There would be drop after drop two or three feet and sometimes six feet apart for a distance, and then a large pool or splash. As soon as the murder became known a lively interest was taken in these blood stains, and they began to be traced. They were soon found to be on both sides of the street, and it was some time before it was seen that the bleeding person had travelled or been carried in a zigzag line.

THE TRAIL WAS EASILY FOLLOWED

down Brady Street for 150 yards to Honey's Mews. In front of this gateway there was a large stain, looking as if the bleeding person had fallen against the wall and lain there. From here to the foot of Buck's Row, in which the body was found, the trail of blood is clearly marked. It was wet yesterday morning, and at noon, although the sun had dried it, and there had been many feet passing over it, it was still plainly discernible. The zigzag direction it took, crossing and recrossing the street, was, and is, a matter of mystery.

In the space of a hundred yards the woman crossed the street twice, and, whenever she crossed, a larger stain of blood, in place of the line of drops, indicated that she had stopped. There are a number of people who early yesterday morning heard the screams of the victim. None of them paid any particular attention to them, however, except Mrs Colwell, who lives between Buck's Row and the next turning. She said, "I was awakened early by my children, who said someone was trying to get into the house. I listened, and heard screams. They were in a woman's voice, and though frightened, were faintlike, as would be natural if she were running. She was screaming, 'Murder, police! Murder, police! Murder, police!' She screamed this five or six times, and seemed to be getting further and further away (toward the bottom of Buck's Row) all the time.

I HEARD NO OTHER VOICE

and no other steps. She seemed to be all alone. I think I would have heard the steps if anybody had been running after her, unless they were running on tiptoe." This is the clearest account of the outrage furnished in Brady Street. It seems to make it evident that the murder was committed there.

How any person gashed as the deceased had been could have run or walked any distance at all, much less a hundred yards, is a mystery, as the loss of blood must have been immediate and exhausting. That the murderer had only partially completed his work and followed her up to finish is a possibility. One fact is certain, however, that the woman could not have reached the gateway in Buck's Row herself, and must have been

CARRIED OR DRAGGED THERE.

That she was carried is more likely, as dragging her would have left more stains than appear on the Buck's Row pavement.

All day long the streets which were the scene of the murder have been crowded. The horrible atrocity of the deed, following so quickly upon the equally horrible tragedy of a few weeks ago, has alarmed all the women in the neighbourhood. The excitement was great, and the more the crowds of women looked at the bloodstains the more excited they became. There was yesterday a general cry for better police protection, and the statement was everywhere made that a policeman is as rare as a wild duck in that district, and somehow is never at hand when anything happens.

THE ONLY CLUE

to the direction taken by the murderer was discovered shortly after noon. While there are plenty of bloodstains in the direction from which the woman was brought, some were found elsewhere. At one o'clock, however, some men searching the pavement in Bucks Row about the gateway found two large spots of blood, each about the size of a shilling. The first was about 25 feet from the gateway, and the second 10 feet beyond. Both were a few inches from the kerb in the roadway, and clearly defined. It is believed that they came either from the hands or

THE CLOTHING OF THE MURDERER

as he went away, and the drops are so large without any others near them that they seemed to have resulted from the squeezing of some blood-soaked clothing. The watchman at the wool factory, whose doorway is a few feet below the doorway where the woman was found, and on the other side of the street, says that at exactly three o'clock he spoke to two men who stopped just outside his gate, and they moved on without any trouble. He says that there was no body lying in the stable gateway at the time, and no one in the street. Moreover he heard no noise from that time forth, and he was wide awake all the time until the police in the street attracted his attention. His statement only emphasises the extreme stealth and care with which the murderer must have acted. The women in a position similar to that of the deceased allege that there is

A MAN KNOWN AS "LEATHER APRON,"

who has more than once attacked unfortunate and defenceless women. His dodge is, it is asserted, to get them into some house on the pretence of offering them money. He then takes whatever little they have and "half kills" them in addition. The woman told her companion that she had been married, but her husband had left her some time ago. She is described as having been quiet for the life she followed.

Source: *Edinburgh Evening News*

SATURDAY 01 SEPTEMBER 1888

A DOCTORS STATEMENT
A GHASTLY SIGHT

Dr Llewellyn has made the following statement; "I was called to Buck's-row about five minutes to four this morning by Police-constable Thane, who said a woman had been murdered. I went to the place at once, and found deceased lying on the ground in front of the stable-yard door. She was lying on her back, with her legs out straight, as though she had been laid down. Police-constable Neil told me that the body had not been touched. The throat was cut from ear to ear, and the woman was quite dead. On feeling the extremities of the body I found that they were still warm, showing that death had not long taken place.

A crowd was now gathering, and as it was undesirable to make a further examination in the street, I ordered the removal of the body to the mortuary, telling the police to send for me again if anything of importance transpired. There was a very small pool of blood on the pathway, which had trickled from the wound in the throat - not more than would fill two wine-glasses, or half-a-pint at the outside. This fact, and the way in which the deceased was lying, made me think at the time that it was at least probable that the murder was committed elsewhere, and the body conveyed to Buck's-row.

There were no marks of blood on deceased's thighs, and at the time I had no idea of the fearful abdominal wounds which had been inflicted on the body. At half-past five I was summoned to the mortuary by the police, and was astonished at finding the other wounds. I have seen many terrible cases, but never such a brutal affair as this. From the nature of the cuts on the throat it is probable that they were inflicted with the left hand.

There is a mark at the point of the jaw on the right side of the deceased's face, as though made by a person's thumb, and a similar bruise on the left side, as if the woman's head had been pushed back and her throat then cut. There is a gash under the left ear reaching nearly to the centre of the throat, and another cut apparently starting from the right ear. The neck is severed back to the vertebrae, which are also slightly injured. Deceased's clothes were loose, and the wounds could have been inflicted while she was dressed."

ACTION BY THE POLICE

Inspector Helson, who has charge of the case, is making every effort to trace the murderer, but there is so little to guide the police that at present there does not seem much likelihood of success. The theory that the murder is the work of a lunatic, who is also the perpetrator of the other two murders of women which have occurred in Whitechapel during the last six months, meets with very general acceptance amongst the inhabitants of the district, the female portion of which are greatly alarmed.

The more probable theory is that the murder has been committed by one or more of a gang of men who are in the habit of frequenting the streets at late hours of the night and levying blackmail on the women. No money was found upon deceased, and all she had in the pocket of her dress was a handkerchief, a small comb, and a piece of looking-glass.

ANOTHER ACCOUNT
IDENTIFICATION OF THE BODY

Another account states:- After the body was removed to the mortuary, steps were taken to secure, if possible, identification, but at first with little prospect of success. As the news of the murder spread, however, first one woman and then another came forward to view the body, and at length it was found that a person answering the description of the murdered woman had lodged in a common lodging-house, 18, Thrawle-street, Spitalfields. Women from that place were fetched, and they identified the deceased as "Polly," who had shared a room with three other females in the place on the usual terms of such houses - nightly payment of 4d each - each having a separate bed.

It was gathered that the deceased had lodged in the house only for about three weeks past. Nothing more was known of her by them but that when she presented herself for her lodging on Thursday night she was turned away by the deputy because she had not the money. She was then the worse for drink, but not drunk, and went away laughing, saying,

"I'll soon get my 'doss' money; see what a jolly bonnet I've got now." She was wearing a bonnet which she had not been seen with before, and left the lodging-house door. A woman of the neighbourhood saw her later, she told the police - even as late as 2.30 on Friday morning - in Whitechapel-road, opposite the church, and at the corner of Osborne-street; and at a quarter to four she was found within 500 yards of the spot, murdered.

The people of the lodging house knew her as "Polly," but at about half past seven last evening a female named Mary Anne Monk, at present an inmate of Lambeth Workhouse, was taken to the mortuary, and identified the body as that of Mary Ann Nicholls, also called "Polly" Nicholls. She knew her, she said, as they were inmates of the Lambeth Workhouse together in April and May last, the deceased having been passed there from another workhouse. On May 12, according to Monk, Nicholls left the workhouse to take a situation as servant at Ingleside, Wandsworth-common. It afterwards became known that Nicholls betrayed her trust as domestic servant by stealing £3 from her employer and absconding. From that time she had been wandering about.

It has been stated that blood could be traced in thick spots and small pools from the spot where the body was found far down Buck's-row to a lateral thoroughfare called Brady-street. The police deny that statement. Inspector Helson states that he walked carefully over the ground soon after 8 o'clock in the morning, and beyond the discolourations ordinarily found on pavements there was no sign of stain. Viewing the spot where the body was found, however, it seems difficult to believe that the woman received her death wounds there. The body must have been nearly drained of blood, but that found in Buck's-row was small in quantity.

THE "HIGH RIP" GANG

The police have no theory with respect to the matter, except that a sort of "High Rip" gang exists in the neighbourhood, which, blackmailing women of the same class as the deceased, takes vengeance on those who do not find money for them. They base that surmise on the fact that within twelve months two other women have been murdered in the district by almost similar means, and left in the gutter of the street in the early hours of the morning.

The other theory is that the woman was murdered in a house, and killed whilst undressed, her clothes being then huddled on the body, which was afterwards conveyed out, to be deposited in the street. Colour is lent to this by the small quantity of blood found on the clothes, and by the fact that they are not cut.

A REPORTED CLUE

Up to one o'clock this afternoon the police had made no arrest in connection with the Whitechapel murder, but they believe they have an important clue. Latest investigations point to the probability of the murder having been committed some distance from the place where the body was found - possibly in a home in the locality.

THE INQUEST TO-DAY

An inquest was opened by Mr Wynne Baxter, this afternoon, on the body of the woman identified as Mary Ann Nicholls.

Edward Walker, Mordwell-street, Albany-road, Camberwell, formerly a smith, identified the body as that of his daughter. She was 42 years old, and married William Nicholls, a painter, 22 years ago. They had been separated for seven or eight years. The husband was still living.

Source: *South Wales Echo*

SATURDAY 1 SEPTEMBER 1888

IN THE DEAD-HOUSE

The news of the terrible tragedy spread like wild-fire amongst the inhabitants of Buck's-row and the neighbourhood, who, filled with morbid curiosity, surrounded Eagle-place, the entrance by which the body was taken into the dead-house. The Whitechapel Mortuary is a little brick building situated right of the large yard used by the Board of Works for the storage of their material. Accompanied by Mr. Edmunds, the keeper, our reporter visited the temporary resting place of the victim on Friday morning.

The first evidence seen of the tragedy on arriving in the yard was a bundle of what were little more than rags, of which the woman had been divested, and which were lying on the flagstones just outside the mortuary. They consisted of a dull red cloak already mentioned, together with a dark bodice and brown skirt, a check flannel petticoat which bore the mark of the Lambeth Workhouse, a pair of dark stockings, and an old pair of dilapidated-looking spring-side boots, together with the little and sadly battered black straw bonnet, minus either ribbons or trimmings.

Contrary to anticipation, beyond the flannel petticoat, and with the exception of a few blood-stains on the cloak, the other clothing was scarcely marked. The petticoat, however, was completely saturated with blood, and altogether presented a sickening spectacle. Entering the deadhouse, with its rows of black coffins, the keeper turned to the one immediately on the right of the door, and lying parallel with the wall.

Opening the lid, he exposed the face of the poor victim. The features were apparently those of a woman of about thirty or thirty-five years, whose hair was still dark. The features were small and delicate, the cheek-bones high, the eyes grey, and the partly-opened mouth disclosed a set of teeth which were little discoloured. The expression on the face was a deeply painful one, and was evidently the result of an agonising death. The gash across the neck was situated very slightly above the breastbone; it was at least six inches in length, over an inch in width, and was clean cut. The hands were still tightly clenched. The lower portion of the body, however, presented the most sickening spectacle of all. Commencing from the lower portion of the abdomen, a terrible gash extended nearly as far as the diaphragm - a gash from which the bowels protruded. There were no rings upon the fingers, and no distinguishing marks either about the face or the body.

The body, with the exception of the face was covered with a white sheet and a blanket.

WHO IS THE VICTIM?

Inspector Helson, of Leman-street, had called earlier, and had taken a description of the woman, together with a list of the articles of clothing. On finding the Lambeth Workhouse mark, he immediately proceeded there, but up to the time of going to Press, he had not gleaned any authoritative information regarding the identity of the woman.

She was unknown either to Police-constable Neale, or any of the officials, as a frequenter of the neighbourhood, and altogether the identity, like that of the victim of the George-yard tragedy, seems likely for a time to be shrouded in mystery. Several people who were waiting outside the mortuary claimed to have friends or acquaintances missing, but when put to the test, the descriptions failed to tally with that of the murdered woman.

WHO WAS THE MURDERER?

There is absolutely no room for doubt that the woman had been the victim of a foul crime. It might have been within the bounds of possibility for a woman to have inflicted the wound across the throat, but the terrible abdominal wound could never have been self-inflicted. Moreover, the wound in the throat, which was evidently the first inflicted, was quite sufficient of itself to have caused almost immediate death. But, while there is, as we have said, but little doubt as to the woman having been murdered, there seems to be but little motive for the murder.

Robbery was certainly not the motive, for the victim appears to have been in extreme poverty. Like poor Martha Tabram, of George-yard, then, the poor "unknown" appears to have been the victim of some fiend. Indeed, the inhabitants of Buck's-row, among whom the murderer was the sole topic of conversation on Friday morning, go so far as to assert that the very similar manner in which both the victims have met their death - both in the dead of the night, both with wounds of a most revolting character, and both without any apparent motive - point to the murder of Martha Tabram having been the murderer also of the poor unknown on Buck's-row.

Near the scene of the murder are the Essex Wharf and several private houses, mostly inhabited by the poorest classes, who either come home very late at night, or have to go out very early in the morning, and yet nobody appears to have been aware of having heard any screaming or other sounds likely to fix the time at which the tragedy was perpetrated - probably judging from the appearance of the dead woman at the time she was found, about two or three o'clock on the Friday morning. The probability is that although the victim did scream, yet, so used are the inhabitants there to drunken brawls and cries of "Murder," that they took no notice of it and that the murderer, whoever he is thus escaped undetected.

Mr. Banks, the coroner's officer, viewed the body early on Friday and communicated the particulars to Mr. George Collier, the coroner, who will probably hold the inquest some time to-day (Saturday).

Source: *East London Observer*

TUESDAY 4 SEPTEMBER 1888

THE WHITECHAPEL MURDER

The inquest was resumed at Whitechapel yesterday on the body of Mary Ann Nichols, who was found murdered on Friday morning in Bucks row. No arrest has yet been made.

Inspector Spratling, J Division, said that at half-past four on Friday morning when in Hackney road he received information of the finding of the body. He went to the mortuary in company with a constable. Witness described the nature of the injuries.

The Inspector was unable to describe the precise condition of the clothes at the time the body was found. It was stated to the coroner that another officer, Inspector Helson, would give evidence on this point. Witness (proceeding) said between 11 o'clock and noon he examined Bucks row, but found no blood stains. Afterwards he examined the London District Railway embankments of the Great Eastern Railway without discovering any traces of blood or any weapon.

Henry Tomkin, horse slaughterer, who was working in Winthorp street, adjoining Bucks row, with two companions, said they heard no suspicious noises during the night, though the gate of the slaughter house was open. They left at about 12.20. On hearing of the murder he and the other two men went to the spot. Witness was of opinion that the woman was murdered in her clothes, and at the place where the body was found.

Inspector Helson, J Division, described the condition of deceased's clothing, and said there was no cut under the stays.

Charles Cross, a carman in the employ of Messrs. Pickford, stated that when he discovered the body on his way to work the clothes were above the knees.

The court adjourned for luncheon, and the inquest was subsequently adjourned for a fortnight.

Source: *Sheffield Daily Telegraph*

THE RIPPER REPORTS

THURSDAY 6 SEPTEMBER 1888

THE EDITOR'S DRAWER
THE WHITECHAPEL MURDER

TO THE EDITOR OF "THE EVENING NEWS"

SIR - Permit me, as an inhabitant of twenty years in Whitechapel, to express on behalf of a number of tradesmen and shopkeepers in Whitechapel our deepest regret and indignation at the shocking and revolting murders which have further disgraced the unfortunate district of Whitechapel of late. The question that now arises is what is to be done, and what can be done to check and prevent the further spreading of such dastardly crimes. In the first place I would suggest that the police force should be strengthened in the East End, and secondly that there should be more gas lights in our back streets, courts, and alleys. There is no doubt but that these unfortunate women were butchered by their bullies (men who gain their livelihood from these unfortunates) and were the police to watch the haunts and dens of these villains and thiefs, no doubt in a short time we should have a decrease of these crimes which have disgraced the capital of England.

There are several supposed clubs in Whitechapel which these villains frequent, which are open all night for the sale of wines, spirits, and beer, and where any non-member can be admitted and served with as much drink as he or she can pay for. It is in these vile dens that the seed of immorality and crime is sown which brings forth the fruits we have just witnessed. The police must know of these places; if not, I am prepared, if required, to give the names of these places to any person in authority.

The East End police are, with a few exceptions, a good and noble body of men who at all times have a hard and difficult duty to perform, and I feel sure that the heads of these police, such gentlemen as Arnold, Fisal, and West, will do their uttermost to stop the breeding of further crimes by these ruffians.

In the second place I suggest more gas lights in our bye-streets, courts, and alleys. We pay rates and taxes, and have a right to have our district properly lighted. Only a little while back a City manufacturer living opposite me was knocked down, beaten, and robbed of a valuable gold chain within a few yards of his own street door, the villains escaping because the spot is dark. My sister also a short time ago was knocked down by some cowards. They also got away, the place being dark.

No, Sir, I hope and trust that the Whitechapel Board of Works and the Commercial Gas Company will awake to their duty, and do their best to have this grievance removed. Apologising for trespassing upon your valuable space, I am, &c.,

ALBERT BACHERT

Gordon House, Newnham-street, Whitechapel, September 5.

Source: *Evening News (London)*

FRIDAY 7 SEPTEMBER 1888

THE WHITECHAPEL MURDER

THE RIPPER REPORTS

The funeral of the unfortunate woman, Mary Ann Nichols, who was murdered in Buck's-row early on Friday last, took place yesterday. The arrangements were of a very simple character. The time at which the cortege was to start was kept a profound secret, and a ruse was perpetrated in order to get the body out of the mortuary where it has lain since the day of the murder. A pair-horsed closed hearse was observed making its way down Hanbury-street, and the crowds, which numbered some thousands, made way for it to go along Old Montague-street, but instead of doing so it passed onto the Whitechapel-road, and, doubling back, entered the mortuary by the back gate, which is situated in Chapman's-court. No one was near besides the undertaker and his men, when the remains, placed in a polished elm coffin, bearing a plate with the inscription, Mary Ann Nichols, aged 42; died August 31, 1888, was removed to the hearse and driven to Hanbury-street, there to await the mourners.

These were late in arriving, and the two coaches were kept waiting some time in a side street. By this time the news had spread that the body was in the hearse, and people flocked round to see the coffin and examine the plate. In this they were, however, frustrated, for a body of police, under Inspector Helson, of the H Division, surrounded the hearse and prevented their approaching too near. At last the procession started towards Ilford, where the last scene in this unfortunate drama took place.

The mourners were Mr. Edward Walker, the father of the victim, and her two children. The procession proceeded along Baker's-row and past the corner of Buck's-row into the main road, where policemen were stationed every few yards. The houses in the neighbourhood had the blinds drawn, and much sympathy was expressed for the relatives.

Up to a late hour last night no arrest has been made in connection with the murder.

THE RIPPER REPORTS

Source: *Morning Post*

SATURDAY 8 SEPTEMBER 1888

THE WHITECHAPEL MURDER

Almost the worst feature about the two really frightful murders which have followed each other in quick succession in Whitechapel is that there are no means of accounting for them. The question of motive is in both cases a baffling one. It is particularly so, perhaps, in the second of the two crimes, the discovery of which was made by a policeman in the small hours of Thursday morning. Was it a maniac, some creature mad with thirst of blood, escaped from a lunatic asylum, who did to death the "unfortunate" - unfortunate in a double sense - Mary Ann Nichols, with such extravagantly superfluous brutality? It certainly looks like the deed of a madman, for who, with a remnant of sense, would murder so miserable a creature for the sake of her empty purse? And not only murder but mutilate her body in a manner so fiendish? The woman was found with her throat ripped out from ear to ear, and her body ripped open from the groin almost to the breast-bone. The whole affair is mysterious.

The place where the body was found was evidently not that where the murder was committed. There were stains and pools of blood at intervals for a considerable distance from the spot where the corpse lay, and at this spot no screams or sounds of any kind were heard by the inhabitants of the street, though a night watchman in a warehouse was at his post close by, and there were people awake in several of the surrounding houses. The woman must have been dragged or carried, or she must have crawled for a distance of more than a hundred yards from the spot where she was first attacked. Probably the murderer did not finish his work where he began it; he must have pursued or dragged her to the place where she lay when the policeman discovered her corpse. The "how" of the hideous deed is plain enough, the "why" is for the present at all events an utter mystery. Nicholls was absolutely penniless, and she is described by those who knew her in the neighbourhood as "quiet for one of her calling." Could any but a madman have done this crime?

And there cannot be any doubt that this murder and the previous one - indeed, the two previous ones, for this is the third Whitechapel murder since a very recent date - were done by the same hand. If, as we imagine, there be a murderous lunatic concealed in the slums of Whitechapel, who issues forth at night, like another Hyde, to prey upon the defenceless women of the "unfortunate" class, we have little doubt that he will be captured. The cunning of the lunatic, especially of the criminal lunatic, is well-known; but a lunatic of this sort can scarcely remain at large for any length of time in the teeming neighbourhood of Whitechapel. The terror which, since Thursday last, has inspired every man and woman in the district, will keep every eye on the watch. A watch should be kept indeed behind the windows in every street in Whitechapel. The murderer must creep out from somewhere; he must patrol the streets in search of his victims. Doubtless he is out night by night. Three successful murders will have the effect of whetting his appetite still further, and unless a watch of the strictest be kept, the murder of Thursday will certainly be followed by a fourth.

The whole of East London is directly interested in bringing the assassin to justice. Every woman in those parts goes in nightly danger of her life as long as he remains at large. In one respect, no doubt, the crowded character of that quarter of the metropolis provides a certain safety for criminals of all kinds; but in a case like this where every inhabitant is bound, from motives of mere personal safety, to become a sort of unauthorised detective, continuously on the alert, the chances of a murderer's escape are fewer than they would be in a more thinly populated region.

Source: *Tower Hamlets Independent and East End Local Advertiser*

SATURDAY 8 SEPTEMBER 1888

THE WHITECHAPEL AND POPLAR MURDERS

William Nicholls, husband of the woman who was found lying dead and fearfully mutilated in Buck's Row, Baker's Row, Whitechapel, early on Friday morning, was, on Saturday afternoon, conducted from his residence at 37 Coburg Road, Old Kent road, to the mortuary, where he recognised the body of the murdered woman as being that of his wife. The son, who resides with his grandfather at 15, Maidwell-street, Albany-street, Camberwell, also identified the remains of his mother. This removed all further doubt as to the deceased being Mary Ann Nicholls. Lately it seems that she had been lodging in a common lodging house in

Thrawle-street, Spitalfields, and it is supposed that she had been leading an immoral life.

The inquest was opened on Saturday night by Mr. W. E. Baxter, the coroner for South-East Middlesex. Evidence of identification, and as to the finding of the body, and the terrible nature of the wounds upon it was given, and the inquiry was adjourned.

Mr. Wynne E. Baxter, the coroner for South-East Middlesex, resumed the inquiry on Monday morning at the Working Lad's Institute, Whitechapel. Inspector Spratling deposed that that about four o'clock on Friday morning, while in the Hackney Road, he received information as to the finding of the body of the deceased. Before he reached the spot the body had been removed the mortuary. While he was taking a description of the body there he discovered the injuries to the abdomen, and at once sent for Dr. Llewellyn. Whilst describing the clothes which were on the body, the witness said that the corsets had no cuts on them.

- The Coroner: Were they fastened when you saw them?
- Witness: Yes, they were fastened at the back.
- The Coroner: Were they fastened at the front? This is a most important point.
- Witness: I did not remove them from the body, so could not say.
- Well, who can give us this information, or shall we have to examine them for ourselves? Inspector Helson can tell you more about it. Witness added that he had examined Buck's Row and Green-street but found no blood stains in either. He subsequently examined the East London District Railway embankment and the Great Eastern Railway yard for bloodstains and weapons, but found none.
- By the jury: It occurred to him that the woman had been murdered with her clothes on; but he could not say whether the clothes bore cuts corresponding with those on the body.

THE RIPPER REPORTS

- The coroner: I have avoided asking the witness questions on the point because he has admitted he did not examine the clothing.

- Henry Tomkins, of 12, Coventry-street, Bethnal Green, said he was at work in the slaughter-house in Winthorp-street about nine o'clock Thursday night, and left off work at about four o'clock on Friday morning. He did not go straight home, as was his usual custom; but went to Buck's Row, as a police-constable passed the slaughter house, and stated that there had been a murder there. The gates of the slaughter house were open all night, so that anyone could walk into the place. None of the men employed there left the building between the hours of one and four o'clock, and none of them heard any unusual noise.

- Inspector Helson gave a description of the deceased's clothing. The back of the bodice of the dress, he said, had absorbed a large quantity of blood, but there was none upon the petticoats. There was no evidence of the body having been washed, and there were no cuts in the clothing. It would have been possible to inflict the wounds while the clothing was on, and without cutting it. There was no cut under the stays. In making a search for blood-stains he saw nothing except some marks in Brady-street, which might have been taken for blood marks.

- By the jury: He was of opinion that the woman was murdered in her clothes and that the murder was committed where the body was found. The clothes were not disarranged, as they would have been if the body had been carried some distance.

- Charles Cross, a carman in the service of Messrs. Pickford, stated that he discovered the body when going to his work. From the position in which the body was lying, his first impression was that the woman had been outraged.

- William Nicholls, of Coburg Road, Old Kent Road, said he was a machinist. The deceased was his wife. They had been living apart for over eight years, and he last saw her alive about three years ago. He did not know what she had been doing during that time.

- Jane Hodden, of 13, Thrawl-street, said the deceased lodged with her for about six weeks, till eight nights ago. On the day of the murder at 2.30 a.m., the witness saw her in Whitechapel Road, when she said that she should leave her lodgings, as they allowed men and women to stay together. The witness did not think the deceased was leading a fast life; in fact she seemed very much afraid of it.

- Mary Ann Monks, an inmate of the Lambeth Workhouse, stated that six or seven years ago the deceased was an inmate of that institution.

- At the conclusion of this witness's evidence the inquiry was adjourned for a fortnight.

Source: *Manchester Times*

THE RIPPER REPORTS

ANNIE CHAPMAN

Died: 8 September 1888

THE RIPPER REPORTS

SUNDAY 9 SEPTEMBER 1888

ANOTHER MURDER IN WHITECHAPEL
A FOURTH VICTIM OF AN UNKNOWN ASSASSIN
FIENDISH MUTILATION OF A WOMAN'S BODY

A fourth murder, of a most brutal nature, has been committed in Whitechapel. At the spot only a very few hundred yards from where the mangled body of the poor woman Nicholls was found just a week ago, the body of another woman, mutilated and horribly disfigured, was found at half-past five yesterday morning. She was lying in the back yard of 29, Hanbury-street, Spitalfields, a house occupied by Mr. Richardson, a packing-case maker. As late as five o'clock yesterday morning it is said that the woman was drinking in a public-house near at hand called the Three Bells. Near the body was discovered a rough piece of iron sharpened like a knife. The wounds upon the poor woman were more fearful than those found upon the body of the woman Nicholls, who was buried on Thursday. The throat was cut in a most horrible manner and the stomach terribly mutilated.

The first discovery of the body was made by John Davis, living on the top floor of 29, Hanbury-street, in the yard of which the body was found. Mr. Davis was crossing the yard between five and six when he saw a horrible-looking mass lying in the corner, partly concealed by the steps. He instantly made for the station and notified the police, without touching the body. Meantime Mrs. Richardson, an old lady sleeping on the first floor front, was aroused by her grandson, Charles Cooksley, who looked out of one of the back windows and screamed that there was a dead body in the corner.

Mrs. Richardson's description makes this murder even more horrible than any of its predecessors. The victim was lying on her back with her legs outstretched. Her throat was cut from ear to ear. Her clothes were pushed up above her waist and her legs bare. The abdomen was exposed, the woman having been ripped up from the groin to the breast-bone as before. Not only this, but the viscera had been pulled out and scattered in all directions, the heart and liver being placed beside her head, and the remainder along her side. No more horrible sight ever met a human eye, for she was covered with blood, and lying in a pool of it.

Mr. And Mrs. Davis occupy the upper story of 29, Hanbury-street, the house consisting of two storeys. When Mr. Davis found the woman she was lying on her back close up to the flight of steps leading into the yard. The throat was cut open in a fearful manner - so deep, in fact, that the murderer, evidently thinking that he had severed the head from the body, tied a handkerchief round it so as to keep it on. It was also found that the body had been ripped open and disembowelled, the heart and abdominal viscera lying by the side. The fiendish work was completed by the murderer tying a portion of the entrails round the victim's neck. There was no blood on the clothes.

Hanbury-street is a long street which runs from Baker's-row to Commercial-street. It consists partly of shops and partly of private houses. In the house in question, in the front room, on the ground floor, Mr. Harderman carries on the business of a seller of catsmeat. At the back of the premises are those of Mr. Richardson, who is a packing-case maker. The other occupants of the house are lodgers. One of the lodgers, named Robert Thompson, who is a carman, went out of the house at half-past three in the morning, but heard no noise. Two girls, who also live in the house, were talking in the passage until half-past 12 with young men, and it is believed that they were the last occupants of the house to retire to rest. It seems that the crime was committed soon after five. At that hour the woman and the man, who in all probability was her murderer, were seen drinking together in The Bells, Brick-lane. But though the murder was committed at this late hour, the murderer - acting, as in the other case, silently and stealthily - managed to make his escape.

On the wall near where the body was found there was, according to one reporter, subsequently discovered written in chalk:-

"FIVE: 15 MORE, AND THEN I GIVE MYSELF UP."

On the place being subsequently visited by our representative this was not to be seen.

ATTEMPT TO LYNCH TWO MEN

Two men passing through Brick-lane yesterday morning were denounced by the crowd as the murderers, and were attacked. They called upon the police for protection and were taken to Bethnal-green and there treated as prisoners. As, however, they made clear statements of their movements, which could not be gainsaid, they were allowed to go. This gave rise to an excited rumour of two arrests.

Source: *Lloyd's Weekly Newspaper*

MONDAY 10 SEPTEMBER 1888

THE HORRIBLE MURDER IN WHITECHAPEL
MUTILATION OF THE VICTIM
PANIC IN THE EAST END
AN ARREST: EXCITING CHASE

As we reported in our last issue, the neighbourhood of Whitechapel was horrified on Saturday to a degree bordering on panic by the discovery of another barbarous murder of a woman at 29, Hanbury Street (late Brown Lane), Spitalfields. Hanbury Street is a thoroughfare running between Commercial Street and Whitechapel Road, the occupants of which are poor and for the most part of Jewish extractions. The circumstances of the murder are of such a revolting character as to point the conclusion that it has been perpetrated by the same hand as committed that in Buck's Row and the two previous murders, all of which have occurred within a stone's throw of each other.

The murdered woman, who appears to have been respectably connected, was known in the neighbourhood by women of the unfortunate class as Annie Sieve, but her real name was Annie Chapman. She is described by those who knew her best as a decent although poor looking woman, about 5ft. 2in. or 5ft. 3in. high, with fair brown wavy hair, blue eyes, large flat nose, and, strange to say, she had two of her front teeth missing, as had Mary Ann Nichols, who was murdered in Buck's Row. When her body was found on Saturday morning it was respectably clad. She wore no head covering,, but simply a skirt and bodice and two light petticoats. A search being made in her pockets nothing was found but an envelope stamped "The Sussex Regiment."

The house in Hanbury Street, in the yard of which the crime was committed, is occupied by a woman named Richardson, who employs several men in the rough packing line. There is a small shop in front at the basement of the house, which is utilised for the purpose of a cat's meat shop. From the upper end of the house there is a passage with a door at either end leading to a small yard, some 13 ft. or 14 ft. square, separated from the adjoining houses by a slight wooden fence. There is no outlet at the back, and any person who gains access must of necessity make his exit from the same end as his entry. In the yard there were recently some packing cases, which had been sent up from the basement of the dwelling, but just behind the lower door there was a clear space left, wherein the murder was undoubtedly committed.

The theory primarily formed was that the unfortunate victim had been first murdered and afterwards dragged through the entry into the back yard; but from an inspection made later in the day it appears that the murder was actually committed in the corner of the yard, which the back door, when open, places in obscurity. There were on Saturday some marks of blood observable in the passage, but it is now known that these were caused during the work of removal of some packing-cases, the edges of which accidentally came in contact with the blood which remained upon the spot from which the unhappy victim was removed.

The evidence which has been collected up to the present shows that the murder was committed shortly before half-past five o'clock in the morning. Albert Cadosch, who lodges next door, had occasion to go into the adjoining yard at the back at 5.25, and states that he heard a conversation on the other side of the palings as if between two people. He caught the word "No," and fancied he subsequently heard a slight scuffle, with the noise of a falling against the palings, but thinking that his neighbours might probably be out in the yard he took no further notice and went to his work. Nothing further can be traced of the dreadful tragedy until shortly before six o'clock, when the man Davies passing into the yard at the back of 29, Hanbury Street, observed a mutilated mass which caused him to go shrieking in affright into the street.

In the house, the back premises of which happened to become the scene of this hideous crime, no fewer than six separate families reside. Some people who live on the ground-floor and are credited with being "light sleepers" stated emphatically that during the night and morning they heard no sound of a suspicious nature, which is likely enough in view of the fact that the passage from the front to the back of the house has been invariably left open for the convenience of dwellers in the building, the traffic being constant. One of the occupants of the house is the man named John Davies, a porter in the Spitalfields Market. When he discovered the body in the yard he made no attempt to ascertain the condition of deceased, but immediately alarmed the other inmates of the house, and then proceeded to acquaint the police at the Commercial Street Station of what had occurred.

In the meantime Mrs. Richardson, the principal occupier of the premises, together with a young woman named Eliza Cooksley, sleeping on the second floor, were aroused, and under the notion that the building was on fire, ran to the back bedroom window, whence they were enabled to see the murdered woman lying on the paved yard, her clothes disarranged, and her person horribly mutilated. On the wall of the court in which the body was found were the words written - "Five: Fifteen more, and then I give myself up."

When the police arrived they found that the woman had been murdered in a terribly brutal fashion. It was obvious both from the marks upon the body and of the splashes of blood upon the palings which separate the dwellings one from the other that the woman while lying down had her throat first cut and then was ripped open and disembowelled. The perpetrator of the ghastly deed undoubtedly occupied some considerable time in doing his victim to death, inasmuch as it appears that he, with fiendish resolve, not only killed the object of his caprice or passion, but afterwards mutilated her body in a terrible manner, leaving the heart and liver lying by the shoulder.

There is on every hand the one opinion prevailing that the Whitechapel murders have been all enacted by the same person. The mortuary in which the body of the murdered woman lies is situated at the corner of Eagle street, a cul de sac ending in a pair of green doors, within which several officers of the police guard the remains of the dead. The body is already in a shell, and the autopsy having been made by Dr. Phillips and his assistants, the portions of flesh and entrails removed by the fiendish hands of the murderer have been so far as possible replaced in their natural positions, and there is little else observable beyond the usual post-mortem indications. The body is that of a fairly nourished woman, but bears traces of rough usage. The corpse is covered with a wrap, and those in custody of it are charged by the police authorities that it shall neither be shown to any person nor disturbed in any way. The district Coroner visited the mortuary on Saturday afternoon, and made arrangements for holding an inquest this morning at 10.30 at the Boys' Refuge, near Whitechapel Station.

The woman's name is Annie Chapman, alias Sieve. She comes from Windsor, and has friends residing at Vauxhall. Her home was a lodging-house at 35, Dorset-street, in Whitechapel. Her husband was a pensioner, who allowed her 10s a week, but he died a twelve month ago and, the pension ceasing, she has since earned her living in the streets. She lived for a time with a man named Sieve. She was identified at the mortuary at half-past seven in the morning by Frederick Simmons, a young man living in the same house with her. Simmons identified her without difficulty, first by her handkerchief and then by her face, and said that she had three rings on when she left the house, one a wedding ring and the other two chased. These had disappeared, having evidently been mistaken for gold and stolen by the assassin.

For the last nine months she has been sleeping at night, or early in the morning rather, at a common lodging house at 35, Dorset-street, Spitalfields, and she was there as recently as 2 o'clock on Saturday morning eating some potatoes. She had not, however, the money to pay for her bed, and at 2 o'clock she left with the remark to the shopkeeper of the place, "I'll soon be back again; I'll soon get the money for my doss." The woman's height is exactly five feet. The complexion is fair, with wavy dark brown hair; the eyes are blue, and two lower teeth have been knocked out. The nose is rather large and prominent. The third finger on the left hand bears signs of rings having been wrenched off, and the hands and arms are considerably bruised.

The deceased had on laced-up boots and striped stockings. She had on two cotton petticoats, and was otherwise respectably dressed. Nothing was found in her pockets but a handkerchief, and two small combs. The only clue of any value is furnished by Mrs. Fiddymont, wife of the proprietor of the Prince Albert public-house, half a mile from the scene of the murder. Mrs Fiddymont states that at 7 o'clock in the morning she was standing in the bar talking with another woman a friend in the first compartment. Suddenly there came into the middle compartment a man whose rough appearance frightened her. He had on a brown stiff hat, a dark coat and no waistcoat. He came in with his hat down over his eyes, and with his face partly concealed, asked for a half pint of four ale. She drew the ale, and meanwhile looked at him through the mirror at the back of the bar. As soon as he saw the woman in the other compartment watching him he turned his back, and got the partition between himself and her.

The thing that struck Mrs. Fiddymont particularly was the fact that there were blood spots on the back of his right hand. This, taken in connection with his appearance, caused her uneasiness. She also noticed that his shirt was torn. As soon as he had drunk the ale, which he swallowed at a gulp, he went out. Her friend went out also to watch him. Her friend is Mrs. Mary Chappell, who lives at 28, Stewart-street, near by. Her story corroborates Mrs. Fiddymont's and is more particular. When the man came in the expression of his eyes caught her attention, his look was so startling and terrifying. It frightened Mrs. Fiddymont so that she requested her to stay. He wore a light blue check shirt, which was torn badly, into rags in fact, on the right shoulder. There was a narrow streak of blood under his right ear, parallel with the edge of his shirt. There was also dried blood between the fingers of his hand. When he went out she slipped out the other door, and watched him as he went towards Bishopsgate-street. She called Joseph Taylor's attention to him, and Joseph Taylor followed him.

Joseph Taylor, a builder at 22, Stewart street, states that as soon as his attention was attracted to the man he followed him. He walked rapidly, and came out alongside him, but did not speak to him. The man was rather thin, about 5ft 8in high, and apparently between 40 and 50 years of age. He had a shabby genteel look, pepper and salt trousers which fitted badly, and dark coat. When Taylor came alongside him the man glanced at him, and Taylor's description of the look was. "His eyes were wild as a hawk's." Taylor is a perfectly reliable man, well known throughout the neighbourhood. The man walked, he says, holding his coat together at the top. He had a nervous and frightened way about him.

He wore a ginger-coloured moustache, and had short, sandy hair. Taylor ceased to follow him, but watched him as far as Halfmoon-street, where he became lost to view. It is said that "Dark Annie," as the woman was called by her companions, was seen drinking at a tavern in Brick-lane with the man supposed to be her murderer. The barmaid says she opened the place at 5 o'clock as is customary on a Saturday morning, as Spitalfields Market is in the near vicinity. She was too busy almost to notice whom she served. She might have served the woman; indeed she has been told by those who knew her that she had, but she had no recollection of it, and certainly could not say whether the unfortunate creature was accompanied by a man.

The terror and excitement were somewhat abating when, at about 11 o'clock the people who had congregated in Commercial-street were thrown into a fresh state of alarm. It was rumoured that about a quarter of an hour previously the man who was supposed to be the murderer, or connected with the murder, had been seen in the locality, but this statement, owing to the want of previous success detecting the perpetrators of the other murders was received with incredulity.

A short time afterwards, however, a young man, apparently about 25 years of age, was seen running down Commercial-street at full speed, followed by a large body of policemen with drawn batons, and a large crowd of persons. The man was gradually gaining on his pursuers, but owing to the cries of the policemen a large body of men and women blocked the street. The man at once grasped the situation, and rushed down a side street. The excitement at this time became intense, as it was thought that the man, who was supposed to be the murderer, would escape.

After an interval of about two minutes, however, a cheer was raised, and shortly afterwards the man was seen between five or six policemen. It would be almost impossible to describe his appearance; he was the picture of terror, the colour of his face being between a ghastly white and yellow. He is about the medium height and was fairly dressed. When the police arrived in Commercial-street the people crowded round, in order to look at the captured man, but they were kept at a distance by a body of policemen. The man was taken to Commercial-street police station. It is thought that in consequence of this arrest a clue will be obtained as to the perpetrators of the dastardly crimes which have thrown the inhabitants of the district into the greatest state of alarm during the last few weeks.

The Press Association says:
- Up to midnight on Saturday no arrest had been made. The police confess they have no clue, but they are making efforts to put an end to the mystery and to bring the criminal to justice. A large number of detectives and police are scouring the neighbourhood. Shortly before midnight the police received information the three rings answering the description of those taken from the murdered woman had been taken in pledge by a pawnbroker in Mile End Road.

A woman who knew deceased well was at once sent to see if she could identify the rings, but she failed to do so. In the meantime the police had ascertained that the person who pledged them had a right to do so. Mrs Fiddymont, the wife of the proprietor of the Prince Albert public house, half a mile from the scene of the murder, states that she will be able to identify the man who entered her house early on Saturday morning with stains of blood on him.

The Press Association telegraphed at midnight last night.
- Hanbury Street, Whitechapel, was this morning in an all but impassable state, owing to the crowds which had assembled in the neighbourhood of the scene of the latest East End tragedy. Some thousands of people passed through the locality during the early part of the day, and the police authorities at Commercial Street Police-station had a number of constables drafted from other parts of the metropolis, and these, as evening advanced were busily occupied in keeping people moving. The public excitement as the day advanced, appeared rather to

grow than diminish, and strong evidence of the fact was apparent in the evening.

Not only did large crowds of the poorer classes loiter in the vicinity of the spot where the murder was committed, but a number of the more well to-do were to be seen either gazing with awe-stricken faces at Mrs. Richardson's house, in the rear of which the mutilated body of the victim was found, or endeavouring to glean some additional particulars as to the circumstances of the tragedy. Up to half-past nine o'clock the police at Commercial Street were unable to say that their investigations had been attended with success, though our reporter elicited a statement regarding which important development might, it is thought, be expected. The Deptford police had made a communication to the effect that a man had been arrested by them under suspicious circumstance.

On the receipt of the information at Commercial Street, Inspector Chandler started at once for Deptford, and at the time of telegraphing he had not returned with his charge, but was momentarily expected. The elapse of a few hours will suffice to know whether the man in custody in Deptford is in any way connected with the crime. The police authorities at Scotland Yard and Whitechapel are fully conscious of the difficult nature of the task they have before him in identifying a particular individual with the series of appalling crimes. "God knows," said an official to our reporter, "but we may have another to-night, though we have men patrolling the whole region of Whitechapel and Spitalfields." That the police are putting forth every possible effort there can be no doubt.

To-night there is a large force on duty. One-third of the men are in plain clothes, and even those entitled to have a leave of absence are retained. That the public are anxious to second their efforts is testified by the presence on the record at Commercial-street of no less than fifty personal statements made with the object of assisting in the work of identification. One officer has been occupied may consecutive hours in writing these statements out, and up to nine o'clock at night they were being supplemented by others. The police are not permitted to make public the written evidence, if evidence it can be called. It is doubtful if it will ultimately prove of much value, but our special representative, in pursuing his investigations last night, heard, in the presence of the police, a statement which, perhaps ought not to be altogether dismissed as unworthy of notice.

The informant was young woman named Lyons, of the class commonly known as unfortunates. She stated that at three o'clock on Sunday afternoon she met a strange man in Flower and Dean Street, one of the worst streets in the East End of London. He asked her to go to the Queen's Head public-house at half-past six and drink with him. Having obtained from the young woman a promise that she would do so, he disappeared, but was at the house at the appointed time. While they were conversing Lyons noticed a large knife in the man's right hand trouser's pocket, and called another woman's attention to that fact.

A moment later Lyons was startled with the remark which the stranger addressed to her, "You are about the same style of woman as the one that was murdered." "What do you know about her," asked the woman; to which the man replied, "You are beginning to smell a rat. Foxes hunt geese, but they don't always find them." Having uttered these words the man hurriedly left. Lyons followed until near Spitalfields Church, and, turning round at this spot, and noticing that the woman was behind him, the stranger ran at a swift pace into Church Street, and was at once lost to view.

One noteworthy fact in this story is that the description of the man's apparel is in all material points identical with the published description of the unknown and, up to the present, undiscovered "Leather Apron." Over two hundred common lodging-houses have been visited by the police with the hope of finding the mysterious and much-talked-of person but he has succeeded in evading arrest. The police have reason for supposing that he is employed in one of the London sweating dens as a slipper maker, and that as it is usual to supply food and lodging in many of these houses he is virtually in hiding. Though "Leather Apron" was a figure well-known to many policemen in the Whitechapel district prior to the murder of Mrs. Nichols in Buck's Row, the man has kept himself out of the way since, and this is regarded as a significant circumstance.

A statement made to an Inspector that a man was heard making use of violent threats towards some woman in a public-house in Hanbury Street on Friday night is not considered to be of much importance, as neither of the parties can be identified.

The police feel strongly that some effort should have been made to detain the man who was alleged to have drunk beer early on Saturday morning in a public bar, with bloodstains upon him. The generally accepted theory is that the whole series of murders are the work of one man, but a medical opinion is that the knife wounds on the woman found in August, in George Yard, may, after all, have been self-inflicted. Whether this was so or not, wounds were not of the kind inflicted on the later victim.

Telegraphing later, the Press Association says that the man arrested at Deptford has not up to the present been brought to Commercial Road Police-station for the purpose of identification, and no further particulars concerning him can be obtained. Inspector Chandler has been to Deptford to see the prisoner, but what the result of his inquiries is is kept secret, but it is understood that not so much importance is attached to the arrest as was the case in the first place.

THE RIPPER REPORTS

Reference is made to a mysterious being bearing the name of "Leather Apron," concerning whom a number of stories have for a week or more been current in Whitechapel. The following is a description of the man:- He is 5ft. 4 or 5 in. in height, and wears a dark close-fitting cap. He is thick-set, and has an unusually thick neck. His hair is black, and closely clipped; his age about 38 or 40. He has a small black moustache. The distinguishing feature of his costume is a leather apron, which he always wears, and from which he gets his nickname. His expression is sinister, and seems to be full of terror for the women who describe it. His eyes are small and glittering. His lips are usually parted in a grin which is not only not re-assuring, but excessively repellent.

He is a slipper-maker by trade, but does not work. His business is blackmailing women late at night. A number of men in Whitechapel follow this degrading profession. He has never cut any-body so far as is known, but always carries a leather knife, presumably as sharp as other knives are wont to be. The knife a number of the women have seen. His name nobody knows, but all are united in the belief that he is a Jew or of Jewish parentage, his face being of a marked Hebrew type. But the most singular characteristic of the man is the universal statement that is moving about he never makes any noise. What he wears on his feet the women do not know, but they agree that he moves noiselessly. His uncanny peculiarity to them is that they never see him or know of his presence till he is close by them.

"Leather Apron" never by any chance attacks a man. He runs away on the slightest appearance of rescue. One woman whom he assailed some time ago boldly prosecuted him for it, and he was sent up for seven days. He has no settled place of residence, but has slept oftenest in a four penny lodging-house of the lowest kind in a disreputable lane leading from Brick Lane. The people at his lodging house denied that he had been there, and appeared disposed to shield him. "Leather Apron's" pal, "Mickeld Joe," was in the house at the time, and his presence had doubtless something to do with the unwillingness to give information. "Leather Apron" was last at this house some weeks ago, though this account may be untrue. He ranges all over London, and rarely assails the same woman twice. He has lately been seen in Leather Lane, which is in the Holborn district.

Source: *Eastern Evening News*

MONDAY 10 SEPTEMBER 1888

ANOTHER MURDER IN WHITECHAPEL
SHOCKING MUTILATION OF THE VICTIM
THE POLICE THEORY
AN ARREST

Once more the neighbourhood of Whitechapel and Spitalfields has been terribly shocked by a brutal and mysterious murder. Before the inquest on Mary Ann Nichols has been concluded, and almost before the grave has closed over her, another woman of the same unhappy class has met a precisely similar fate, and, as before no possible trace of the murderer can be found. "For all we can tell," said an agitated woman in the crowd yesterday assembled before the house at which the body had been found, "he may be one of the mob listening to the speechifying about it." It is anything but improbable. That the assassin should have been there would have been quite in keeping with the cool audacity which must of necessity be characteristic of the man who, in all probability, has perpetrated all four of the murders which have so shooked this locality.

It seems to be pretty conclusively established that the victim in this case is Annie Chapman, the widow of a veterinary surgeon who died about a year and a half ago at Windsor. She had long been separated from her husband, who appears to have allowed her ten shillings a week while he lived, and she has been known for the past six years among the lodging houses of the neighbourhood in which she met her death. She appears to have maintained herself to some extent by making antimacassars or selling articles in the street, but there is little room for doubt that her earnings in this way were eked out by less creditable courses. She cohabited, it is said, for a time with a sieve maker, commonly known as Jack Sivvy, and hence she has been generally known of late as Annie Sivvy, and the name appearing in the summonses for the inquest is "Annie Siffey." Those who knew her best spoke of her as a quiet, inoffensive creature, not given to drink, and earning her living respectably in so far as she could. She had relatives; and a friend who had lodged with her, and had been in the habit of writing her letters for her says that last week she expressed her intention of going hop-picking if she could get her sister to provide her with a pair of boots. She had, it is said, a sister and a mother, and also two children - a daughter travelling with a circus company in France, and a crippled boy about four years of age at some sort of charity school near Windsor.

Judging by the appearance of the woman as she lay in the mortuary on Saturday she must have been somewhere about five and forty years of age. She was a little over five feet in height, well and strongly built, with dark hair, and features somewhat plain and unprepossessing, her nose being especially flat and broad. For some months past she has been in the habit of frequenting a lodging house in Dorset-street, Spitalfields, an extremely low and turbulent spot, just in front of Spitalfields Church, on the opposite side of Commercial-street. The deputy of the lodging-house, No. 35, states that she had been there for the past four months and on Saturday evenings usually came with a pensioner or a soldier. The man generally left on Monday and Chapman would stay in the place for the early part of the week, paying eight pence a night. Last Monday night the two left together, and she was not seen again till about half-past eleven last Friday night, when she reappeared, and in answer to inquiries said she had been in the infirmary. This was probably the truth, as the deputy of the lodging house had during her absence found letters which showed she had been under medical treatment at St. Bartholomew's Hospital. She had probably come out of the infirmary with little or nothing in her pocket, and after putting in an appearance at the lodging house passed out into the street till just before two on the fatal Saturday morning, when she returned eating baked potatoes, and according to the deputy somewhat the worse for drink. This we have some reason to believe was a mistake on his part. The woman was probably quite sober and wanted a bed. She passed downstairs into the kitchen, and a demand was made for payment for the bed. "I haven't got enough," she replied, and turned to go out again into the street. "Keep my bed for me," said the poor creature, "I shan't be long; I won't be long Brummy," she added to the watchman as she passed out; "See that Jim keeps my doss for me." That was just before two o'clock last Saturday morning. About a quarter before six she was found in a dirty little yard up in a muddy corner beneath some broken palings, her head nearly severed from her body, and her person mutilated in a manner too horrible for description.

How came she there, and who was her assassin? These are the questions that are now being discussed over the East of London with a degree of excitement and agitation quite distressing in its intensity, and as we shall presently show, with effects in themselves not a little serious and alarming.

THE RIPPER REPORTS

There can be little reasonable doubt that the unfortunate woman went out into the streets to obtain the price of her bed; that she went in the ordinary way of her outcast sisterhood into this little back yard, as it is likely enough her wont had been, and there in the grey dawn, under the back windows of houses crowded with people she suddenly found herself in the clutches of a homicidal maniac. Before she had time to utter so much as a cry or make a resisting movement, her throat was cut. She was treated, in fact, precisely as poor Nichols had been in a neighbouring street within a few days. So far as can be made out, there is really no reason whatever to suppose the murder was committed elsewhere and the victim carried here, or that any "gang" was concerned in it. In all human probability the hundred and fifty police who, we are credibly informed, have been drafted down into this neighbourhood for special duty in connection with this shocking affair to have pit their wit against the ferocious cunning of a monomaniac, who in all ordinary respects is, it may be, perfectly sane and seemingly quiet and inoffensive. The marvellous astuteness and deep cunning of certain phases of madness are of course perfectly familiar to doctors, and the very fact of a person's being taken by lunacy out of the range of the motives, the fears, and the agitations which would beset a sane mind, if we can conceive a sane mind planning and executing such a scheme, would no doubt tend to give the calm audacity which has hitherto baffled all attempts to solve these frightful riddles.

Number 29, Hanbury-street, is a house let out to various tenants, like a great many of the houses about there. The different occupants fasten their own doors if they think proper; but as they come home at night and got out in the morning at all sorts of hours, according to their occupations, the front door is left unfastened. Anybody is free to walk through the house passage into the back yard, and it is not uncommon in all parts of London for homeless persons to creep in and sleep in passages and staircases thus left. In this very house only a short time since one of the residents says a man slept on the stairs certainly one night, and probably more than one. Under such circumstances, of course anybody passing through into the yard would attract no attention. One lodger went out at four, and saw nothing amiss. The landlady's son, who is engaged in Spitalfields Market, is said to have looked round the yard before going to his business at ten minutes to five, as there had been some sort of robbery there recently, and at the time there was nothing noticeable. About six o'clock, however, John Davis, who lives at the top of the house, before setting out to his work happened to go into the yard, and the found the body of the woman rushed frantically off for the police. His alarm soon routed general excitement, and in the horror and agitation which ensued there were, it appears, imaginative minds capable of adding a gruesome touch or two even to such a tragedy. The body undoubtedly was dreadfully mutilated, but some of the details published are unquestionably exaggerations, to say the least of it. But beyond all question the poor creature was out and gashed horribly, and presented a sight indescribably shocking. The police and the divisional surgeon soon arrived on the scene, and the body was borne away on a stretcher to the very mortuary from which only a day or two before Mary Anne Nichols had been carried out.

The excitement has been intense. The house and the mortuary were besieged by people, and it is said that during a part of Saturday people flocked in in great numbers to see the blood-stained spot in the yard, paying a penny each. In the White-chapel-road "Lines on the Terrible Tragedy" were being sold, and men with the verses round their hats were singing them to the tune of "My Village Home." A wretched waxwork show had some horrible picture out in front, and people were paying their pence to see representations of the murdered woman within. The result of all this sort of thing working up the excitement natural to the shocking tragedy is startlingly illustrated by the experience of the divisional surgeon of the police, Mr. Phillips says that he and his assistant were out of their beds nearly all Saturday night in attendance of cases of assault, some of them of the most serious character, arising directly or indirectly out of the intense excitement occasioned by the discussion of this affair. Unless Mr. Phillip's experience is different from that of other medical men in the locality, this certainly shows that even so dreadful a murder as that which has just taken place is the only part of the mischief such an occurrence originates.

Another account says that at five minutes to six on Saturday morning a man named John Davis, living at 29, Hanbury-street, Spitalfields, discovered that a woman had been murdered in the yard at the rear of that house, and that when the police were called in the circumstances attending her murder made it clear that she was another victim of the miscreant who murdered Mary Ann Nichols in Buck's-row, Whitechapel, only a week previously. The same horrible ferocity had been exhibited in the commission of the crime, and the victim was again an "unfortunate," so poor that robbery could scarcely be suggested as a motive for the murder. The house, 29, Hanbury-street (which is not half a mile from Buck's row) is let out by rooms to several people, all very poor and struggling. The front parlour is in the occupation of a Mrs. Harriman, who uses it as a shop for the sale of cats' meat. She and her son also sleep in the room. The back parlour is a sort of sitting room for the landlady and her family, and looks out upon a yard, at the further side of which stands a shed. The passage of the house leads directly to the yard, passing the door of the front parlour, the yard being about four feet below the level of the passage, and reached by two stone steps. The position of the steps creates a recess on their left, the fence between the yard and the next house being about three feet from the steps. In this recess John Davis, as he crossed the yard at five minutes to six o'clock, saw the body of a woman, horribly mutilated, and her throat so terribly gashed that the head was severed from the trunk. Davis seems at once to have run out and called in Police-constable Pinnock, 238 H, who sent information to the station in Commercial-street. Inspector Chandler, on duty, with others, hurried to the place, and before the body was removed from its position the divisional surgeon, Mr. George Bagster Phillips; of Spital-square, was called to examine it. The fiendish character of the mutilation then became revealed. There was no doubt, he said that the throat was first cut and the stomach subsequently mutilated. As in the case of Mary Ann Nichols, in Buck's-row the body had been ripped up. The body was removed as soon as possible to the mortuary of the parishes of Whitechapel and Spitalfields, in Old Montague-street, and placed in a shell - the same in which a week before the corpse of the previous victim had been placed. The precise description of the body was quickly made out and before ten o'clock it was identified as that of Annie Chapman alias "Sivvey," a name by which she had become known through living with a sieve maker. One of the same class as Mary Ann Nichols, her usual places of abode were also in the common lodging-houses of Spitalfields and Whitechapel. A stout, well-proportioned woman of about five feet in height, who was described as quiet and as one who had "even letter days."

Detective Inspector Abberline of Scotland-yard, who had been detailed to make special inquiries as to the murder of Mary Ann Nichols, at once took up the inquiries with regard to the new crime, the two being obviously the work of the same hands. He held a consultation with Detective Inspector Henson, J division, in whose district the murder in Buck's-row was committed, and with Acting Superintendent West, in charge of the H division. The result of that consultation was an agreement in the belief that the crimes were the work of one individual only, and that, notwithstanding many misleading statements and rumours - the majority of which in the excitement of the time had been printed as facts - the murders were committed where the bodies had been found, and that no "gang" were the perpetrators. It having been stated that the woman must have been murdered elsewhere and her body deposited in the yard, the house door giving access to the passage and the yard being never locked, the most careful examination was made of the flooring of the passage and the walls, but not a trace of blood was found to support such a theory. It is moreover considered impossible that a body could have been carried in without arousing from their sleep Mrs. Harriman and her son, past whose bedroom door the murderer had to go. There is no doubt that the deceased was acquainted with the fact that the house door was always open or ajar, and that she and her murderer stealthily passed into the yard. Although, as in the case of Mary Ann Nichols, a very small quantity of blood was found on the ground (which would lead to the supposition that the murder was committed elsewhere), its absence is accounted for by the quantity the clothes would absorb. The throat being so completely severed, it is the opinion of medical experts, would preclude the slightest cry, and the tenants of the house agree that nothing was heard to create alarm. The back room on the first floor, which had an uninterrupted view of all the yard, is a bedroom, and was tenanted by a man named Alfred Walker and his father, neither of whom "heard a sound." John Richardson, living in the house, stated that he, in accordance with his usual practice, entered the place which on his way to work at Leadenhall Market, and at that time, 4.50, he was certain no one was in the yard. Albert Cadosh, who lodges next door, had occasion to go into the adjourning yard at the back at 5.25, and states that he heard a conversation on the other side of the palings, as if between two people. He caught the word "No," and fancied he subsequently heard a slight scuffle, with the noise of a falling against the palings, but thinking that his neighbours might probably be out in the yard, he took no further notice and went to his work. The police have been unable to discover any person who saw the deceased alive after two a.m. about which time she left the lodging-house, 35, Dorset-street, because she had not 4d. to pay for her bed. No corroboration of the reported statement that she was served in a public-house at Spitalfields Market, on its opening at 5 a.m., could be gained, nor of the sensational report that the murderer left a message on a wall in the yard, which was made out to read "Five: 15 more, and then I give myself up." With respect to the statement that a knife and apron were discovered beneath the body of Annie Chapman, it may be said that there was no knife; and though an apron was found it belonged to a man in the house, and no importance is attached to the fact, the police not having taken possession of it. It seems certain that the deceased was robbed of three rings she wore on the left hand, and which the murderer mistook for gold, though it is said that to a woman in the lodging house she admitted they were only brass. It is possible of course that the murderer before discovering the fact may endeavour to dispose of the rings, and the police will be glad to receive any information on such a matter.

The Deptford police yesterday made a communication to the effect that a man had been arrested by them under suspicious circumstances. Up to a late hour, however, he had not been brought up to Commercial-street police station for the purpose of identification.

Amongst other statements, the following has been made: John Davis, who was first to make the shocking discovery says - Having had a cup of tea at about six o'clock, I went down stairs. When I got to the end of the passage I saw a female lying down, her clothing disarranged, and her face covered with blood. I heard no noise, nor had my missus. I saw Mr. Bailey's men waiting at the back of the Black Swan ready to go into their work - making packing cases. I said to them, "Here's a sight! A woman must have been murdered!" I then ran to the police station in Commercial-road, and I told them there what I had seen, and some constables came back with me. I did not examine the woman when I saw her - I was too frightened at the dreadful sight. Our front door at 29, Hanbury-street is never bolted, and anyone has only to push it open and walk through to the gate at the back yard. Immoral women have at times gone there. No lock has ever been placed on the front door; at least, I have never seen one; but it is only a fortnight ago that I came to lodge there. I have known people open the passage door and walk through into the yard when they have had no right there. There are about fifteen altogether living in the house.

Mrs. Richardson, the landlady at 29, Hanbury-street, the house where the body of deceased was found, in the course of an interview said: "I have lived at this house fifteen years, and my lodgers are poor but hardworking people. Some have lodged with me as long as twelve years. They mostly work at the fish market or the Spitalfields market. Some of the carmen in the fish market go out to work as early as 1 a.m., while others go out at 4 and 5, so that the place is open all night, and anyone can get in. It is certain that the deceased came voluntarily into the yard, as if there had been any struggle it must have been heard. Several lodgers sleep at the back of the house, and some had their windows open, but no noise was heard from the yard. One of my lodgers, a carman, named Thompson, employed at Goodson's, in Brick-lane, went out at 4 o'clock in the morning. He did not go into the yard, but he did not notice anything particular in the passage as he went out. My son John came in at ten minutes to 5, and he gave a look round before he went to market. He went through the yard, but no one was there then, and everything was right. Just before 6 o'clock, when Mr. Davis, another of my lodgers, came down, he found the deceased lying in the corner of the yard, close to the house and by the side of the step. The lower part of her body was uncovered. There was not the slightest sign of a struggle, and the pool of blood which flowed from the throat after it was cut, was close to the step where she lay. She does not appear to have moved an inch after the fiend struck her with the knife. She must have died instantly. The murderer must have gone away from the spot covered with blood. There was an earthenware pan containing water in the yard, but this was not discoloured, and could not, therefore, have been used by the murderer. The only possible clue that I can think of is that Mr. Thompson's wife met a man about a month ago lying on the stairs. This was about four o'clock in the morning. He looked like a Jew, and spoke with a foreign accent. When asked what he was doing there, he replied he was waiting to do a "doss" before the market opened. He slept on the stairs that night, and I believe he has slept on the stairs on other nights. Mrs. Thompson is certain she could recognise the man again both by his personal appearance and his peculiar voice. The police have taken a full and careful description of the man."

The deputy of a lodging house at 30, Dorset-street, stated that Annie Chapman used to lodge there about two years ago with a man called Jack "Sivvy," a sieve maker; hence her nickname Annie Sivvy. She appeared to be a quiet woman, and not given to drinking; in fact, he was quite surprised to hear that she had been drinking the night before her murder. The woman had two children to his knowledge - a boy who was a cripple, and who he believed was at some charitable school, and a daughter who was somewhere in France.

Timothy Donovan, the deputy at the lodging-house, 36, Dorset-street, where the deceased frequently stayed, states that the deceased stayed there on Sunday night last. She had been in the habit of coming there for the past four months. She was a quiet woman, and gave no trouble. He had heard her say she wished she was as well off as her relations, but she never told him who her friends were or where they lived. A pensioner or a soldier usually came to the lodging-house with her on Saturday nights, and generally he stayed until the Monday morning. He would be able to identify the man instantly if he saw him. After the man left on Monday deceased would usually keep in the room for some days longer, the charge being eight pence per night. This man stayed at the house the Saturday to Monday, and when he went the deceased went with him. She was not seen at the house again until Friday night last about half-past eleven o'clock, when she passed the doorway, and Donovan, calling out, asked her where she had been since Monday, and why she had not sleep there, and she replied, "I have been in the infirmary." Then she went on her way in the direction of Bishopsgate-street. About 1.40 a.m., on Saturday morning she came again to the lodging-house and asked for a bed. The message was brought upstairs to him, and he sent downstairs to ask for the money. The woman replied "I haven't enough now, but keep my bed for me. I shan't be long." Then as she was going away she said to John Evans, the watchman. "Brummy, I won't be long. See that Jim keeps my bed for me." She was the worse for drink at the time, and was eating some baked potatoes. He saw nothing of her again until he was called to the mortuary on Saturday morning, when he identified the deceased by her features and her wavy hair, which was turning grey. After the deceased left on Monday last he found two large bottles in the room, one containing medicine, and labelled as follows: "St Bartholomew's Hospital. Take two tablespoonfuls three times a day." The other bottle contained a milky lotion, and was labelled. "St Bartholomew's Hospital. The lotion. Poison." This confirmed her statement that she had been under medical treatment.

A woman named Amelia Farmer gave important information that she had been a fellow lodger with the deceased, and had known her for some considerable time. She stated that the deceased was Annie

Chapman, the wife of a veterinary surgeon, who had died at Windsor about eighteen months ago. She was accordingly taken to the mortuary at half-past eleven o'clock, and immediately recognised her friend, apparently being much touched at the dreadful spectacle. Later on she made a statement of what she knew of the history of the murdered woman. Annie Chapman had for a long time been separated from her husband, a veterinary surgeon at Windsor, by mutual agreement, and had been allowed 10s. a week by him for her maintenance. The money had been sent by post-office order, made payable at the Commercial-street Post-office, and had always come regularly. About eighteen months ago the instalments suddenly ceased, and, upon inquiry being made, it was found that the husband had died. Annie Chapman had two children, but where they were she could not say. The deceased had a mother and sister, who were living in the neighbourhood of Brompton or Fulham. Farmer had been in the habit of writing letters for her friend, but could not remember the exact address of the mother or sister, but thought it was near the Brompton Hospital. Last Monday Chapman had intimated her intention of communicating with her sister saying. "If I can get a pair of boots from my sister I shall go hop picking." Another relation, a brother-in-law of the deceased, living somewhere in or near Oxford-street. Farmer asserted that her murdered friend was apparently a sober, steady-going sort of woman, and one who seldom took any drink. For some time past she had been living occasionally with a man named Ted Stonley, who had been in the militia, but was now working at some neighbouring brewery. Ted Stonley was a good-tempered man, rather tall, about 5ft. 10in., fair, and of florid complexion. He was the last man in the world to have quarrelled with Chapman, nor would he have injured her in any way. At the beginning of the week the deceased had been rather severely knocked about in the breast and face by another woman of the locality through jealousy in connection with Ted Stonley.

As a regular means of livelihood she had not been in the habit of frequenting the streets, but had made antimacassars for sale. Sometimes she would buy flowers or matches with which to pick up a living. Farmer was perfectly certain that on Friday night the murdered woman had worn three rings, which were not genuine, but were imitations, as otherwise she would not have troubled to go out and find money for her lodgings.

Another clue which may prove of value was furnished by Mrs. Fiddymont, wife of the proprietor of the Prince Albert public-house, better known as the "Clean House," at the corner of Brushfield and Stewart streets, half a mile from the scene of the murder. Mrs. Fiddymont states that at seven o'clock on Saturday morning she was standing in the bar talking with another friend, in the first compartment. Suddenly there came into the middle compartment a man whose rough appearance frightened her. He had on a brown stiff hat, a dark coat, and no waistcoat. He came in with his hat down over his eyes, and with his face partly concealed asked for half a pint of four ale. She drew the ale, and meanwhile looked at him through the mirror at the back of the bar. As soon as she saw the woman in the other compartment watching him he turned his back, and got the partition between himself and her. The thing that struck Mrs. Fiddymont particularly was the fact that there were blood spots on the back of his right hand. This, taken in connection with his appearance, caused her uneasiness. She also noticed that his shirt was torn. As soon as he had drunk the ale, which he swallowed at a gulp, he went out. Her friend went out also to watch him.

Great weight is attached to the statement as to the rings which were on the woman's hand before the murder was committed, but which are supposed to have been wrenched off by the murderer before he made good his escape. On Saturday evening a further clue had been gained. It was ascertained that a pawnbroker in Mile-end-road had detained rings which had been presented to him for pledge, but which on being tested had not been found genuine. Should these rings proved to be taken from Annie Chapman, and should Amelia Farmer be able to identify them, a solid trace of the murderer will be obtained which may lead to his capture.

All day yesterday five policemen guarded the scene of the crime in Hanbury-street. No one was admitted unless he resided in the house. In the street half-a-dozen coster mongers took up their stand and did a brisk business in fruit and refreshments. Thousands of respectably dressed persons visited the scene, and occasionally the road became so crowded that the constables had to clear it by making a series of raids upon the spectators. The windows of the adjoining houses were full of persons watching the crowd below. A number of people also visited the house in Dorset-street where the murdered woman lodged.

In the course of the day nearly a dozen persons were arrested and conveyed to the Commercial-street police-station. In the afternoon a vast crowd had collected about the streets, and as each apprehension was made they rushed pell-mell towards the station, obviously under the idea that the murderer of the woman had been caught.

The following is the official telegram wired to every station throughout the metropolis and suburbs:-

"Commercial-street, 8.20 p.m.- Description of a man wanted who entered a passage of the house at which the murder was committed of a prostitute at 2 a.m. the 7th. Age 37; height 5ft. 7in. Rather dark beard and moustache. Dress: Shirt, dark jacket, dark vest and trousers, black scarf and black felt hat. Spoke with a foreign accent."

An inquest will be opened to-day at 10 o'clock at the Lad's Industrial Institute.

Source: *London Daily News*

MONDAY 10 SEPTEMBER 1888

THE SPITALFIELDS MURDER ARREST OF "LEATHER APRON"

The Press Association says:- About nine o'clock this morning a detective arrested the man known as "Leather Apron, "who was wanted in connection with the Whitechapel murder at 22, Mulberry-street, Commercial-street. The real name of the man arrested is John Piser; but his friends deny that he has ever been known under the nickname of "Leather Apron." When the detective called at the house the door was opened by Piser himself. "Just the man I want," said the detective, who charged him on suspicion of being connected with the murder of the woman "Sivey."

The detective searched the house and took away some finishing tools, which Piser is in the habit of using in his work. By trade he is a boot finisher, and for some time has been living at Mulberry-street with his step-mother and a married brother, who works as a cabinet-maker. When he was arrested by the detective this morning his brother was at work, and the only inmates of the house were the prisoner's step-mother, his sister-in-law, and a Mr. Nathan, for whom he has worked.

His mother and his sister-in-law declared positively to a representative of the Press Association that Piser came home at half-past ten on Thursday night and had not left the house since. They further stated that Piser is unable to do much work on account of ill-health, and that he is by no means a strong person, as some time ago he was seriously injured. About six weeks ago he left a convalescent home of which he had been an inmate on account of a carbuncle on his neck. He is about thirty-five years of age.

At the Leman-street police-station, to which Piser was taken, a large force of police were kept in readiness with drawn staves. Only a few persons amongst the crowd outside seemed aware that an arrest had been made; and so quietly did the police act in Mulberry-street that few even in the neighbourhood connected the arrest with the murder.
The police at Leman-street refuse to give any information, and some officials who had come from Scotland-yard denied that such an arrest had been made; but this statement was incorrect.

We learn on inquiry at Scotland-yard that the man known as "Leather Apron" has undoubtedly been arrested; though it is impossible to say, so far, with what offence he is to be charged, or indeed whether any specific charge can be made against him. In all probability he would still be at large, had it not been for the suspicions so widely made known in the public press.

Source: *St James's Gazette*

WEDNESDAY 12 SEPTEMBER 1888

PIZER SET AT LIBERTY
LIGHT ON THE MURDERER'S

THE RIPPER REPORTS

MOVEMENTS

The latest reports as to the search for the murderer are not of a hopeful character. A half-Spaniard and half-Bulgarian, who gave the name of Emanuel Delbast Violenia, waited on the police yesterday. He stated that he, his wife, and two children tramped from Manchester to London with the view of being able to emigrate to Australia, and took up their abode in one of the lodging houses in Hanbury-street. Early last Saturday morning, walking alone along Hanbury-street, he noticed a man and a woman quarrelling in a very excited manner. Violenia distinctly heard the man threaten to kill the woman by sticking a knife into her. They passed on, and Violenia went to his lodging. After the murder he communicated what he had seen to the police.

At one o'clock yesterday afternoon Sergeant Thicke, assisted by Inspector Cansby, placed about a dozen men, the greater portion of whom were Jews, in the yard of the Leman-street police-station. Pizer was the brought out and allowed to place himself where he thought proper among the assembled men. He is a man of short stature, with black whiskers and shaven chin. Violenia was then brought into the yard. Having keenly scrutinised all the faces before him, he went up to Pizer and identified him as the man whom he heard threaten a woman on the night of the murder. Subsequently, cross-examination so discredited Violenia's evidence that it was wholly distrusted by the police, and Pizer was set at liberty.

An important discovery, however, which throws some light upon the movements of the murderer immediately after the committal of the crime, was made yesterday afternoon. In the backyard of the house, 25, Hanbury-street, the next house but one to the scene of the murder, a little girl noticed peculiar marks on the wall and on the ground. She communicated the discovery to Detective-Inspector Chandler, who had just called at the house in order to make a plan of the back premises of the three houses for the use of the coroner at the inquest. The whole of the yard was then carefully examined, with the result that a bloody trail was found distinctly marked for a distance of five or six feet in the direction of the back door of the house. Further investigation left no doubt that the trail was that of the murderer, who, it was evident, after finishing his work, had passed through or over the dividing fence between Nos. 29 and 27, and thence into the garden of No. 25. On the wall of the last house there was found a curious mark, between a smear and a sprinkle, which had probably been made by the murderer, who, alarmed by the blood-soaked state of his coat, took off that garment and knocked it against the wall. Abutting on the end of the yard of this establishment, is an out-of-the-way corner, the police yesterday afternoon found some crumbled paper almost saturated with blood. It was evident that the murderer had found the paper in the yard of 25 and had wiped his hands with it, afterwards throwing it over the wall into Bailey's premises. The general appearance of the bloody trail and other circumstances seem to show that the murderer intended to make his way as rapidly as possible into the street through the house next door but one, being frightened by some noise or light in No. 29 from retreating by the way by which he came.

Some further particulars are forthcoming respecting the strange conduct of Pigott, the man who was apprehended at Gravesend. He was first seen in Gravesend on Sunday afternoon about four o'clock. He then asked four young men, who were standing in the London-road, near Prince-street, where he could get a glass of beer, he having walked from Whitechapel. The young men told him. Following their directions he jumped into a tram car going towards North-Fleet. The young men noticed that he had a bad hand, and that he carried a black bag. He was without this bag when subsequently seen. He left a paper parcel at a fish shop, stating that he was going across the water to Tilbury. Instead of doing so he went to the Pope's Head public house, where his conversation about his hatred of women aroused suspicion, and led to his being detained by the police authorities. Superintendent Berry found the paper parcel at the fish shop to contain two shirts and a pair of stockings, one of the shirts, a blue-striped one, being torn about the breast, and having marks of blood upon it. At the police-station, Pigott first said he knocked down the woman who had bitten his hand in a yard at the back of a lodging house in Whitechapel, but he subsequently said the occurrence took place in Brick-lane. What has become of the black bag which Pigott was seen to have in Gravesend on Sunday is not known. Pigott of late years has followed the business of a publican, and seven or eight years ago he was in a good position, giving £8,000 to go into a house at Hoxton.

THE MORAL OF THE WHITECHAPEL MURDERS

"Not half enough is being done for the wretched." - Morning Post.

The Morning Post, the organ of the Conservative party, has been stirred to write an article on the conditions of the poor in Whitechapel, which shows that a murder sometimes touches a heart indifferent to less violent reminders. Our contemporary says:-

HOW THE POOR LIVE

The veil has been drawn aside that covered up the hideous condition in which thousands, tens of thousands, of our fellow-creatures live, in this boasted nineteenth century, and in the very heart of the wealthiest, the healthiest, the most civilised city in the world. We have all known for many years that deplorable misery, gross crime, and unspeakable vice - mixed and matted together - lie just off the main roads that lead through the industrial quarters of the metropolis. The daily sins, the nightly agonies, the hourly sorrows that haunt and poison and corrupt the ill-fated tenants and sojourners in these homes of degradation and disease have again and again described with more or less truth and force by popular writers; but it is when some crime or accident, more than usually horrible, has given vividness and reality to the previously unrealised picture, that we are brought to feel - what our keenest powers failed adequately to conceive before - how parts of our great capital are honeycombed with cells, hidden from the light of day, where men are brutalised, women are demonised, and children are brought into the world only to be inoculated with corruption, reared in terror, and trained in sin, till punishment and shame overtake them too, and thrust them down to the black depths where their parents lie already lost, or dead to every hope or change of moral recovery and social rescue. Then comes a terrible crime, bringing a revelation that fills every soul with horror, and makes us ask why sleeps the thunder, and how these things can be?

A SAMPLE SLUM

The answer is in the facts disclosed. Take the latest as a sample of the rest. A wretched back street is rowed with houses of the most miserable class. Nearly all of them are let out in lodgings, of a single room, or part of a room. The house where the murder was committed had no less than six families, all toilers for daily bread, some of questionable honesty or sobriety, and all, we may be sure, contaminated in greater or less degree by the vicious surroundings of their distressed home. Loose women have as free run in these abodes as rabbits in a warren. There is a continual coming and going. Precepts of decency are not observed, the standard of propriety is low, the whole moral atmosphere is pestilential. Poverty in its direst form haunts some dwellings, ghastly profligacy defiles others, and this in street after street, alley after alley, cul de sac after cul de sac, garret after garret, and cellar after cellar. Amid such gross surroundings who can be good? With this atrocious miasma continually brooding over them and settling down among them, who can rise to anything better. Morally these people are not only lost - they are dead and buried.

CLAMOURING FOR IMMEDIATE CONSIDERATION

This is the part of the subject that clamours for immediate consideration, these are miseries that need immediate remedy, these are the lamentable conditions of human existence, which may well tax the wisest counsels and the most philanthropic consideration of the best men and women of the day. Side by side with all the luxury, the ease, the magnificence, and abounding plenty of our vast metropolis, are all these pitiable ground-down people bowed with misery, and steeped in crime. Happily there are here and there, like far oft stars in darkest nights, exceptional instances of honesty. What can be done? How shall the help, the sympathy, the succour or the better circumstanced, the wealthy, and the well-to-do, be brought to bear with sweet reclaiming power among these lost ones?

WHAT IS WANTED

It is not so much the truncheon of the policemen that is wanted as the wand, magical in its power and healing in its touch, of higher moral ministries - some centres at intervals in their very midst where the gentle ministrations of Christian love shall never be sought by the weary and heavy laden in vain, where the veriest outcast may knock and feel that there at least are pitying hearts and open hands, the instruments of God in the recovery of man. We take into the reckoning all that is being nobly done for the wretched people, but what we want to urge is that it is not half enough. The saddening sight of pent-up misery which the recent four murders disclose confirm our complaint, that the better off classes have not yet risen to the height of self-denial and charity which the hardness of the lot of these close-packed, hard-working, much-suffering poor require to enable them to break through the fetters that bind them down and gall their necks till they are fain to let things drift, while they, like Lazarus in his grave, are without the wish or power to rise to anything better.

Source: *Pall Mall Gazette*

SATURDAY 15 SEPTEMBER 1888

HANBURY-STREET MURDER

Great excitement was caused in the neighbourhood of Commercial-street Police Station during Monday afternoon on account of the arrival from Gravesend of a suspect whose appearance was alleged to resemble in some respects that of "Leather Apron." This man, whose name is William Henry Pigott, was taken into custody on Sunday night at the Pope's Head public-house Gravesend. Attention was first attracted to Pigott because he had some bloodstains on his clothes.

On approaching the man, who seemed in a dazed condition, the sergeant of police saw that one of his hands bore several recently-made wounds. Being interrogated as to the cause of this Pigott made a somewhat rambling statement to the effect that while going down Brick-lane, Whitechapel, at half past four on Saturday morning he saw a woman fall in a fit. He stooped to pick her up, and she bit his hand. Exasperated at this he struck her, but seeing two policemen coming up he then ran away.

Mrs. Fiddymont, who is responsible for the statement respecting a man with blood-stained hand resembling "Leather Apron" being at the Prince Albert public-house on Saturday, was sent for, as were also other witnesses likely to be able to identify the prisoner; but after a very brief scrutiny, it was the unanimous opinion that Pigott was not "Leather Apron." Pigott's mind was found to be unhinged.

AT THE INQUEST

On the body of the poor woman, on Monday, Mr. Wynne E. Baxter, the Coroner, was commendably acute. For instance, he promptly said two witnesses of importance ought to be forthcoming. These were two men who worked for Mr. Bailey, packing-case maker, of Hanbury-street, and who were called by John Davis to see the dead body in the back yard, and did so from the passage.

Evans, night watchman at the place where Annie Chapman lodged, said a pensioner who visited the woman called last Saturday afternoon to inquire about her, and left when he heard of her death. Tim Donovan, the deputy, described the pensioner as about forty-five years of age and about 5ft. 8in. in height. At times he had the appearance of a dock labourer and at others the appearance of something better. The inquest was resumed on Wednesday.

THE RIPPER REPORTS

THE TRAIL OF BLOOD

The police ought surely to have discovered themselves what a little girl found out on Tuesday - via., the peculiar marks in the yard of 25, Hanbury-street, two doors from the scene of murder. These marks led to the discovery of a trail of blood from No. 25, against the wall of which a blood-stoned coat had been smeared; to the finding in the yard of Mr. Bailey, the packing-case maker, of some crumpled paper saturated with blood, presumably used by the murderer. On reaching the yard of No. 25 he, it is believed, made for the back door, and then, suddenly remembering his bloodstained appearance, he must have hesitated a moment, and then, catching sight of the pieces of paper lying about, doubtless retraced his steps to the end of the yard, and there sought to remove the bloodstains.

THE MAN "WANTED"

The following official notice has been circulated throughout the metropolitan police district and all police-stations throughout the country: - "Description of a man who entered a passage of the house at which the murder was committed at two a.m. on the 8th. - Age, thirty-seven; height, 5ft. 7in.; rather dark beard and moustache. Dress. - Shirt, dark jacket, dark vest and trousers, black scarf, and black felt hat. Spoke with a foreign accent."

From inquiries which have been made in Windsor it seems that the deceased was the widow of a coachman in service at Clewer.

Source: *Penny Illustrated Paper*

THE RIPPER REPORTS

MONDAY 24 SEPTEMBER 1888

THE POLICE AND THE EAST-END TRAGEDIES

The Daily News, commenting on the proceedings at the adjourned inquest on the body of Mary Ann Nicholls, on Saturday points out that the Coroner rejected the theory of either robbery or jealousy. So far as can be gathered from his summing-up he is disposed to attribute these outrages to a kind of anatomical body snatcher, who wished to carry away some part of the remains, and who, in Chapman's case, apparently succeeded in his object. These are hardly to be dignified with the name of speculations. They are the merest guesses.

We are all at fault, the police, of course, more conspicuously than the rest of us. They have nothing to suggest, and in the case of Nicholls, to judge by an observation of Inspector Helson on Saturday, they have no hope of further evidence. The evidence they have offered is of the most elementary description. It hardly extends beyond the finding of the body. It exemplifies their worst fault in its want of constructive ingenuity. They cannot put two and two together and proceed from one ascertained fact to a number of hypotheses that might lead them to the next stage of a demonstration. The French police, according to what is related of them, at any rate according to what is fabled by M. Gaborian, have this power in an eminent degree. We all know what M. Lecoq made of a few foot-prints. The Australian savage, it has been said, can follow a trail if only it has been brushed by a rabbit's foot. The London police are not like the Australian savage. They prefer the footprint of the elephant. At Whitechapel the clue must start from a space not more than 200 yards square. Can no one find it? The committee of residents might do worse than invite a private agency to try.

The Daily Chronicle remarks that is has been supposed by some people that all the four murders committed within the last few months at the East-end of London might safely be attributed to the same person or persons. "There are no grounds, though, that we can discover for connecting the stabbing of Emma Elizabeth Smith last Easter Monday with the three crimes that followed after a somewhat long interval. Smith herself lived long enough to state that her fatal injuries were the work of several men, who robbed her.

We cannot believe, after the surgical evidence which has been given, that there was more than one man engaged in the awful scene enacted in Hanbury-street at all events; and Martha Tabram's murder on the landing of an inhabited house also forbids the assumption that she went thither in company with more than one person."

Source: *The Globe*

SATURDAY 29 SEPTEMBER 1888

CORONER WYNNE-BAXTER ON THE WHITECHAPEL MURDERS

The able Coroner for South-east Middlesex, Mr. Wynne E. Baxter, last Saturday brought to a close the inquiry into the death of Mary Ann Nichols, the discovery of whose dead body in a Whitechapel street was depicted in The Penny Illustrated Paper of Sept.8.

Coming to a consideration of the perpetrator of the murder, the shrewd Coroner said: It seems astonishing at first though that

THE CULPRIT

should have escaped detection, for there must surely have been marks of blood about his person. If, however, blood was principally on his hands, the presence of so many slaughter-houses in the neighbourhood would make the frequenters of this spot familiar with blood-stained clothes and hands, and his appearance might in that way have failed to attract attention while he passed from Buck's-row in the twilight into Whitechapel-road, and was lost sight of in the morning's market traffic. We cannot altogether leave unnoticed the fact that the death that you have been investigating is one of four presenting many points of similarity, all of which have occurred within the space of about five months, and all within a very short distance of the place where we are sitting.

ALL FOUR VICTIMS

were women of middle age, all were married, and had lived apart from their husbands in consequence of intemperate habits, and were at the time of their death leading an irregular life, and eking out a miserable and precarious existence in common lodging-houses. In each case there were abdominal as well as other injuries. In each case the injuries were inflicted after midnight, and in places of public resort, where it would appear impossible but that almost immediate detection should follow the crime; and in each case the inhuman and dastardly criminals are at large in society.

EMMA ELIZABETH SMITH,

who received her injuries in Osborn-street on the early morning of Easter Tuesday, April 3, survived in the London Hospital for upwards of twenty-four hours, and was able to state that she had been followed by some men, robbed and mutilated, and even to describe imperfectly one of them.

MARTHA TABRAM

was found at three a.m. on Tuesday, Aug. 7, on the first-floor landing of George-yard-buildings, Wentworth-street, with thirty-nine punctured wounds on her body. In addition to these, and the case under your consideration, there is the case of

ANNIE CHAPMAN,

still in the hands of another jury. The instruments used in the two earlier cases are dissimilar. In the first it was a blunt instrument, such as a walking-stick; in the second, some of the wounds were thought to have been made by a dagger; but in the two recent cases the instruments suggested by the medical witnesses are not so different. Dr. Llewellyn says

THE INJURIES OF NICHOLS

could have been produced by a strong-bladed instrument, moderately sharp. Dr. Phillips is of opinion that those on Chapman were by a very sharp knife, probably with a thin, narrow blade, at least six to eight inches in length, probably longer. The similarity of the injuries in the two cases is considerable. There are bruises about the face in both cases; the head is nearly severed from the body in both cases; and those injuries again, have each case been

PERFORMED WITH ANATOMICAL KNOWLEDGE.

Dr. Llewellyn seems to incline to the opinion that the abdominal injuries were first, and caused instantaneous death; but, if so, it seems difficult to understand the object of such desperate injuries to the throat, or how it comes about that there was so little bleeding from the several arteries that the clothing on the upper surface was not stained, and, indeed, very much less bleeding from the abdomen than from the neck. Surely it may well be that, as in the case of Chapman, the dreadful wounds to the throat were inflicted first and the others afterwards. This is a matter of some importance when we come to consider what possible motive there can be for all this ferocity. Robbery is out of the question; and there is nothing to suggest jealousy; there could not have been any quarrel, or it would have been heard. I suggest to you as a possibility that these two women may have been

MURDERED BY THE SAME MAN WITH THE SAME OBJECT,

and in the case of Nichols the wretch was disturbed before he had accomplished his object; and having failed in the open street he tries again, within a week of his failure, in a more secluded place. If this should be correct, the audacity and daring are equal to its maniacal fanaticism and abhorrent wickedness. But this surmise may or may not be correct, the suggested motive may be the wrong one; but one thing is very clear - that a murder of a most atrocious character has been committed.

REPETITION OF THE WHITECHAPEL MURDER AT GATESHEAD

THE RIPPER REPORTS

We regret to have to report that Jane Beatmoor, twenty-eight years of age, was murdered at Birtley, near Gateshead, last Saturday night or Sunday morning. It appears that she was in delicate health, and had been at the Gateshead Dispensary on Saturday for medicine, and that on the road home she called at several farms.

At half-past seven o'clock she left the house of an acquaintance, Mrs. Newall, evidently with the intention of returning home. She had not arrived at eleven o'clock, and her mother and stepfather went to look for her, without success.

Early on Sunday morning, a miner named John Fish, going to work, found the body of the young woman at the bottom of a railway embankment in a horribly mutilated condition. The lower part of her body had been cut open, and the entrails torn out. She was also cut about the face. The doctor expressed the opinion that the cuts had been made with a knife.

The affair caused quite a panic in the district, the resemblance to the Whitechapel murders at first encouraging the idea that the murderer who has been at work in London has travelled down to the north of England.

Source: *Penny Illustrated Paper*

THE RIPPER REPORTS

ELIZABETH STRIDE

Died: 30 September 1888

CATHERINE EDDOWES

Died: 30 September 1888

THE DOUBLE EVENT

MONDAY 1 OCTOBER 1888

THE WHITECHAPEL ATROCITIES
TWO MORE WOMEN MURDERED
HORRIBLE MUTILATION
DESCRIPTION OF THE SUPPOSED CULPRIT

Yesterday morning the Metropolis was thrown into a state of renewed consternation by the announcement that the bodies of two more murdered women had been discovered in the East End. This report, unhappily, proved to be too true, and the terrible character of the crimes is intensified by the circumstance that the locality and manner in which the murders were committed point very strongly to the conclusion that the miscreant who was responsible for at least two of the previous murders is also guilty of those crimes. It will be remembered that the

FIRST OF THE SERIES

of murders was committed so far back as last Christmas, when a woman, whose identity was never discovered, was found murdered in or contiguous to the district known as Whitechapel. There were circumstances of peculiar barbarity about the mode in which the body was treated. This fact did not attract so much attention at the time as it did when, on August 7th last, a woman named Martha Turner, aged 35 years, was found dead on the first-floor landing of some model dwellings in Spitalfields, with thirty-nine bayonet or dagger wounds on the body. On the 31st of the same month the woman Nichols, an unfortunate, was found dead in Buck's-row, Whitechapel. With this probably begins

THE SERIES OF CRIMES

which have lately horrified and terrified the public, for the mutilation of the body was done with so much technical skill and audacity as to suggest a definite but extraordinary, and at that time unexplained, purpose. What that object was, the Coroner recently suggested in the summing up at the inquest on the woman Chapman, who was murdered in the same district and under similar circumstances on September 8. That crime created almost a panic, which had scarcely died away, when it became known yesterday that two more murders of apparently the same kind had been committed under circumstances detailed hereunder.

THE MITRE SQUARE TRAGEDY

The Central News says:- The circumstances connected with the murders committed on Saturday night or early on Sunday morning do not differ materially from those of recent occurrence, except perhaps that the Mitre Square crime was perpetrated with bestial ferocity and reckless daring and rapidity exceeding that exhibited by the fiend who despatched and mutilated poor Annie Chapman in the gloomy backyard in Hanbury Street on the 8th September. Mitre Square is a sort of huge yard about 120 feet square, and there are three entrances to it, the principal being from Mitre Street, which is broad enough to accommodate two vehicles abreast. There is also a short covered court, about twenty yards long, leading into St. James's Place, another square, popularly known as

THE "ORANGE MARKET"

in the centre of which is a urinal, a street fire station, consisting simply of a waggon on wheels, and also a permanent street fire station in course of erection. There is also a fire-escape there at night, and three men of the Metropolitan Brigade are always on duty until daylight. Another passage, thirty to forty yards long, open to the sky, known as Church Passage, leads into Duke Street. Two sides of Mitre Square are occupied by the warehouse of Messrs Kearney and Tonges, tea and coffee merchants, and a private house occupied by a city constable named Pearce. The third side is occupied by the warehouse of Messrs Horner and Sons, drug merchants. On the fourth side where the roadway leads into Mitre Street one corner is occupied by Messrs Walter Williams and Co., and the opposite corner is

USED AS A WORKSHOP,

and is locked up at night. Next to it are three empty houses, the backs of which look into the square. During business hours the square is extensively used, but after six o'clock is comparatively deserted, and, according to people in the vicinity, it is about as quiet a place as could be found in the City of London. it may be added that the square is well lighted, there being one standard lamp in the square itself, another fixed to the wall at the left hand entrance from Mitre Street, a third at the corner of the court at the St. James's Place end, and two more fixed in the wall in Church Passage, one being placed at each end, so that altogether there are five lamps throwing their light into the square.

DISCOVERY OF THE BODY

At a quarter to two o'clock yesterday morning, City Constable Watkins, 881, was on his beat, and as he passed through Mitre Square he saw a body lying in the south-west corner. He had passed through the square about fifteen minutes previously, and he is certain that then there was nobody there. The corpse was that of a woman, and it was lying on its back in the south-west corner of the foot way, with the head toward a hoarding, and her feet to the carriageway. The head was inclined on the left side and both the arms were extended outward, the left leg was extended straight out and the right leg was bent away from the body. After the first shock of the discovery, the constable bent down and felt the body, which was found to be quite warm.

BLOOD WAS ALL AROUND

and on the body, but it had not congealed. Watkins immediately ran across to George James Norris, a night watchman, in the employ of Messrs Kearney, and sent him to Dr Sequeira's at 34 Jewry Street, and then proceeded to call up Constable Pearce, who lives in one of the houses in the square itself. The constables then returned to the southwest corner, and, throwing the light of their lanterns fully upon it, found to their horror that the woman's throat was cut from ear to ear and half way round the head. The clothes had been raised to the chest, and more horrible still, the body had been completely ripped up from the pelvis right up to the chest, the flaps of flesh being turned back and revealing the intestines. In addition to these fearful injuries a portion of the right ear was also cut off, and

THE NOSE WAS SLASHED

half way through. The face was also slashed and cut about in the most brutal fashion, and a portion of the intestines was also placed on the neck. Dr. Sequeira arrived at five minutes to two o'clock, and shortly after that time Major Smith, Assistant Chief Commissioner of the City Police; Detective-Inspector McWilliam, chief of the City Detective Department; Superintendent Forster and Inspector Collard, of Bishopsgate Street Station, were on the spot. They had been preceded, however, by Dr Brown, surgeon to the City Police force, while Dr. Phillips, of Spital Square, surgeon to the H division of Metropolitan Police, who had previously examined the body of the woman found in Berner Street was also present. The doctors proceeded at once to make an examination of the body. It was

LYING IN A POOL OF BLOOD,

which had flowed from the terrible wound in the throat, and there was also a considerable quantity round the abdomen. The ground around was eagerly examined by the police, but it soon became clear that the murderer had carefully avoided treading in the blood, and consequently no footmarks could be seen. At the conclusion of this preliminary examination the body was removed to the City Mortuary of Golden Lane, where in the course of the afternoon, an exhaustive post mortem examination was made. As soon as the corpse had been removed from Mitre Square, the south-west corner was carefully washed down, in order to disappoint morbid sightseers, and it was not long before all traces of the awful crime had been removed. A sketch of the place was also made under the direction of the police in charge of the case.

THE VICTIM

The following is the official description of the body and clothing of the woman:- "Age about 40, length 5 feet, dark auburn hair, hazel eyes. Dress - Black jacket, with imitation fur collar, three large metal buttons; brown bodice, dark green chintz (with Michaelmas and Gordon lily pattern) skirt, three flounces; thin white vest, light drab lindsey underskirt, dark green alpaca petticoat, whith chemise; brown ribbed stockings, mended at feet with piece of white stocking, black straw bonnet, trimmed with black beads and green and black velvet; large white handkerchief round neck, a pair of men's old lace boots and a piece of coarse white apron. The deceased had "O" on left forearm tattooed in blue.

THE BERNER ST. MURDER

The scene of the other outrage, says the Press Association, is a narrow court in Berner Street, a quiet thoroughfare running from Commercial Road down to the London, Tilbury, and Southend Railway. At the entrance to the court are a pair of large wooden gates, in one of which is a small wicket for use when the gates are closed. At the hour when the murderer accomplished his purpose these gates were open; indeed, according to the testimony of those living near the entrance to the court they are seldom closed. For a distance of 18 or 20 feet from the street there is a dead wall on each side of the court, the effect of which is to enshroud the intervening space in absolute darkness after sunset. Further back some light is thrown into the court from the windows of

A WORKMEN'S CLUB,

which occupies the whole length of the court on the right, and from a number of cottages occupied mainly by tailors and cigarette makers on the left. At the time when the murder was committed, however, the lights in all the dwelling-houses in question had been extinguished, whilst such illumination as came from the club being from the upper story would fall on the cottages opposite and would only serve to intensify the gloom in the rest of the court. From the position in which the body was found it is believed that the moment the murderer had got his victim in the dark shadow near the entrance to the court, he threw her to the ground, and with one gash severed her throat from ear to ear. The hypothesis that the wound was inflicted after and not before the woman fell is supported by the fact that there are

SEVERAL BRUISES

on her left temple and left cheek, thus showing that force must have been used to prostrate her, which would not have been necessary had her throat been already cut. When discovered the body was lying as if the woman had fallen forward, her feet being a couple of yards from the street, and her head in a gutter which runs down the right hand side of the court close to the wall. The woman lay on her left side, face downwards, her position being such that, although the court at that part is only nine feet wide, a person walking up the middle might have passed the recumbent body without notice. The condition of the corpse, however, proves pretty conclusively that no considerable period elapsed between the committal of the murder and the discovery of the body; in fact it is conjectured that

THE ASSASSIN WAS DISTURBED

while at his ghastly work, and made off before he had completed his designs. All the features of the case go to connect the tragedy with that which took place three-quarters of an hour later, a few streets distant. The obvious poverty of the woman, her total lack of jewellery and ornaments, and the soiled condition of her clothing, are entirely opposed to the theory that robbery could have been the motive, and the secrecy and despatch with which the crime was effected are equally good evidence that the murder was not the result of an ordinary street brawl. At the club referred to above the International Workmen's Educational Club, which is an offshoot of the Socialist League, and a rendezvous of a number of foreign residents, chiefly Russians, Poles and

CONTINENTAL JEWS

of various nationalities, it is customary on Saturday nights to have friendly discussions on topics of mutual interest, and to wind up the evening's entertainment with songs, &c. The proceedings commenced on Saturday about 8.30 with the discussion on "The necessity for Socialism amongst Jews." This was kept up until about eleven o'clock, when a considerable portion of the company left for their respective homes. Between twenty and thirty remained behind, and the usual concert which followed was not concluded when the intelligence was brought in by the steward of the club that a woman had been done to death within a few yards of them, and within earshot of their jovial songs. The people residing in the cottages on the other side of the court were all indoors, and most of them

IN BED BY MIDNIGHT.

Several of these persons remember lying awake and listening to the singing, and they also remember the concert coming to an abrupt termination, but, during the whole of the time from retiring to rest until the body was discovered, no one heard anything in the nature of a scream or a woman's cry of distress. It was Lewis Diemschutz, the steward of the club, who found the body. Diemschutz, who is a traveller in cheap jewellery, had spent the day at Westow Hill Market, near the Crystal Palace, in pursuance of his avocation, and had driven home at his usual hour, reaching Berner Street at one o'clock. On turning into the gateway he had some difficulty with his pony, the animal being apparently determined to avoid the right-hand wall. For the moment

DIEMSCHUTZ

did not think much of the occurrence, because he knew the pony was given to shying, and he thought some mud or refuse was in the way. The pony, however, obstinately refused to go straight, so the driver pulled him up to see what was in the way. Failing to discern anything in the darkness. Diemschutz poked about with the handle of the whip, and immediately discovered that some large obstacle was in his path. To jump down and strike a match was the work of a second, and then it became at once apparent that something serious had taken place. Without waiting to see whether the woman whose body he saw was drunk or dead, Diemschutz entered the club by the side door higher up the court, and informed those in the concert-room upstairs that

SOMETHING HAD HAPPENED

in the yard. A member of the club named Kozebrodski, but familarly known as Isaacs, returned with Diemschutz into the court, and the former struck a match while the latter lifted the body up. It was at once apparent that the woman was dead. The body was still warm, and the clothing enveloping it was wet from the recent rain, but the heart had ceased to beat, and the stream of blood in the gutter terminating in a hideous pool near the club door showed but too plainly what had happened. Both men ran off without delay to find a policeman, and at the same time other members of the club who had by this time found their way into the court went off with the same object in different directions. The search was for some time fruitless.

THE POLICE SUMMONED

At last, however, after considerable delay, a Constable was found in Commercial Road. With the aid of a policeman's whistle more constables were quickly on the spot, and the gates at the entrance to the Court having been closed, and a guard set on all the exits of the club and the cottages, the superintendent of the district and the divisional surgeon were sent for. In a few minutes Dr. Phillips was at the scene of the murder, and a brief examination sufficed to show that life had been extinct some minutes. Careful note having been taken of the position of the body, it was removed to the parish mortuary of St. George's-in-the-East, Cable Street, to await identification.

DESCRIPTION OF THE BODY

A representative of the Press Association, who has seen the corpse, stats that the woman appears to be about 30 years of age. Her hair is very dark, with a tendency to curl, and her complexion is also dark. Her features are sharp and somewhat pinched, as though she had endured considerable privations recently - an impression confirmed by the entire absence of the kind of ornaments commonly affected by women of her station. She wore a rusty black dress of a cheap kind of sateen, with a velveteen bodice, over which was a black diagonal worsted jacket with fur trimming. Her bonnet, which had fallen from her head when she was found in the yard was of black crape, and inside, apparently with the object of making the article fit closer to the head, was folded

A COPY OF THE "STAR"

newspaper. In her right hand was tightly clasped some grapes, and in her left hand she held a number of sweet meats. Both the jacket and the bodice were open towards the top, but in other respects the clothes were not disarranged. The linen was clean, and in tolerably good repair, but some articles were missing. The cut in the woman's throat, which was the cause of death, was evidently effected with a very sharp instrument, and was made with one rapid incision. The weapon was apparently drawn across the throat rather obliquely from left to right, the gash being about three inches long and nearly the same depth.

THE BODY IDENTIFIED

A telegram received early this morning says:- The woman murdered in Berner Street has been identified as Elizabeth Stride, who, it seems, had been leading a gay life, and had resisted latterly in Flower and Dean Street. Inquiries made amongst her associates elicit the fact that the deceased, who was commonly known as "Long Liz," left the house between six and seven o'clock on Saturday night. She then said she was not going to meet anyone in particular. It is stated she was of calm temperament, rarely quarrelling with anyone; in fact she was so good-natured that she would "do a good turn for anyone." Her occupation was that of a charwoman. She had the misfortune of losing her husband in the Princess Alice disaster on the Thames some years ago. She had lost her teeth and suffered from a throat affection.

Source: *Shields Daily Gazette*

MONDAY 1 OCTOBER 1888

MORE HORRORS IN THE EAST-END
TWO WOMEN MURDERED
THE SAME FEARFUL MUTILATION

In the early hours of yesterday morning two more horrible murders were committed in the East-end of London, the victim in both cases belonging, it is believed, to the same unfortunate class. No doubt seems to be entertained by the police that these terrible crimes were the work of the same fiendish hands which committed the outrages which had already made Whitechapel so painfully notorious.

The scenes of the two murders just brought to light are within a quarter of an hour's walk of each other, the earlier discovered crime having been committed in a yard in Berner-street, a thoroughfare out of the Commercial-road, while the second outrage was perpetrated within the City boundary, in Mitre-square, Aldgate. In neither case can robbery have been the motive, nor can the deed be set down as the outcome of an ordinary street brawl. Both have unquestionably been murders deliberately planned, and carried out by the hand of some one who has been no novice to the work; and again it must be added that no reliable clue has yet been obtained.

THE BERNER STREET MURDER

Berner-street is a narrow, badly-lighted, but tolerably respectable street, turning out of the Commercial road, a short distance down on the right-hand side going from Aldgate. It is a street mainly consisting of small houses, but which has lately been brightened and embellished by one of the fine new buildings of the London School Board. Just opposite this is an "International and Educational Club", domiciled in a private house, standing at the corner of a gateway leading into a yard in which are small manufacturing premises and four small houses occupied by Jewish families. The yard gates are usually closed at night, a wicket affording admission to the lodgers and others residing in the houses.

The club was on Saturday evening winding up the Jewish holidays by a lecture on "Judaism and Socialism". A discussion followed, which carried on the proceedings to about half-past twelve, and then followed a general jollification, accompanied, as the neighbours say, by a noise that would effectually have prevented any cries for help being heard by those around. The mirth however was brought to a sudden and dreadful stop.

The steward of the club, who lives in one of the small houses in the yard, and had been out with some sort of a market cart, returned home just before one (Sunday morning). He turned into the gateway, when he observed some object lying in his way under the wall of the club. Unable to see clearly what it was, he struck a match and found that it was a woman. He thought at first she was drunk, and went into the club. Some of the members went out with him and struck another light, and were horrified to find the woman's head nearly severed from her body and blood streaming down the gutter.

The police were summoned, and the poor creature was borne to the St. George's dead house.

IDENTIFICATION OF THE VICTIM

The corpse was still warm, and in the opinion of the medical experts, who were promptly summoned to the place, the deed of blood must have been done not many minutes before. The probability seems to be that the murderer was interrupted by the arrival of the cart, and that he made his escape unobserved, under the shelter of the darkness, which was almost total at the spot. The efforts of the police to trace the murderer have been without result as yet.

The body has been identified as that of a woman named Elizabeth Stride, who had been living in a common lodging-house in Flower and Dean street, and had been in the habit of frequenting this neighbourhood, where it appears she was familiarly known as Long Lizzie. She has a sister living somewhere in Holborn, and her husband, from whom she has been separated for some years, is said to be living at Bath.

The body when found was quite warm. In one hand was clutched a box of sweets, and at her breast were pinned two dahlias; she was respectably dressed for her class, and appears to be about thirty-five years of age. Her height is 5 ft. 5 in. and her complexion and hair are dark. She wore a jacket made of dark diagonal cloth, feather trimmings, a black skirt, velveteen bodice, crape bonnet, side-spring boots, and white stockings. Medical men were busy yesterday in minutely examining the body, and this morning about eleven Mr. Wynne E. Baxter opened an inquest.

The woman's movements have been traced up to a certain point. She left her lodgings in Flower and Dean street between six and seven o'clock on Saturday evening, saying that she was not going to meet any one in particular. From that hour there is nothing certainly known about her up to the time at which her body was found, lifeless indeed, but not otherwise mutilated than by the gash in the throat, which had severed the jugular vein and must have caused instantaneous death.

THE MITRE SQUARE MURDER

At the precise moment that the police were gathering about the place of slaughter in Berner-street, another and more horrible shambles was being provided for their inspection scarcely half a mile away. Shortly before two o'clock Police Constable Watkins (No. 881), of the City Police, was going round his beat, when, turning his lantern upon the darkest corner of Mitre-square, Aldgate, he saw the body of a woman, apparently lifeless, in a pool of blood.

He at once blew his whistle, and several persons being attracted to the spot, he despatched messengers for medical and police aid. Inspector Collard, who was in command at the time at Bishopsgate police-station, but a short distance off, quickly arrived, followed a few moments after by Mr. G. W. Sequeira, surgeon, of 35, Jewry-street, and Dr. Gordon Brown, the divisional police doctor of Finsbury-circus. Chief Superintendent Major Smith, Superintendent Foster, Inspector McWilliams, and Inspector Collard immediately organized a "scouting" brigade, to detect and arrest any suspicious looking character, but no one was taken into custody.

THE RIPPER REPORTS

A SHOCKING SIGHT

In the meantime, Dr. Sequeira and Dr. Gordon Brown made an examination of the body. The sight was a most shocking one. The woman's throat had been cut from the left side, the knife severing the main artery and other parts of the neck. Blood had flowed freely, both from the neck and body, on the pavement. Apparently, the weapon had been thrust into the upper part of the abdomen and drawn completely down, ripping open the body, and, in addition, both thighs had been cut across. The intestines had been torn from the body, and some of them lodged in the wound on the right side of the neck. The woman was lying on her back, with her head to the south-west corner, and her feet towards the carriage way, her clothes being thrown up on to her chest. Both hands were outstretched by her side.

Near where she was lying two or three buttons were picked up, and a small cardboard box containing two pawntickets. The supposition is that her pockets were hastily turned out, either for robbery or to evade suspicion as to the motive for the crime. Dr. Brown having taken a pencil sketch of the exact position in which the body was found, at three o'clock it was removed to the City Mortuary, Golden-lane, to await a coroner's inquest.

DESCRIPTION OF THE DECEASED

The following is the description of the deceased issued by the police authorities with a view to identification:-

"Age about forty, no rings on fingers, black cloth jacket, three large metal buttons down the front, brown bodice, dark green chintz dress, with Michaelmas daisies, golden lily pattern; three flounces, dark linsey skirt, thin white skirt, white chemise, brown ribbed stockings - feet mended with white material, a large white neckerchief round neck, a pair of men's old lace-up boots. Tattoo marks on right forearm, 'T. C.,' the whole of the clothing being very old. She wore also a black straw bonnet, trimmed with black beads." It may be remarked that the police rely principally on the tattoo marks as a means of identification.

RECOGNITION ALMOST IMPOSSIBLE

For several hours yesterday Detective Sergeant Outram, accompanied by another officer, was engaged in making inquiries in the lodging-houses in and around Spitalfields, his object being principally to trace the antecedents of the victim. The pawnbroker's duplicates found near the body bear the dates 31st August and the 28th September. The names given on the tickets were Emily Burrell and Jane Kelly, and the addresses Dorset-street and White's-row, Whitechapel, both being fictitious.

Yesterday afternoon Sergeant Outram accompanied two women and a man from a lodging-house in Spitalfields to the mortuary, one of the former stating her belief that the victim was a Mrs. Kelly. After carefully scrutinizing the features for some time, however, they were unable to give a decided opinion on the matter. It may be mentioned that the tattoo marks on the arm are slightly obscured from view unless the arm is almost fully exposed; and, further, that the nose and face are hacked about to such an extent as to render recognition almost impossible.

STREET SCENES ON SUNDAY

On approaching the scene of the murders yesterday morning it was easy to see, no nearer than a mile away, that something unusual was in the air. Along all the main thoroughfares a constant stream of passengers, all impelled by the same motive of horrified curiosity, was rolling towards the district. The scanty details which had then transpired were eagerly passed from mouth to mouth. There was but one topic of conversation. The few acres of streets and houses between Mitre-square and Berner-street seemed to be a goal for which all London was making.

At the actual places the scene was naturally even more remarkable. The two adits to Mitre-square were blocked by hundreds, and during part of the day thousands, of persons struggling for a place where they could look on the fatal spot. A bar of police kept the crowd outside the square. As one of these was heard inquiring, "What did they want to see? The body had been taken away long ago, and even the blood was all washed away." However, the barren satisfaction of trying to peer round the fatal corner continued to be enjoyed by long lines of men, women, and children, going and returning.

After a glance at one place, the spectators hurried away to the other. From Commercial-road, Berner-street seemed a sea of heads from end to end. At both places on the fringe of the crowd the opportunity for business was seized by costers with barrows of nuts and fruit, a shop even being opened for the purpose in Mitre-street. One remark, overhead in Commercial-road, was in this strain: "Well, it brings some trade down this end anyway."

At nightfall the stream ran the other way. There seemed to be an exodus of dis-reputability from the East. Along the two great avenues leading westward the miserable creatures who apparently have most to fear from the mysterious criminal seemed to be migrating to a safer and better-lit quarter of the metropolis. The noisy groups fleeing before the approaching terrors of night were conspicuous among the better-dressed wayfarers in Holborn and the Strand.

MATTHEWS AND WARREN CALLED UPON TO RESIGN

At three o'clock yesterday afternoon a meeting of nearly one thousand persons took place in Victoria Park, under the chairmanship of Mr. Edward Barrow, of the Bethnal-green-road. After several speeches upon the conduct of the Home Secretary and Sir Charles Warren, a resolution was unanimously passed that it was high time both officers should resign and make way for some officers who would leave no stone unturned for the purpose of bringing the murderers to justice, instead of allowing them to run riot in a civilized city like London. On Mile-end-waste during the day four meetings of the same kind were held and similar resolutions passed. The Whitechapel Vigilance Committee have addressed the Queen a petition praying that, in the interests of the public at large, her Majesty will direct an immediate offer of a large reward for the capture of the murderer.

THE HELPLESS, HEEDLESS, USELESS FIGURE AT THE HOME OFFICE

And where, forsooth, is Mr. Matthews all this while? (asks the Daily Telegraph.) What has her Majesty's Secretary of State for Home Affairs been doing about these very disquieting "home affairs"? We do not even know whether these regularly repeated assassinations of helpless fallen women have sufficed to bring Mr. Matthews up to town, except that the issue of a letter on the subject of offering a ward for the detection of the criminal appears to prove that our Home Secretary has at last heard of what is happening. Truly, the public generally would like at last to know whether Mr. Secretary Matthews still sees "nothing in the present case to justify a departure from the rule."

Justice - personified unhappily just now in the helpless, heedless, useless figure of the Right Honourable Henry Matthews - ought at length to arouse herself, and scour the capital, obliterate the slums, search between the very bricks and mortar, in order to unearth this unspeakable villain whose deeds appall a whole kingdom. If it be of any avail, we would once more urge Mr. Matthews to wake up and do his duty. If it be of no avail then the protest gainst his ineptitude will assuredly become a clamour, a demand, an insistence; and Lord Salisbury will have to dismiss the Minister who has not good sense enough to resign.

Source: *Pall Mall Gazette*

MONDAY 01 OCTOBER 1888

THE DEVON EVENING EXPRESS

The catalogue of horrors perpetrated in the East End of London was painfully augmented yesterday morning, when it was discovered that during the night two women had fallen victim to the fiend who has long since become a terror to the whole neighbourhood. The first body was discovered in a yard in Berner-street, St. George's not far from the locality where the last of the four Whitechapel tragedies had been committed. The body was not mutilated, but the head was nearly severed.

The second body, which was found about half-an-hour later in Mitre-square, Houndsditch, was shockingly mutilated. One of the dead women was identified last night. The police have made one arrest, but taken into custody was released this morning. As in the previous cases, the authorities appear to be entirely without a clue. The "Central News" has telegraphed copies of some extraordinary letters received from an individual signing himself "Jack, the Ripper."

On behalf of the inhabitants of the East-end of London a petition was forwarded to her Majesty on Saturday, urging that a reward should be offered for the detection of the murderer or murderers of the four women who up to date have been killed in Whitechapel, and expressing the conviction that the offender, if undiscovered, would sooner or later commit other crimes of a like nature.

The inadequacy of words was never more widely realised than now, when men find it impossible to express the feelings aroused by the renewal of the Whitechapel murder horrors. The similarity of the circumstances, their loathsomeness, their frightful completeness, and the apparent powerlessness of the police combine to appall the public imagination. But a state of perpetual panic is an impossibility. If people come to entertain the belief that the recognised resources of the Executive are unequal to the work of affording protection, they will resort to the primitive means of individual self-defence.

That would give the lie direct to the existence of our boasted civilisation, and at the same time to accentuate the prevailing sense of the impotence of the metropolitan police system. Next to the feeling of horror inspired by the butcheries themselves is the indignation everywhere felt that, despite the cost involved in their maintenance - despite their number, and the facilities at their disposal - the London police should have failed to run to earth the culprit or culprits concerned in the series of murderous mutilation of which Whitechapel has been the scene.

It will be remembered with what fancied consciousness of superiority most of us joined in censuring the French police for their supposed apathy in connexion with the murder of Mr. O'Neill, a journalist, at Boulogne; how it was said upon all hands that had such an occurrence taken place in this country our detectives would within very few hours, have secured the criminal. This sort of argument, or comment rather, employed to the disparagement of the French police, was, not many months since, very common in the pages of English newspapers. Any egotism upon the score in question has, we think, been pretty well killed out of the country by this time.

There is a great deal to be effected before our own house can be said to be even approximately in order. The British metropolis requires policemen, not the mechanical instruments of a spurious militarism. Let us hope that the official disgrace already incurred will not be augmented; it is impossible that it should be wholly wiped away.

MORE EAST LONDON TRAGEDIES

TWO VICTIMS
ONE BODY MUTILATED
NO ARREST AND NO CLUE
INTENSE EXCITEMENT

Two women were found murdered in two different localities of the East End of London at an early hour yesterday morning. There is little doubt that both crimes were perpetrated by one hand - that which has already in Whitechapel committed many horrible deeds. The police have, however, no evidence of any kind actually establishing it as a fact that the two murders were committed by the same hand. It is just within the bounds of possibility that the two deeds may have been done by different persons, and that their happening within an hour in point of time, and within a distance of about a mile of each other, may be mere coincidences.

But from the fact of the two cases, as well as from what has gone before, it will be perceived that the presumption is almost overwhelming in favour of the supposition that the two are connected, and that these and the previous murders are the work of the same inhuman creature. The facts that have thus far been established are, as in the previous cases, in one sense meagre in the extreme. All that is really known is that two women have been barbarously murdered.

The first of the two murders in point of time took place in Berner-street, a narrow, badly lighted, but tolerably respectable street, turning out of the Commercial-road, a short distance down on the right hand side going from Aldgate. It is a street mainly consisting of small houses, but which has lately been brightened and embellished by one of the fine new buildings of the London School Board. Just opposite this is an "International and Educational Club," domiciled in a private home, standing at the corner of a gateway leading into a yard, in which are small manufacturing premises and four small houses occupied by Jewish families.

The yard gates are usually closed at night, a wicket affording admission to the lodgers and others residing in the houses. Friday or Saturday, however, brought round the close of the Jewish holiday season, and down in this part of London, where the people are largely composed of foreign Jews, some departure from regular habits was more or less general. The International and Educational Club was on Saturday evening winding up the holidays by a lecture on "Judaism and Socialism."

A discussion followed, which carried on proceedings to about half-past twelve, and then followed a sing-song and a general jollification, accompanied, as the neighbours say, by a noise that would effectually have prevented any cries for help by those around. The hilarious mirth, however, was brought to a sudden and dreadful stop. The steward of the club, who lives in one of the small houses in the yard, and had been out with some sort of market cart, returned home just before one. He turned into the gateway, where he observed some object lying in his way, under the wall of the club, and without getting down first prodded it with his whip.

Unable to see clearly what it was, he struck a match, and found it was a woman. He thought at first she was drunk, and went into the club. Some members went out with him and struck another light, and were horrified to find the woman's head nearly severed from her body and blood streaming down the gutter. The police were summoned, and amid intense excitement of the few who were out and about at this unhallowed hour, the poor creature was borne to the St George's dead-house.

That is really all that was known of the matter up till a late hour yesterday, when the body of the murdered woman was identified as that of a woman who has been living in a common lodging-house in Flower and Dean-street, and had been in the habit of frequenting this neighbourhood, where it appears she was familiarly known as Long Lizzie. It subsequently became known that her name was Elizabeth Stride. She has a sister living somewhere in Holborn, and her husband, from whom she has been separated some years, is said to be living at Bath.

Anything beyond this the police superintendent of the H division, at a late hour last evening, said they had been unable to discover. As to the circumstances under which the murder was committed, or the motive for it, they are entirely conjectural, and not the faintest clue to the murderer has been discovered. The body when found was quite warm. In one hand was clutched a box of sweets, and at her breast were pinned two dahlias; she was respectably dressed for her class, and appears to be about 35 years of age, about 5ft. 5in. in height, and of dark complexion. The theory of the police is, and it is generally endorsed by those who have inquired into the matter on the spot, that precisely the same thing was attempted as in the case of the Hanbury street murder, and that but for interruption the same ghastly mutilation would have been perpetrated.

In some way, however, the fiendish assailant was disturbed, as it is assumed the same individual was disturbed in Buck's-row. It is supposed that finding he had not time to complete what he had intended without running the risk of capture, he left his victim very possibly, as it would seem, with little or none of her blood upon him. He may simply have seized her by the pink scarf round her neck, pulled her head hard, and given one horrible gash across the throat from behind, severing the windpipe, and thus at once putting it out of the power of his victim to cry for help, though, as we have seen, even though she had cried out, it is quite possible that no one could have heard it.

All this, however, is mere speculation. Medical men were busy yesterday in minutely examining the body, and this morning at eleven o'clock Mr. Wynne E. Baxter opened an inquest.

It is announced by the police that in all probability the wretch was disturbed in his work, and made off in the direction of the City with the ghoulish thirst for blood still blazing within him; that he beguiled another hapless victim into a dark secluded spot, and then again fell to his butchery.

It is certain at least that within a time just above sufficient to cover the distance in the leisurely manner necessary for the inveiglement of another victim, another victim was found, this time not only was the throat cut but with the face slashed and the bowels frightfully ripped, apparently by two desperate strokes of a strong stout blade. There had been apparently one frightful stab in the breast and a cut downwards, and there had been another gash from below upwards. There seems, in the opinion of the police, reason to believe that in this case the throat was cut as the woman lay on the ground, the flow of the blood from each side of the neck seeming to indicate that she had died without movement, after the cut across the neck, though the part of the face here so slashed - the nose being nearly cut off and a wound having been received under one eye - is thought to show that the unfortunate woman had some premonition of her assailant's purpose, and made a struggle for it.

Struggles, however, were in vain, and so must have been any shriek for help, for the murderer had again selected his spot with a cunning and astuteness that are in themselves among the most bewildering features of these mysterious crimes. If the East of London had been searched for a spot in which to do such a deed, it would have been difficult to find one better adapted.

Between Mitre-street and Duke-street, Aldgate, there is an exceedingly dull, badly-lighted square, having however, three ways out of it. There is an open way into Mitre-street, a long narrow passage leading into Duke-street, and a third leading out into St. James's-street. By either of these, therefore, the assassin could have made his exit had he been again disturbed.

THE RIPPER REPORTS

The spot, though close to Adgate main thoroughfare and lying between two streets busy enough at times, would any morning between one and two of course be quiet enough. Duke-street has long been known as the Jews fruit market, but the property all round has long been undergoing change, and warehouses have taken the place of residences or small shops. This particular square is as dull and lonely a spot as can be found anywhere in London, and it was up in a dark corner of this gloomy retreat that at about a quarter to two a constable of the City Police, who should have patrolled the spot, and, as he affirms, did so not more than twenty minutes previously, found the murdered woman.

The face was gashed, her hair matted in the blood that flooded the pavement, her clothes were thrown up over the body, and the body itself mutilated as we have described. This was the dreadful sight that the constable flashed his lantern upon, and once more it is distressing to have to write that flood of light revealed pretty nearly everything that is positively known upon the subject. Whether the monster this time finished the business he set about, or whether again he was disturbed and fled before he had complete his butchery, can only be conjectured.

He has left no trace, nobody appears to have caught even momentary sight of him, and whether he has this time committed the same mutilation of the unhappy woman can be known only when the results of the post-mortem examination have been made public. So far, however, as the rough examination of the police have enabled them to judge, this was not attempted. It is a simple case of butchery, inhuman beyond the power of words to express, and absolutely purposeless.

Several surgeons were yesterday engaged in the post mortem examination, but, of course, nothing has been allowed to transpire as to the conclusion arrived at. It will be observed that this time the City Police have devolved upon them the principal share in the responsibility for the discovery of the criminal, the crime having been committed within their precincts.

With reference to the Mitre-square tragedy, Police-constable Watkin, 881, says that at half-past one o'clock yesterday morning he went round the square and saw nothing unusual. The place is ill-lighted, for there is only one lamp post and a lantern lamp which projects from the corner of the buildings on one side of the Church-passage. In the City, where the police supervision is as perfect as could possibly be expected, the beats are short, and it is the testimony of the residents that the constable diligently perform their duty.

The constables are under supervision of a sergeant, who is constantly on the alert, and unexpected surveys of the beats are also made by the inspector and the superintendent. There is no reason to doubt that Watkins went into the square at the hour mentioned, and further that a quarter of an hour later, that is, at 1 45 a.m., he re-entered it and then made the fearful discovery. As he was walking near to the south-west corner, quite twenty-five yards removed from the nearest gaslight, he saw the body of a woman, with the clothes disarranged, and with dreadful injuries to the abdomen and to the face.

During the day the police thoroughly searched the empty houses in Mitre-street, and also the yard where the body was found, and took up a grating near the spot where the woman was found. Nothing, however, in the shape of a weapon was found, nor did the investigations lead to anything to throw light upon the matter. The public were not admitted to the square until late in the afternoon, after an official plan of the square had been made for production at the inquest.

As soon as the Berner-street murder was discovered, a messenger was despatched to the police-station in Leman-street, and some constables quickly arrived on the scene with an ambulance, the superintendent and an inspector of the H Division speedily following.

The first precaution taken was to close the doors of the yard and the entrance of the club, the members of which were informed that they could not leave until each individual had been searched and his belongings examined - a process which occupied until nearly five o'clock in the morning, when the men were told that they were free to depart, no clue to the murder having been met with.

Meanwhile, Dr. Phillips, the divisional police surgeon, was fetched from his residence in Spital-square, and shortly after two o'clock that gentleman came upon the scene, accompanied by Drs. Blackwell and Kaye. It was then obvious that the jugular vein and the windpipe had been severed; that the wound, which was nearly three inches long, and ran from left to right, had been caused by a very sharp instrument; and that death must have been instantaneous.

The deceased appeared to be between 35 and 40 years of age, and about 5ft 4in in height. She was of dark complexion, and her hair black and curly. She wore a short black jacket, which was opened at the bosom, as was also her old black velveteen bodice, thus exposing her stays and chemise. Her dress, which was saturated with rain, was of a common black material. She had on two petticoats, one made of poor material resembling sacking, and white cotton stockings; but the clothes were in no way disarranged. Eventually the corpse was conveyed on an ambulance to the parish mortuary of St. George-in-the-East, where it remained in charge of the police. No ring or jewellry of any sort was on the deceased, but two handkerchiefs - one large and one small - were found in her pockets, together with a common brass thimble and a skein of black worsted. Part of an old evening newspaper was found crammed into her bonnet. During the day several women of the unfortunate class saw the body, but failed to identify it, although some of them stated that the features of the poor creature seemed to be familiar to them.

Various theories have been started as to the manner in which the assassin accomplished his purpose, but the hypothesis which finds most favourite is that the miscreant tempted his victim into the darkness of the courtyard, and at an opportune moment put his left around round her neck, cutting her throat with his right. It is believed that no considerable interval elapsed between the committal of the murder and the discovery of the body, and, as previously stated, it is conjectured that the fiendish wretch was disturbed, and was obliged to decamp before completing his ghastly work.

The obvious poverty of the woman and her total lack of valuables destroy the possibility of robbery having been contemplated, and the expedition with which the crime was effected demonstrates that it was the work of no ordinary hand. Indeed, though there is no positive proof, all the circumstances tend to strengthen the supposition that this murderer was also the perpetrator of the horrible deed subsequently committed within the precincts of the city. It is remarkable that the crime could have been done so silently; but a slight scream or cry of distress would probably have been drowned by the noise of the singing at the Workman's Club.

Both Scotland-yard and the City detectives are still busy making inquiries and search, which they hope may throw light on the murders. There is an idea that if the criminal is not a member of a gang he must be a homicidal maniac, lurking alone in some wretched den or untenanted house, otherwise his blood-stained hands and clothing must have attracted attention. There are many such places about Whitechapel, and a search is to be made amongst them, in case such a being should be in existence. The body of the victim of the Mitre-court outrage has not yet been identified.

THE MEDICAL EXAMINATIONS

The post-mortem examination of the woman found in Mitre-square, was made yesterday afternoon at the city mortuary, Golden-lane. The proceedings lasted from 2 30 until 6 o'clock. Dr. Brown, of 17, Finsbury-circus, surgeon to the city police force, conducted the operations, and was assisted by Dr. Seguira, of 34 Jewry-street, and Dr. G. E. Phillips of 3, Spital-square. Dr. Sedgwick Saunders was also present. The doctors decline to say whether any portion of the body is missing, or to give any information as to the autopsy until the inquest is held. This will probably be on Tuesday at the mortuary in Golden-lane.

The "Central News," however, understands that as the result of the post-mortem examination of the body of the woman found in Mitre-square it is shown that the details of the mutilation are almost exactly the same as in the case of Annie Chapman, a certain portion of whose body, it would be remembered, was missing. Up to a late hour last night the victim had not been identified.

With regard to the Berners-street murder, Dr. Blackwell states that he was called to Berners-street by a policeman at ten minutes past one. The woman could not have been dead more than twenty minutes, the body being perfectly warm. Her head had almost been severed from her body, and Dr. Blackwell is of the opinion that the same man committed both the murders, and that he is a maniac who has been accustomed to the use of the knife.

The head of the deceased had evidently been dragged back by means of a silk handkerchief which she wore round her neck, and the throat then cut. The woman's windpipe being completely cut through she was unable to make any sound. Dr. Blackwell thinks that it does not follow that the murderer would be bespattered with blood, for as he was sufficiently cunning in other things he could contrive to avoid coming in contact with the blood by reaching well forward.

THE RIPPER REPORTS

A REMARKABLE LETTER

The "Central News" says that on Thursday last the following letter, bearing the E.C. postmark and directed in red ink, was delivered to this agency: -

"25th September, 1888.

"Dear Boss,

"I keep on hearing the police have caught me, but they won't find me just yet. I have laughed when they look so clever and talk about being on the right track. That joke about Leather Apron gave me real fits. I am down on w——s, and I shan't quit ripping them till I do get buckled. Grand work the last job was I gave the lady no time to squeal. How can they catch me now? I love my work, and I want to start again. You will soon hear of me with my funny little games. I saved some of the proper red stuff in a ginger-beer bottle over the last job to write with, but it went thick, and I can't use it. Red ink is fit enough, I hope. Ha! Ha! The next job I do I shall clip the lady's ears off and send to the police officers, just for folly, wouldn't you? Keep this letter back till I do a bit more work. Then give it out straight. My knife's so nice and sharp I want to get a chance. Good luck

"Yours truly, "Jack the Ripper."

"Don't mind me giving the trade name. Was not good enough to post this before I got all the red ink off my hands, curse it. No luck yet. They say I am a doctor now. Ha! Ha!"

The whole of this extraordinary epistle is written in red ink, in a free, bold, clerkly hand. It was, of course, treated as the work of a practical joker, but it is singular to note that the latest murders have been committed within a few days of the receipt of this letter, that apparently in the case of his last victim the murderer made an attempt to cut off the ears and that he actually did mutilate the face in a matter which he has never before attempted. The letter is now in the hands of the Scotland-yard authorities.

HOMICIDAL MANIA

Dr. George H. Savage, discussing the whole subject of homicidal mania in the "Fortnightly," while admitting that he has never seen among the many murderers he has known a man filled with the purely destructive passion, and resembling in his lust for blood the man-eating tiger, tells of a patient who seems to have been demoralised by bull fights in Spain. He would constantly attempt murder, twice having sharpened the handle of his toothbrush to a weapon. "He would quietly smoke a cigarette the moment before his attack, and would resume his smoking when he had delivered his blow."

Something of this easy nonchalance must surely characterise the Whitechapel murderer. He must be capable of retuning to the society, whatever it may be, in which he moves without showing any trace of the sanguinary passion that possesses him. On the other hand, the coroner's theory is borne out by the fact that having in one instance failed to perform the post-mortem operation which makes these murders so horrible, the murder as though he would not lose the time he had devoted to the purpose, proceeded straightway to gain his purpose by a successful attack upon another victim.

His power of invisibility is remarkable. In no case has he given the slightest sign by which he could be traced. He has given none now. The police promised themselves that when he resumed his work he would be caught. He has resumed his work but has not been caught, and he seems to be as safe from arrest as when he began the series of dreadful acts which have so stirred public minds.

INDIGNATION MEETINGS

At three o'clock yesterday afternoon a meeting of nearly 1,000 persons took place in Victoria-park, under the chairmanship of Mr. Edward Barrow, of the Bethnal-green-road, and after several speeches upon the conduct of the Home Secretary and Sir Charles Warren in reference to the murders, a resolution was unanimously passed that it was high time that both functionaries should resign and make way for some officers who would leave no stone unturned for the purpose of bringing murderers to justice, instead of allowing them to run riot in a civilized city like London.

On Mile-end-waste during the day four meetings of the same kind were held and similar resolution passed, and at half past eight last evening a large meeting of the Vigilance Committee took place at 74, Mile-end-road, where Mr. Aarons, Mr. Reeves, Mr. Lawton, Mr. B. Harris, and other gentlemen spoke for some time upon the subject of a Government reward.

AN ARREST

Shortly before midnight a man was arrested in the Borough on suspicion of being the perpetrator of the murders in the East End yesterday morning. A tall, dark man, wearing an American hat, entered a lodging house in Union-street, known as Albert-chambers. He stayed there throughout the day, and his peculiar manner riveted the attention of his fellow lodgers. He displayed great willingness to converse with them, and certain observations he made regarding the topic of the day aroused their suspicions.

Last night this mysterious individual attracted the notice of the deputy-keeper of the lodging house, whose suspicions became so strong that he sent for a policeman. On the arrival of the officer the stranger was questioned as to his recent wanderings, but he could give no intelligible account of them, though he said he had spent the previous night on Blackfriars-bridge. He was conveyed to the Stones'-end Police Station, Blackman-street, Borough.

The "Daily News" rightly argues that the police have done nothing, they have thought of nothing, and in their detective capacity they have shown themselves distinctly inferior to the bloodhounds which a few years ago, in the provinces, tracked the mysterious murderer of a little girl to his doom. The trail must run true and clear from Berner-street to Mitre-square, and beyond, for those who have the true instinct of the detective calling. None of the accepted apologies for the shortcomings of the Force will cover their repeated failure in these extraordinary cases. The inadequacy of their numbers, though it is absolute in regard to the Metropolitan district taken as a whole, is but relative in regard to the limited area which is the scene of these crimes.

In the quarter of these crimes, apparently, whatever changes there may have been in the frequency, there has been no change in the manner of the patrol. There has been no sudden doubling on the beat to baffle the calculations of the murderer. The policemen tramps slowly by as he tramped before and to those who have an interest in the calculation his returning tread may be timed with the same certainly as the movements of a planetary body. The entire management of this business, on the part of the representatives of law and order, exhibits what, under the circumstances, may justly be called an appalling lack of resource.

THE RIPPER REPORTS

There has been no sign of an especial cunning of device to meet the terrible emergencies of the case. There has been no hearty co-operation with the Press which, on a hundred occasions, has saved the Detective Department from the worst consequences of its own mistakes. There must be something incurably faulty in the organisation and engagement of the Force, and, to all appearance, the gallant soldier who is at the head of it will never be able to tell what it is.

The public are fast coming to the belief that it is its military organization, and the absence of local interest and control, which makes our Metropolitan Police so inefficient in the very first of their duties - that of preventing violence and crime. The most agonising of the East-end mysteries is the mystery of the utter paralysis of energy and intelligence on the part of the Police.

Again (says the "Daily Telegraph") this vast metropolis has been horror-stricken by a repetition of the hideous murders and mutilations of which the East-end of London, four times in succession, has already been the scene during the past few months. On this occasion a double crime, in all its leading characteristics so closely resembling its predecessors as to leave little doubt that it was committed by the same merciless hand which deliberately slaughtered and mangled Mary Ann Smith, Ann Tabram, Mary Ann Nicholls, and Annie Chapman, has been added to the dread list of assassinations perpetrated with impunity in the chief city of the civilised world.

The latest victims to the incredible blood-lust of an unknown malefactor, or gang of malefactors, have not as yet been identified with certainty, but their appearance, the hour at which they were barbarously slain, and the obscure, sordid character of the localities in which their bodies were discovered, justify the presumption that they belonged to the class of poor and pitiable "unfortunates" upon whom the ruthless and wily assassin had previously wreaked his homicidal fury.

THE RIPPER REPORTS

Yesterday morning's twofold murder only differs from those preceding it in the respect that its victims were done to death at an hour when the streets of the populous district in which the crimes were committed had by no means lapsed into the stillness of early morn, but were still frequented by a considerable number of persons belonging to the Whitechapel district. In the East-end, as in the majority of poor London neighbourhoods, a good deal of open-air business is transacted on Saturday nights, with the effect of keeping up buyers and sellers alike to a later hour than that on which they seek their homes on ordinary week-nights.

In Berner-street, St George's, within hearing of the woman murdered there shortly after midnight, the members of a working-men's club were singing songs and indulging in other convivial recreations whilst the assassin was doing his deadly work. Mitre-square, the scene of another crime perpetrated, in all probability, about half-an-hour later than that of Berner-street, as an open space surrounded by warehouses and accessible by three thoroughfares. During daytime it is a busy spot, much occupied by vendors of fruit, porters, and miscellaneous idlers. Yet within its small precincts, approachable from Mitre street, Duke-street, and St. Jame's-place, a woman was butchered in cold blood, not fifty yards from the quarters of a night watchman, who heard no sound of a struggle or even of footsteps, although he had alleged that, "as a rule, he can hear the tread of the policeman passing on his beat every quarter of an hour."

Thus, between midnight and one o'clock, two murders were effected at places half a mile distant from one another, without hindrance, noise, or detection, and obviously by one and the same hand. It seems probably that the assassin, having cut the throat of his first victim in Berner-street, was alarmed by the sound of some approaching footstep, possibly that of a member of the club above alluded to, and took to flight foregoing his ghastly purpose of mutilation for the moment.

Having reached the purlieus of Mitre-square on his homeward way, and being unsated with the blood he had already shed, he found another opportunity of carrying out his revolting resolve to its uttermost atrocity of detail, induced a second luckless waif of the night to accompany him into the still, deserted little enclosure hard at hand, and there slaughtered her with more than the savagery of a wild beast, hacking her face to pieces, and mutilating her lifeless body in a manner that is all but indescribable.

The darksome, appalling deeds, done in the centre of a thickly-populated metropolitan district, and at a time of night when hundreds of people were still perambulating streets in the immediate vicinity of the thoroughfares in which the butchered women were found weltering in their blood, have cast a shadow of gloom and horror over this vast city. It cannot but be a deep humiliation to every Londoner who has heretofore taken a just pride in the many evidences of a high civilisation abounding in the English capital to recognise the terrible fact that murder after murder can be perpetrated in our very midst, so to speak, undetected and unpunished, braving successfully all the efforts of our huge police force to bring the guilty to justice.

In the East-end, selected by the author or authors of these inhuman crimes as the scene of their operations, consternation is rapidly turning into wrath, the consequences of which may at any moment prove disastrous to any person, innocent or culpable, upon whom popular suspicion may fall. It could hardly be wondered at where people so desperately exasperated as the East-enders have reason to be by this appalling recurrence of brutal bloodshed in their district, to take the law into their own hands, having lost faith in the capacity of the Executive to exorcise the grim spectre by which they are haunted.

Significant enough of the state of feeling prevailing throughout the East-end are the facts that the Vigilance Committee constituted by Whitechapel ratepayers has offered a reward for the apprehension of the murderer or murderers, and that its President, Mr. George Lusk, on Saturday evening - several hours, therefore, before the discovery of the two corpses that make up the tale of the Whitechapel assassinations to the formidable number of six - has forwarded to her Majesty the Queen a petition, "on behalf of the inhabitants of the East-end of London," imploring our gracious Sovereign to reverse the decision lately arrived at by the Home Secretary, and to direct that that Government reward, "sufficient in amount to meet the peculiar exigencies if the case, may immediately be offered."

It is a momentous and unwelcome novelty in the history of the present right that a large body of Londoners should be driven by the sheer force of calamitous circumstances to entreat their Queen to remedy the shortcomings of one of her own Cabinet Ministers, above all of the Secretary of State for the Home Department!

LATEST DETAILS
ANOTHER EXTRAORDINARY EPISTLE
[BY TELEGRAPH]

On enquiry in the East End at 7 o'clock this morning a representative of the "Central News" was informed that up to that hour that neither the City Police nor the Metropolitan Police had succeeded in capturing anyone against whom well founded suspicions rested in the matter of the East End murders.

THE RIPPER REPORTS

The mysterious man arrested in Southwark lodging-house last night was soon able to prove his innocence to the police. Such awkward incidents as these are, in present circumstances, unavoidable.

Upon enquiry at 10 o'clock this morning the "Central News" was informed that not withstanding the most searching enquiries which has been prosecuted during the night, that the police have been unable to make any arrests.

The body of the woman murdered in Mitre-square had not been identified up to that hour.

The "Central News" says: - A postcard bearing the stamp, "London, E., October 1st," was received this morning, addressed to the "Central News" Office, the address and subject matter being written in red ink, undoubtedly by the same person who wrote the sensational letter already published as having been received on Thursday last. Like the previous missive, this also had reference to the horrible tragedies in East London, forming, indeed, a sequel to the first letter.

"I was not codding, dear old Boss, when I gave you the tip. You'll hear about 'Saucy Jacky's' work to-morrow. Double event this time. Number one squealed a bit. Could'nt finish straight off. Had not time to get ears for police. Thanks for keeping the last letter back till I got to work again. - Jack the Ripper"

The card is smeared on both sides with blood, which has evidently been impressed thereon by the thumb or finger of the writer, the corrugated surface of the skin being plainly shown. Upon the back of the card some words are nearly obliterated by a bloody smear. It is not necessarily assumed that this has been the work of the murderer, the idea that naturally occurs being that the whole thing is a practical joke. At the same time the writing of the previous letter immediately before the commission of the murders of yesterday was so singular a coincidence that it does not seem unreasonable to suppose that the cool, calculating villain, who is responsible for the crimes, has chosen to make the post a medium through which to convey to the Press his grimly diabolical humour.

A man was arrested last night at a coffee shop opposite the Thurnow Arms public house, at West Norwood, on suspicion of being connected with the Whitechapel murders. Suspicion appears to have been excited by his face being much scratched and by marks, apparently of blood, upon his clothes. No guilt, either of complicity or of the actual commission of the crime, has, however, yet been proved against him.

SUBSEQUENT ARRESTS

Three men are still detained at Leman-street and Commercial-street Police stations pending enquiries as to their whereabouts on Sunday night. The excitement amongst residents in the East End shows no signs of abating. A street row such as is only too frequent in the district occurred in the Great Garden-street early this morning. The rumour soon spread that another murder had been attempted, and that fiend had been captured. A great crowd collected and the police had considerable trouble in clearing the mob away.

Just before daylight an arrest was made between Cannon-street-road and back of Church-lane, the person taken into custody being apparently a woman. On being taken to Leman-street Station it was found that the prisoner was a well-known local reporter, who had dressed in female attire and had walked over from Leytonstone in the hope that in this disguise he might gather some important information. He was shortly afterwards released from custody.

Mitre Square and the surrounding streets are this morning thronged with people, the idle ones standing in groups discussing the murders. The Square itself is lively enough, business being in full swing. The spot where the body was found is surrounded by a morbid crowd, who appear to derive satisfaction from standing upon the flagstones where the horrid deed was done.

A PRACTICAL STEP

The feeling of indignation against the Home Secretary for not offering a reward has immensely increased since the discovery of the last two murders. The following practical letter has been forwarded to the Home Office:

"The 'Financial News,' London, October 1st, 1888,

The Right Hon. Henry Matthews, Q.C., M.P., Secretary of State for the Home Department.

Sir,

In view of your refusal to offer a reward out of the Government funds for the discovery of the perpetrator or perpetrators of the recent murders in the East End of London, I am instructed on behalf of several readers of the "Financial News," whose names and addresses I enclose, to forward you the accompanying cheque for £300 and to request you to offer that sum for this purpose in the name of the Government.

Awaiting the favour of your reply I have the honour to be your obedient servant (signed) Harry H. Marks."

MEDICAL OPINION ON THE MURDERS

This morning a representative of the "Central News" interviewed two eminent London physicians for the purposes of ascertaining whether they could throw any scientific light on the East End murders.

THE RIPPER REPORTS

Sir James Risdon Bennett, of Cavendish Square, West, in the course of a conversation with the reporter, said: - I have no desire to promulgate any theory in reference to these murders. My purpose in writing to the "Times" the other day was simply to demonstrate the absurdity of the theory that the crimes were being committed for the purpose of supplying an American physiologist with uteruses. I cannot believe for a moment that any commission has been given out for the collection of uteruses. It would be extremely easy here or in America either for a physiologist to secure this portion of the intestines. All he would have to do would be to apply to the public Hospitals, where there are always many paupers or unclaimed persons who are made the subjects of experiments and his demands would be easily met.

Supposing, for instance, that a specialist proposed to lecture in the Theatre of his Institutions upon the uterus, he would communicate with the surgeon, who would have no difficulty in providing him with a sufficient number of specimens for all his purposes. The notion that the uteruses were wanted in order that they might be sent out along with copies of a medical publication is ridiculous; not only ridiculous indeed but absolutely impossible of realisation. I attach no importance whatever to that. If one sane man had instructed another sane man to procure a number of specimens of the uterus, the modus operandi would have been very different from that which has been pursued in these cases. The murderer has run a fearful and a quite unnecessary risk. The mutilations which be contended were, to a great extent, wanton, and did not assist him in the accomplishment of his intention.

My impression is that the miscreant is a homicidal maniac. He has a specific delusion, and that delusion is erratic. Of course, we have at this moment very little evidence indeed, in fact I may say no evidence at all as to the state of the man's mind, except so far as is suggested by the character of the injuries which he has inflicted upon his victims.

I repeat that my impression is that he is suffering under an erratic delusion, but it may be that he is a religious lunatic. It is possible that he is labouring under the delusion that he has a mandate from the Almighty to purge the world of prostitutes, and in the prosecution of his mad theory he has determined upon a crusade against the unfortunates of London, whom he seeks to mutilate by deprivation of the uterus.

There are, on the other hand, a number of theories which might be speculated upon as to the particular form that this mania takes, but inasmuch as we have no knowledge of the man himself, but only of the characteristics which surround the commission of his crimes wherewith to guide us, I come to the conclusion that his delusion has reference to matters of a sexual character. The two crimes which were perpetrated yesterday morning do not lead me to modify my opinion that the assassin is a lunatic.

Even if it should transpire that in the case of the Mitre-square victim the uterus is missing, I should not be disposed to favour what I may call the American theory in the slightest degree, and I must confess that it was with considerable surprise that I noticed in certain newspapers a disposition to readily accept the theory which the coroner who investigated the circumstances attending the murder of the woman Chapman first suggested.

It is my opinion that if any person wanted a number of specimens of the uterus, and was a man possessed of surgical skill, he would himself undertake to secure them rather than employ an agent. No love of gain could possibly induce a sane man to commit such atrocities as these, and besides this there is the circumstance remaining, as I have previously said, that they might all be secured at the medical institutions either of England or America - that if they were needed for legitimate purposes - practically without any consideration at all. It has been said - and it is a very natural observation - that if the murderer were a lunatic he could not commit these crimes and escape with impunity. That is a comment which any person, not fully acquainted with the peculiarities of lunatic subjects, might very well make. In my view, however, the extraordinary cunning evinced by the homicide is a convincing proof of his insanity. No sane man could have escaped in just the same fashion as this man seems to have done. He must almost necessarily have betrayed himself.

It is a matter of common knowledge, however, amongst "mad doctors" that lunatics display a wonderful intelligence, if it may be called so, in their criminal operation, and I have little doubt that, if the murderer were other than a madman he would, ere this, have been captured by the police. In many instances a madman's delusion is directed to only one subject, and he is mad upon that subject alone. I doubt, however, that the murderer of these women is other than a man suffering from acute mania, and, that being so, his infirmity would be obvious to almost every person with whom he came into contact. That is to say, if he were in the presence of either of us, we should say, "Oh, he's a madman." There are many instances in which the common test is for the doctor to enter into conversation with the suspect, to touch upon a variety of topics, and then as if by accident to mention the matter in regard to which the patient has a specific delusion.

Then the person's madness is manifested, although upon every other point he converses rationally. But here the disease is mental and I should say that those persons with whom he comes into daily contact cannot regard him as a sane person. Dr. Phillips has stated that the injuries inflicted upon these women have been apparently performed by a person possessing some anatomical knowledge.

That is likely enough, but would not a butcher be quite capable of treating the body in this way? Since I wrote my letter to the "Times" I have received several communications in support of my views. One of these comes from the Bishop of Bedford, who agrees with me that the theory of the American physiologies, has no claim to credit. I only wish to have it understood that my only desire is to remove from the public mind the evil impression which has been by the suggestion that a member of the medical profession is more or less responsible for these murders. I have never believed in that theory, and these two last murders confirm me in the opinion that they are the work of a man suffering from acute mania, to whom the ordinary rules of motive and procedure do not apply.

Dr. Forbes Winslow, the eminent specialist in lunacy cases, said to our representative: - I am more certain than ever that these murders are committed by a homicidal maniac, and there is no moral doubt in my mind that the assassin in each case is the same man. I have carefully read the reports in the morning papers, and they confirm me in the opinion which I had previously formed. While I am clearly of opinion that the murderer is a homicidal lunatic, I also believe him to be a mono-maniac, and I see no reason why he should not, excepting at periods when the fit is upon him, exhibit a cool and rational exterior.

I have here in my book - a work on physiology - a case in which a man had a lust for blood, as in this case, and he was generally a person of bland and pleasant exterior. In all probability the whole of the murders have been committed by the same hand, but I may point out that the imitative faculty is very strong in persons of unsound mind, and that is the reason why there has been a sort of epidemic of knives. We shall probably find that a good many knives will be displayed to the people within the next few weeks. Still, all the evidence that is forthcoming up to the present moment shows clearly enough that the Whitechapel crimes have been perpetrated by the same hand. My idea is that, under the circumstances, the police out to employ, for the protection of the neighbourhood, and with the view of detecting the criminal, a number of officers who have been in the habit of guarding lunatics. That is to say, warders from asylums, and other persons who have charge of the insane.

These men, if properly disposed in the neighbourhood, would assuredly note any person who was of unsound mind. I have sent a letter embodying this suggestion to Sir Charles Warren, but I have received only a formal communication acknowledging its receipt. It is not easy to prevail upon the police to accept a suggestion from outside sources. This I discovered the other day, when a man in emulation of the Whitechapel murder, drew a knife and sharpened it in the presence of a relative of mine at Brighton, under circumstances which have been published in the newspapers.

When I made a statement to the police on that occasion they though very little of it. Indeed I attach not the less importance to the American physiologist story. It is a theory which is utterly untenable, and I should think there were very few medical men who ever entertained it seriously. All that has recently happened appears to me to be a strong confirmation of the views which I have previously given expression to upon this subject - that the murder is a homicidal monomaniac of infinite cunning, and I fear he would not be brought to justice, unless he be caught while engaged in the commission of one of his awful crimes.

A REWARD OF £500 OFFERED

The "Central News" says Mr. Phillips, a member of the Common Council of London, has given notice of his intention to move at the next Council meeting that the Corporation offer a reward of £250 for the detection of the murderer or the woman found in Mitre-square, which is within the City precincts. This has, however, been anticipated by the Lord Mayor, who has, on behalf of the Corporation, issued an offer of £500 reward for the apprehension of the criminal.

OPINIONS OF THE PRESS

Commenting on the Whitechapel murders, the "St. James's Gazette" says: "What may be called ordinary precautions, frequency of patrolling, and closeness of watch, have been taken already, but they have manifestly not been taken effectually enough, and more are wanted. When the murderers of Lord F. Cavendish and Mr. Burke were being hunted down, marines in plain clothes were freely employed to drive them into a corner. The same measures might be taken again. The offer of a reward seems to us decidedly a step which ought to be taken. We have never thought the reasons given for ceasing to work on the cupidity of the associates of criminals were sufficient.

The "Pall Mall Gazette" says: The only practical thing to be done is to keep a sharp look out, and to dismiss once and for all the Coroner's theory as to the motive of the murder.

The "Globe" says: We have no doubt the police will do all they can to track and seize the criminal, but it has often been noted that the duties imposed upon police take them from their proper business, and that new duties of a really objectionable nature have recently been invented. What the public demand, and must have in such a thorough and astute inquiry into these shameful atrocities as shall lead to the arrest and punishment of this superlative delinquent. If it cannot be done by the Police it must be done by the people."

THE INQUEST

THE RIPPER REPORTS

Mr. Wynne Baxter opened the inquest on the body of the woman Elizabeth Stride, who was found with her throat cut in Berner-street, on Sunday morning, at the Vestry Hall, Cable-street, this morning.

William West, of 2, William-street, said he was at the International Working Men's Club on Sunday night. He gave a description of the premises, and stated that the wooden gates were not closed until late at night as a rule. Witness worked at the printing office during the evening, and went into the Club afterwards, where he remained until twenty minutes past twelve. He went into the yard, and noticed that the gates were open. He did not notice any body lying there, but it might have been there without his observing it. There was no lamp in the yard. He then went into the Club again, and called his brother and Louis Selso, and they left together by the front door. On only one occasion, about twelve months ago, he had noticed a man and woman in the yard, and they walked away when he went towards them.

Maurice Eagle, of 4, New-road, Commercial-road, stated that he left the Club about 11.30, and returned about 12.40. He went in through the yard, as the front door was closed, but did not notice anything in the yard. He was certain he should have noticed a man and a woman if they had been there He was in the habit of going through the yard occasionally, but had never noticed any men and women there. He remained in the club about twenty minutes. A man named Gilleman came upstairs and said there was a dead woman lying in the yard.

He went down and struck a match, and saw a woman lying in a pool of blood on the ground, near the gateway. He did not touch the body, and went down towards Commercial-road for the police. He found two constables and informed them of the murder, and they returned with him to the yard, where a number of people had assembled. One of the policemen sent him to the Station for the Inspector. He could not say if the woman's clothes were disturbed. He thought people in the club would have heard a cry of murder.

Lewis Diemschitz, steward of the International Working Men's Educational Club, was the next witness. He stated that he left the Club about 11 30 on Saturday morning. He had a costermonger's barrow and pony, and drove into the yard. Both gates were wide open. It was very dark. His pony shied, and he looked down on to the ground and saw something lying there, but could not see what it was. He jumped down and struck a match, but being windy he could only see it was some person lying there.

He went into the club, and in the front room he found several members and told them a woman was lying in the yard. He got a candle and went out at once and discovered a quantity of blood around the body. He did not touch the body, but at once went for the police. He passed several streets without seeing a policeman, and returned without one. A man named Isaacs was with him, and they were both shouting for the police. Another man returned with them into the yard and took hold of the woman's head. Witness then first saw a wound in the throat.

The doctor arrived about ten minutes after the constables. The police searched everywhere and took the names and addresses of those present. The deceased's clothes were in order. She was lying on her side with her face towards the wall. The doctor put his hand on her bosom and said she was still quite warm. Witness estimated that about two quarts of blood were around the body. He had never seen men and women in the yard.

The inquiry was adjourned until two o'clock tomorrow.

Source: *Express and Echo*

THE RIPPER REPORTS

TUESDAY 02 OCT 1888

THE EAST-END MURDERS INQUEST ON ELIZABETH STRIDE OFFER OF REWARDS

The excitement of Sunday in the neighbourhood of the last two of the six Whitechapel murders which are now generally regarded as the work of one hand, had not abated yesterday. On the contrary it seemed to have increased, and the subject was the one topic of conversation and speculation in the metropolis. In the provinces, too, a great sensation has been produced, and in all the large towns the local newspapers have published copious telegrams, which have been eagerly read.

The police seem to be as far from a real clue as ever, and several arrests were made during the course of yesterday, only to be followed by the unconditional release of the persons said to be suspected. Theories, of course, abound, and everybody who can twist the most ordinary occurrence so that it may appear to have the remotest connection with the crimes hastens to communicate it to a police officer. This, of course, is as it should be, even though it invariably turns out that the information is worthless.

It may be observed that the officers and constables of the Metropolitan force, who have previously been studiously reticent not to say brusque, in the manner in which they met the inquiries of newspaper representatives, have during the last 24 hours shown a more communicative disposition - so far as it is prudent to say anything - presumably in obedience to orders from headquarters. They really, however, have little or nothing to tell; for the daring of the murderer is only equalled by the skill with which he has avoided leaving any traces of his crime.

Dissatisfaction at the inaction of the authorities in the matter of offering a reward for information continues to be loudly expressed. One of the murders having taken place within the confines of the city of London, led Mr. Phillips, a member of the Court of Common Council, promptly to give notice that he would move the council at its next meeting to offer a reward of £250. This step, however will be unnecessary, owing to the issue of the following notice by Colonel Sir James Fraser, the Commissioner of the City Police:-

MURDER - £500 REWARD

"Whereas at 1.45 a.m. on Sunday, the 30th of September last, a woman, name unknown, was found brutally murdered in Mitre-square, Aldgate, in this City, a reward of £500 will be paid by the Commissioner of Police of the City of London, to any person (other than a person belonging to a police force in the United Kingdom) who shall give such information as shall lead to the discovery and conviction of the murderer or murderers. Information to be given to the inspector of the Detective Department, 26, Old Jewry, or at any police station.

"James Fraser, Colonel, Commissioner.

"City of London Police-office, 26, Old Jewry, Oct. 1, 1888."

Outside the City steps in a similar direction have been taken by public bodies and private individuals. A meeting of the Vigilance Committee which has lately been formed in Whitechapel was held yesterday morning, and a resolution was passed calling upon the Home-office to offer a substantial Government reward. A sum of £300 has been forwarded to the same department on behalf of several readers of the Financial News with a request that it may be offered in the name of the Government. To this request the following reply has been received:-

THE RIPPER REPORTS

"October 1, 1888.

My dear Sir, - I am directed by Mr. Matthews to acknowledge the receipt of your letter of this date, containing a cheque for £300, which you say has been contributed on behalf of several readers of the Financial News, and which you are desirous should be offered as a reward for the discover of the recent murders in the East-end of London. If Mr. Matthews had been of opinion that the offer of a reward in these cases would have been attended by any useful result he would himself have at once made such an offer but he is not of that opinion. Under these circumstances, I am directed to return to you the cheques (which I enclose), and to thank you and the gentlemen whose names you have forwarded for the liberality of their offer, which Mr. Matthews much regrets he is unable to accept. - I am, sir, your very obedient servant,

"Harry H. Marks, Esq."

"E. Leigh Pemberton."

The above, with other sums - including the £100 offered by Mr. Samuel Montagu, M.P., and the £200 collected by the Vigilance Committee - make an aggregate sum of £1,200, sufficient to excite the cupidity even of an accomplice, and to sharpen the wits of the dullest of detectives. It is, however, more than probable that the reward will be increased to £2,000, as the Lord Mayor has been urged to open a subscription list, and the members of the Stock Exchange seem disposed to take the matter up. Colonel Sir Alfred Kirby, the officer commanding the Tower Hamlets Battalion Royal Engineers, has offered on behalf of his officers an additional reward of £100.

Sir Alfred Kirby is also willing to place the services of not more than 50 members of his corps at the disposal of the authorities, to be utilised in assisting them in any way they may consider desirable at this juncture, either for the protection of the public or finding out the criminal. Of course the volunteers will have to be made use of as citizens, and not in a quasi-military capacity. Finally, there is talk of holding "a great indignation meeting" on the subject of the murders and the attitude of the Home-office thereto, over which Mr. S. Montagu, the member for the division, will preside.

Naturally the sightseers and curiosity-mongers crowded the neighbourhood of Berner-street and Mitre-square all day yesterday, but they got nothing for their pains, every trace of the crimes having been removed by the police. A large additional force of constabulary has been posted at both points, and in the immediate vicinities. Had this precaution not been taken in Berner-street it is probable that the crowds would have broken down the gates of the yard in which the body of the woman Stride was found. In connection with the Mitre-square murder, a startling discovery was made during the afternoon.

Sargeant Dudman had his attention drawn to 36, Mitre-street, a house a short distance from the spot where the murdered woman was found, and there he saw what appeared to be blood-stains upon the doorway and underneath the window, as if a person had wiped his fingers on the window-ledge, and drawn a bloodstained knife down the part of the door-way. Mr. Hurtig, who lives on the premises, said he had only just before noticed the stains, and then quite by accident. Almost immediately afterwards the same police officer had his attention drawn to similar marks on the plate glass window of Mr. William Smith, at the corner of Mitre-square, but Mr. Smith scouted the idea that they could have anything to do with the murders as the windows were covered at night by shutters.

The discovery, notwithstanding, caused increased excitement for a time in the locality. The only other trace left by the murderer was a portion of an apron, which, as was mentioned yesterday, was picked up in Goldston-street, and which corresponded with a piece left on the body of the Mitre-square victim. This seemed to show that the murderer had escaped in the direction of Whitechapel.

It has been definitely ascertained that Mrs. Stride, better known as "Long Liz," left the lodging-house at 32, Flower and Dean-street, Commercial-street, where she had been staying since the previous Tuesday, at seven o'clock on Saturday night. At the time of her departure she was quite cheerful and in good health. As to her movements after that hour nothing reliable has been obtained, nor has anyone yet been able positively to vouch that since then she has been seen alive. Her usual haunts of a night were the Commercial-road East, Stratford, and Bow, the latter especially, and it is quite possible that from her old acquaintances information may yet be forthcoming as to her later movements on that night.

At the lodging-house in Flower and Dean-street, which from time to time she has made her home during the last five or six years, since the death of her husband. "Long Liz" is spoken of almost in terms of affection. The occupants describe her as a good-natured, hardworking, clean woman, who only took to the streets when she was unable to obtain employment as a charwoman. It is feared, however, that some difficulty will be experienced in ascertaining the identity of the woman murdered in Mitre-square. The face is badly mutilated, and it wears an unnatural appearance. Many persons have been admitted to the mortuary in Golden-lane, and up to last night no one had recognised the dead woman as bearing the slightest resemblance to anyone with whom they were acquainted.

During the afternoon a female called at the mortuary, and after viewing the body said she thought it was that of her sister. The female admitted, however, that she had not seen her sister for a number of years, and altogether the recognition was of such a hesitating character that not much importance is attached to it. The inquest on this woman has, in consequence of the lack of identification, been deferred until Thursday, when Dr. Langham will open an inquiry at eleven o'clock at the mortuary.

The authorities have under consideration the practicability of shortening the time of the patrol beats, which in the metropolitan district are much too long for effective police duty. The resources of the force are, however, already taxed to their utmost, and if the beats are to be shortened the number of policemen must be considerably increased, or special constables sworn in. The latter course finds much favour, and it is certain that an official call for volunteers would be responded to with enthusiasm.

THE INQUEST

Mr. Wynne E. Baxter, coroner for South-East Middlesex, opened the inquiry yesterday morning at the Vectry-hall St. George's-in-the-East on the body of Elizabeth Stride, the woman who was murdered in Berner-street, Commercial-road, on Sunday morning.

The first witness called was William West, of 40, Berner-street, Commercial-road, printer. He said - I live on the premises; it is the International Working Men's Educational Club. There are two windows on the ground floor facing the street, and the door opens into the same street. At the side of the house there is a passage into the yard, and there are two wooden gates at the entrance to the yard; they open into the street. The first passage into the club leads into a room, and the door opens out of this passage. The gates are open at all hours of the day, but are mostly closed at night. The door is not closed till the members leave. There is no particular person to look after it. The room contains three doors leading into the yard. There is no other way out of the yard except through the gate. Opposite the gate there is a workshop, which belongs to a sack manufacturer.

There is a stable on the left-hand side before you come to the club. One room is used as a printing-office; the men from which left, I should think, about two o'clock in the afternoon. It is a Socialist club, and any working man, whatever his nationality who professes Socialism, can be a member. I left the club for home at a quarter past twelve o'clock. In the evening there had been a discussion going on in the large room on the first floor, in which there are two windows looking into the street. About 100 persons were present on Saturday.

When did the discussion cease? - About midnight, and the bulk of the people left the premises then.

Which way did they go out? - Through the street door, which is the most convenient. Some of the members, about 30, remained behind. These latter were singing, and discussing various questions.

Were the windows open? - Partly.

Where did you go when you left? - To my lodgings, 2, William-street, Canon-street-road.

Which way did you go out of the club? I went out of the yard passage. I noticed the gates were open, so I went that way.

Is there any light in the yard? - None whatever.

Are there any lamps in the street that light the yard? - There are lamps, but not opposite.

How is the yard lighted? - By the light of the club windows.

When you left the club did anything attract your attention? - No, sir; I noticed nothing as I looked towards the gates.

Was there anything on the ground? - I can't say.

Might there have been? - I don't know, it was rather dark, so there might have been.

Did you notice anyone in the yard? - No, sir.

Did you meet anybody in Berner-street? - I can't recollect, but as I went along Fairclough-street, close by, I noticed some men and women standing together.

Did you see no one nearer? - No, sir.

Have you ever seen a man and woman in the yard? - About 12 months ago I happened to go into the yard and heard someone chatting near the gate, and I at once went there and shut the gate.

Morris Eagle, 4, New-road, Commercial-road, said - I am a traveller and a member of the Socialist Club. I was at the club on Saturday night, and did not leave till after the discussion. I went through the front door on my way out at a quarter-past twelve, but returned to the club about 20 to one. When I returned the front door was closed, so I went in at the back door in the yard and along the passage into the club.

Did you notice anything lying on the ground? - No, I did not notice anything as I came in.

Could anything have lain there and you not seen it? - I don't think so.

How wide is the passage? - About 9ft.

Can you say whether the body was lying there then? - I could not say for certain; it was very dark near the gates, and only the lights from the club shone into the yard.

If a man and woman had been there would you have seen them? - Oh, yes, I should certainly have seen them.

When did you hear of the murder? A member named Gidlemann came up and said there was a dead woman in the yard. I went, and saw a woman lying on the ground in much blood. Her feet were about 6ft. or 7ft. from the gate.

Was she against the club wall? - Yes, sir.

Her head towards the yard? - Yes her feet to the gate and her head to the yard. I stuck a light and saw her covered in blood. I could not look at her long, so I ran for the police. Another man went for them at the same time. We could not find one at first; but when we got to the corner of Grove-street, Commercial-road, I found two constables, and I told them there was a woman murdered in Berner-street. There were lots of people present in the yard at the time we returned. One of the constables said to his companion, "Go for a doctor," and turning to me he said, "Go to the police-station for the inspector."

Did anyone appear to be touching the body? - The policeman touched the body; not those standing close by. The people seemed afraid to go near it.

Can you fix the time the discovery was made? - About one o'clock was the time that I first saw the body. I did not notice the time, but I have calculated it from the time I left home to return to the club.

By a Juror - On Saturday night there is a free discussion at the club, and any one can go in. There were some women there on Saturday night. There were only those we knew, no strange women. It was not a dancing night, but there may have been a little dancing among the members after the discussion.

The Coroner - If there were singing and dancing going on would you have been likely to have heard the cry of a woman in great distress - a cry of murder, for instance - from the yard? - Oh, we should certainly have heard such a cry.

Lewis Diemschitz said - I live at 40, Berner-street, and am steward of the International Working Men's Educational Club. I am married, and my wife lives there too. She assists in the management of the club. I left home about half-past eleven on Saturday morning, and returned home exactly one o'clock on Sunday morning. I noticed the time at Harris's tobacco shop at the corner of Commercial-road and Berner-street. It was one o'clock. I had a barrow, something like a costermonger's, with me. I was sitting in it, and a pony was drawing it. It is a two-wheeled barrow.

The pony is kept at George-yard, Cable-street. I do not keep it in the yard of the club. I was driving home to leave my goods. I drove into the yard. Both gates were wide open. It was rather dark in there. I drove in as usual, and, all at once, as I came into the gate my pony shied to the left. That caused me to turn my head down to the ground on my right to see what it was that had made him shy.

Could you see anything? - I could see there was something unusual on the pavement. I could not see what it was. It was a dark object. There was nothing white about it. I did not get off the barrow, but I tried with my whip handle to feel what it was. I tried to lift it up, but I could not. I jumped down at once and struck a match, and as it was rather windy I could not get sufficient light to see exactly what it was. I could, however, see that there was the figure of some person lying there. I could tell by the dress that it was a woman. I did not disturb it. I went into the club, and asked where my missus was. I saw her in the front room on the ground floor.

There were several members in the front room, where my wife was, and I told them all, "There is a woman lying in the yard, but I could not say whether she was drunk or dead." I then took a candle and went out at once, and by the candlelight I could see that there was blood about before I reached the body. I did not touch the body, but went off at once for the police. We passed several streets without meeting a policeman, and we returned without one. All the men who were with me halloed as loud as they could for the police, but no one came. When I returned a man that we met in Grove-street, and who came back with us, took hold of the head, and as we lifted it up I first saw the wound in the throat.

At the very same time Eagle and the constable arrived. I noticed nothing unusual on my approach to the club, and met no one that looked at all suspicious. The doctor arrived about 1 minutes after the constable arrived. The police afterwards took our names and addresses, and searched everybody.

Did you notice if her clothes were in order? - In perfect order, as far as I could see.

How was she lying? - She was lying on her side, with her face towards the wall of the club. I could not say whether the body was on its side, but her face was. As soon as the police came I ceased to take any interest in the matter. I did not notice in what position her hands were. I only noticed when the doctor came up he undid the first buttons of her dress next the neck, and put his hand in. He then told the constable that she was quite warm yet.

He told the constable to put his hand in and feel the body, and he did so. There appeared to me to have been about two quarts of blood on the ground, and it seemed to have run up the yard from her neck. The body was lying, I should say, about a foot from the club wall. The gutter of the yard passage is made of paving stones, the centre being of irregular boulders. The body was lying half on the paving stones.

Have you ever seen men and women in the yard? - Never.

Have you ever heard anyone say that they have found men and women in there? - I have not.

By a Juror - Was there room for you to have passed the body with your cart? - Oh, yes. Mine is not a very wide cart; it only took up the centre of the passage. If my pony had not shied, perhaps I would not have noticed it at all. When I got down my cart passed the body. The barrow was past the body when I got down to see what it was.

Another Juror - Was any one left in charge of the body while you went for the police? - I cannot say, but there were several about when I came back. I cannot say positively, but I do not believe any one touched the body.

THE RIPPER REPORTS

Detective-Inspector Reid - All the people who came into the yard were detained and searched? - Yes, and their names and addresses were taken. The first question was whether they had any knives. They were then asked to account for their presence there.

By a Juror - Would it have been possible for any one to have escaped from the yard if he had been hiding there while you went into the club to inform the members? - Yes, it would have been possible; but as soon as I informed the members every one went out, and I do not think it would have been possible for any one to get out then.

If any one had run up the yard, you would have seen him? - Yes, because it is dark just in the gateway; but further up the yard you could see anybody running or walking by the lights of the club.

Do you think any one could have come out of the gateway without you seeing them? - No, I think they could not.

Detective-Inspector Reid stated that the body had not been identified yet.

The Coroner - It has been partially identified; but it is a mistake to say that she has been identified by one of her relatives. It is known, however, where she lived.

At this stage the inquiry was adjourned till two o'clock this afternoon.

At a meeting of the Whitechapel District Board of Works last evening - Mr. Robert Gladding presiding - Mr. Catmur said he thought that the board, as the local authority, should express their horror and abhorrence of the crime which had been perpetrated in the district, and that although it was not within their province to suggest anything, it would be right that they should address the authorities really responsible.

Proceeding, Mr. Catmur spoke of the evil effect which had resulted in the district in the loss of trade. Evening business had become practically extinct in many trades, women finding themselves unable to pass through the streets without an escort. Moreover, the inefficiency of the police was shown in the striking circumstances that but an hour or two later than the murders in Berner-street and Mitre-square the post-office in the immediate vicinity was broken into and property of the value of £100 taken from it. - Mr. Nicholson said that while the local authority might not be responsible for the efficiency of the police, they were responsible for the proper lighting of the district.

In one instance, which he mentioned, a court had been absolutely without light for nearly a week. - Mr. Abrahams said he could not agree with the wholesale condemnation of the police, nor with any resolution which did not indicate a means of reform. He could, however, vouch from his own personal experience that the effect of these murders had been most injurious to the business in Whitechapel; indeed it was the most disastrous blow to the trade of the district that he had known in his experience of a quarter of a century. - The Rev. Daniel Greatorex said the emigrant's houses of call were feeling the panic to such an extent that emigrants refused to locate themselves in Whitechapel, even temporarily. The new system of police, whereby constables were frequently changed from one district to another, kept the policemen ignorant of their beats.

This was one great cause of police inefficiency, and the inspectors themselves testified that what he said was correct. In days gone by constables were acquainted not only with the streets in their districts but also with all the houses, - The chairman said that local bodies had no responsibility in these matters, as the management of the police had been taken away from them. - Mr Telfer said the fact that four or five murders having taken place was no reason why there should be universal hysteria. In fact, the new method of murder suggested the reverse, the victims in every case having chosen to place themselves before their murderers. No increase of the force of the police could secure that the quiet of the nooks and crannies of a great city were protected for those who themselves sought solitude.

It was, however, to be hoped that these recent crimes would result in a reversion to the old system by which constables were acquainted with every corner of their local beats. - Mr. G. F. Brown said that the weak part of the London police system was the want of a proper detective element in dealing with the criminal portion of the community, and there was also a large amount of disaffection running throughout the whole force. The Government itself should be appealed to in the matter rather than the Home Secretary or Chief of Police, who were themselves really only upon their trial. - Mr Caramelli said the change in the condition of Whitechapel in recent years would suggest an entire revision of the police arrangements.

Whitechapel was now a place for the residuum of the whole country and the Continent as well, but it was not so a generation ago. - After further discussion the following resolution was carried, on that motion of Mr. Catmur, seconded by Mr. Barham: - "That this board regards with horror and alarm the several atrocious murders recently perpetrated within the district of Whitechapel and its vicinity, and calls upon Sir Charles Warren so to locate and strengthen the police force in the neighbourhood as to guard against any repetition of such atrocities; and that the Home Secretary be addressed in the same terms."

The most important clue which has yet been discovered with regard to the perpetrators of the inhuman murders in Whitechapel, came to light yesterday through information given by Mr. Thomas Ryan, who has charge of the Cabmen's Reading-room, at 43, Pickering-place, Westbourne-grove. Mr. Ryan is a teetotaler, and is the secretary of the Cabmen's Branch of the Church of England Temperance Society. He has been stationed at Pickering-place for about six years, and is widely known throughout the metropolis and in the country as an earnest temperance advocate.

Ryan says that on Sunday afternoon, while he was in his shelter, the street attendant brought a gentlemanly-looking man to him, and said, "This 'ere gentleman wants a chop, guv'nor; can you cook one for him? He says he's 'most perished with cold." The gentleman in question, Ryan says, was about 5ft. 6in. in height, and wore an Oxford cap on his head, and a light check ulster, with a tippet buttoned to his throat, which he did not loosen all the time he was in the shelter. He had a thick moustache, but no beard; was roundheaded, his eyes very restless, and clean white hands. Ryan said, "Come in, I'll cook one for you with pleasure." This was about four o'clock in the afternoon.

Several cabmen were in the shelter at the time, and they were talking of the new murders discovered that morning at Whitechapel. Ryan exclaimed, "I'd gladly do seven days and nights if I could only find the fellow who did them." This was said directly to the stranger, who, looking into Ryan's face quietly said, "Do you know who committed the murders?" and then calmly went on to say, "I did them. I've had a lot of trouble lately. I came back from India and got into trouble at once. I lost my watch and chain and £10." Ryan was greatly taken aback at the man's statement, and fancied he was just recovering from a drinking bout; so he replied, "If that's correct you must consider yourself engaged." But he then went on to speak to him about temperance work and the evils wrought by drink. Meanwhile, the chop was cooking, the vegetables were already waiting, and the stranger began eating.

During the meal the conversation was kept up with Ryan and others in the shelter, all of whom thought the man was recovering from a heavy drinking bout and that his remarks as to his being the murderer were all nonsense. Ryan reasoned with him as to the folly of his drinking, and at last he expressed his willingness to sign the pledge, a book containing pledges being shown him. This the stranger examined, and at length filled up one page, writing on the counterfoil as well as on the body of the pledge. In the hand of a gentleman he wrote the following words:

"J. Duncan, doctor, residence, Cabman's Shelter, 30th Sept., 1888." After doing this he said, "I could tell a tale if I wanted." Ryan called his attention to the fact that he had not filled in his proper residence, and the man replied, "I have no fixed place of abode at present. I'm living anywhere." While Duncan was eating his chop he again asked for something to drink, and water was brought him, but then he said he would have ginger beer, and when that was brought him, he filled up the glass with the liquid from a bottle he had in his pocket.

"This he drank," said Ryan, "differently to what people usually drink, he literally gulped it down." In answer to further conversation about teetotalism, Duncan accepted an invitation to go with Ryan to church that evening, and said he would return to the shelter in an hour, but he never came back. Duncan carried a stick, and looked a sinewy fellow, just such a one as was capable of putting forth considerable energy when necessary.

In connection with the letter received on Thursday last by the Central News and published yesterday, the agency says that a postcard bearing the stamp "London, E., October 1," was received yesterday morning, addressed to their office, the address and subject matter being written in red, and undoubtedly by the same person from whom the former letter was received. It runs as follows:- "I was not codding, dear old Boss, when I gave you the tip. You'll hear about Saucy Jacky's work to-morrow. Double event this time. Number One squealed a bit; couldn't finish straight off.

Had not time to get ears for police. Thanks for keeping last letter back till I got to work again. - Jack the Ripper." The card is smeared on both sides with blood, which has evidently been impressed thereon by the thumb or finger of the writer, the corrugated surface of the skin being plainly shown. Upon the back of the card some words are nearly obliterated by a bloody smear. It is not necessarily assumed that this has been the work of the murderer, the idea that naturally occurs being that the whole thing is a practical joke. At the same time the writing of the previous letter immediately before the commission of the murders of Sunday was so singular a coincidence, that it does not seem unreasonable to suppose that the cool calculating villain who is responsible for the crimes has chosen to make the post a medium through which to convey to the Press his grimly diabolical humour.

TO THE EDITOR OF THE MORNING POST

Sir, - I was very glad to read your remarks to-day on the recent horrible tragedies in Whitechapel, and to learn that the theory, as originally started by myself, was accepted by your journal. I have been in communication with the authorities on the subject, and from time to time have expressed a strong opinion as to the murders, and believe what has been suggested by me has been followed out to the letter. I do not know, however, whether, what I recently advised, has been accepted.

This was to employ, in addition to the police, several skilled and trained asylum attendants, who knew the cunning and the ways of insane people, and, being as a rule either old soldiers or old policemen, could bring additional weight to bear in finding this dangerous lunatic now at large in London. All the crimes point to one individual. It must not be lost sight of that the imitative genius is great among persons of unsound mind. It frequently happens that after some extraordinary event which is clearly of an irrational nature many are found to attempt to outvie it. Some years ago a lunatic jumped off the Duke of York's Column. A few days after another one did the same from the Monument, and so on.

One insane person is at large flourishing a knife, many more are to be found doing the same thing; but those in whom, however, the idea has been dormant until being reminded of it.

The opinion I entertain of the murders is as follows: - That the murderer is one and the same person; that he has committed the crimes suffering from homicidal monomania of a religious description, and labouring under a morbid belief that the delusion entertained by him has direct reference to the part of the bodies removed. That under the delusion, and desiring to directly influence the morality of the world, and under the delusion that he has a certain destiny to fulfil, he has chosen a certain class of society to vent his vengeance on, still acting under his morbid religious belief. "If thine eye offends thee pluck it out," is a text of Scripture I have frequently known lunatics act strictly up to. Religious homicidal monomania is of the most obstinate description, and the person who is guilty of these crimes is such an individual, who imagines that it is his design to wipe a social blot from the face of the earth. Yours, &c.,

L. FORBES WINSLOW

Source: *Morning Post, London*

WEDNESDAY 3 OCTOBER 1888

NOTES

THE RIPPER REPORTS

With the usual logic of persons in a fright, a good many people are beginning to argue that as we cannot hang the Whitechapel murderer we had better hang somebody else. Opinion seems to differ as to whether the victim should be Sir Charles Warren or Mr. Matthews or both; while there is a certain tendency on the part of gentlemen of the Separatist fashion to include Lord Salisbury's Government as a whole. All this is very absurd; and some of it is very unscrupulous.

But, all the same, those in authority should take note of it. For men in a panic reason hastily, and, irrational as it may be, the recent outrages (especially if they are renewed, or if more mutilated bodies are discovered in odd places) may reflect seriously on those in power and authority. We hope that Scotland-yard and the Home Office are straining every nerve to discover the miscreant. But can it be really true that Dr. Anderson, the new head of the detective department, is away on his holiday at this crisis?

Not wanting to add to the strangeness and mystery of the Whitechapel tragedies. Mrs. Malcolm who thinks she has identified the woman murdered in Berner-street as her sister, said at the inquest yesterday: "I was lying on my bed about twenty minutes past one o'clock on Sunday morning, and I felt a pressure on my bed, and I heard three kisses quite distinctly." She thought it was her sister - the sister who had gone so fatally "wrong" - and had a presentiment that she was in trouble. Mrs. Malcolm is perhaps mistaken in her identification; but it was a curious and pathetic story altogether that she told.

Among the plenitude of suggestions offered by the amateur detectives of crime, it is not common to find one so sensible as that contained in a letter to us from "H. F. W.": - Since it is, at the least possible that the person signing himself "Jack the Ripper," who wrote the letter and postcard published yesterday, is really the murderer he claims to be, would it not be well that the press should be enabled and requested by the police to furnish a facsimile of his handwriting? Should he indeed be identical with the assassin, the detection of the latter would be rendered probably, if not certain, by such a course. Should he prove to be but an infamous buffoon, his exposure to universal contempt would surely serve the end of hindering other similar jesters from like diabolical folly.

Source: *St James's Gazette*

THURSDAY 4 OCTOBER 1888

THE WHITECHAPEL TRAGEDIES FURTHER ARRESTS

Some further arrests were made last night in connection with the East-End murders but it is not yet certain whether the murderer is among the prisoners.

Sir C. Warren writes to the Whitechapel District Board, pointing out that the police are doing their utmost to prevent further murders, and urging the Board to warn women not to trust themselves with strangers in lonely places.

A story was widely circulated in London this morning that "Jack the Ripper" had been caught, after a desperate struggle, in which a constable was terribly injured.

[The following telegram was obligingly handed to us by a gentleman who received it, from London, early this morning.]

"Think Whitechapel murderer caught. Killed a policeman."

M. LATER.

The police received similar information, but after a searching inquiry, the whole affair was proved to be a fabrication.

The London Evening News publishes a story related to two private detectives, whose inquiries have, they claim, provided an accurate description of the Berner-street murder, as well as other important clues.

The American arrested last night was released this morning.

A drunken man who confessed to the murder was arrested in Kilburn last night, but was discharged to-day. There is now not a single person on arrest.

THE MITRE-SQUARE MURDER INQUEST

John Kelly, who lived with the deceased, said she used to hawk things about the streets for a living. He was last in her company at 2 o'clock on Saturday afternoon, she then said she was going to Bermondsey to find her daughter. She sometimes drank to excess, but she usually returned to her lodgings early at night. They were on good terms.

Mr. Frederick Wilkinson, deputy at a lodging-house, said John Kelly and deceased were old intimate friends and paid regularly, and were on good terms. He said deceased was not often intoxicated, and was a very jolly woman, and fond of singing. He could not remember whether any stranger came to the house early Sunday morning. Wilkinson will be further examined.

THE BERNER STREET MURDER
THE MITRE-SQUARE VICTIM
SINGULAR EVIDENCE OF IDENTIFICATION
NOTICE ISSUED BY THE POLICE
ARRESTS AND CONFESSIONS

The inquest on the body of Elizabeth Stride, who was on Tuesday identified as Elizabeth Watts, was resumed at the Vestry Hall, Cable-street, yesterday, at one o'clock before Mr. Wynne Baxter, the coroner. Elizabeth Tanner, Flower-and-Dean Street, said she was the deputy of a common lodging-house. She had seen the body in the mortuary, and recognised it as that of "Long Liz," who had lodged at her house on and off for six years.

Michael Kidney, of Dorset-street, waterside labourer, identified the body at the mortuary as that of the woman he had been living with who was known as Elizabeth Stride. He had known her about three years, and she had lived with him nearly all that time. She was thirty-eight years of age, and had told him she was born three miles from Stockholm. She informed him that her husband was drowned when the Princess Alice went down. The witness last saw the deceased alive on Tuesday week. She was in the habit of going away at time; and during the time he had known her she had been absent five months.

This evidence entirely upsets Mrs. Malcom's depositions, given at the inquest on Monday, who declared that deceased was her sister.

According to a statement in the Times, a labouring man, giving the name of John Kelly, 55, Flower and Dean-street - a common lodging-house - entered the Bishopsgate police-station on Tuesday night, and stated that from what he had been reading in the newspapers he believed that the woman who had been murdered in Mitre-square was his "wife." He was at once taken by Sargent Miles to the mortuary in Golden-lane, and there identified her as the woman, to whom he subsequently admitted he was not married, but with home he had cohabited for seven years. Major Henry Smith, the Assistant-Commissioner for the City Police, and Superintendent Foster were telegraphed for, and immediately went to the Bishopsgate-street station. Kelly, who was considerably affected, spoke quite unreservedly, and gave a full statement to his own movements and those of the ill-fated woman, as to whose identity he was quite positive. In this statement he was borne out by the deputy of the lodging-house, Frederick Wilkinson, who knew the woman well, and who had just seen the body.

So far the bodies of the last two victims have been identified.

There is no doubt in the minds of the police that the man Kelly's identification of the woman murdered in Mitre-square as Kate Conway is correct. In order that the matter may be fully cleared up, however, it has been deemed advisable to send the man Kelly, in company with Sergeant Outram and other officers, to find the victim's two daughters and her sister.

The police yesterday morning made a house-to-house visitation in Whitechapel, distributing a handbill worded as follows:-

"Police notice to the occupier. On the mornings of Friday, 31st August; Saturday, 8th; and Sunday, 30th September, 1888, women were murdered in Whitechapel, it is supposed by some one residing in the immediate neighbourhood. Should you know of any person to whom suspicion is attached, you are earnestly requested to communicate at once with the nearest police station.

Metropolitan Police Office,
30th September, 1888."

THE RIPPER REPORTS

William Bull, 27, describing himself as a medical student, of Stannard-road, Dalston, was charged before Mr. Alderman Stone, at the Guildhall Police-court, yesterday, on his own confession, with committing the murder in Mitre-square, Aldgate, on Sunday morning last. The Prisoner appeared to be recovering from the effects of intoxication.

Inspector George Izzard, of the City Police, deposed: Last night at twenty minutes to eleven o'clock the Prisoner came into the charge-room of the Bishopsgate Police-station, and made a statement. After cautioning him two or three times, I wrote down his statement, which I now produce, and with your Worship's permission, will read it.

Mr. Alderman Stone desired it to be read, and Witness read as follows:-

"My name is William Bull. I reside at 6, Stannard-road, Dalston, and am a medical student at the London Hospital. I wish to give myself up for the murder in Aldgate on Saturday night last or Sunday morning. About two o'clock, I think, I met the woman in Aldgate. I went with her up a narrow street. I promised to give her half a crown, which I did. While walking along together there was a second man, who came up and took the half-crown from her. I cannot endure this any longer. My poor head." Prisoner here put his hand to his head on the front of the desk, and cried, or pretended to cry, "I shall go mad. I have done it, and I must put up with it." I asked him what he had done with his clothing that he was wearing on the night of the murder, and he said, "If you wish to know, they are in the Lea, and the knife I threw away," At this point he declined to say anything more. He was drunk. Part of his statement was heard by Major H. Smith. Inquiries were made by Serjt. Myles, and he was told that no such person was known at the London Hospital and no such name. His father is a most respectable man, and says that his son was at home on Saturday night.

Mr. Alderman Stone: Do you ask any questions, Bull? - Prisoner: No. When I stated what I did I was mad drunk. I could not do it.

Inspector Izzard: I should like a few days' remand to make inquiries, your worship.

The Alderman: Very well. I shall remand him.

Prisoner: Can I have bail? - The Alderman: No I shall not allow bail.

Two arrests were made on Wednesday afternoon in connection with the murders. In one case a man went up to a police-office in the street, and said he "had assisted in the Mitre-square job." The constable took him to the Leman-street Police-station, where it was found that he was suffering from delirium tremens, and he was accordingly detailed in order that further inquiries might be made. About 3 o'clock a man went into a lodging-house in the High-street, Whitechapel, and asked permission to wash his hands. The suspicion of the inmates having been aroused by the stranger's behaviour, they communicated with the police, and the man was taken into custody. At Leman street he declared that he had only just been discharged from the workhouse, and an officer was instructed to accompany him to investigate the truth of his statements.

Source: *The Star*

WEDNESDAY 3 OCTOBER 1888

LONDON NEWS

THE RIPPER REPORTS

An arrest was made on Monday in connection with the murder of Jane Beatmoor at Birtely Fell, near Gateshead, on Saturday week. Dr. Phillips, the medical gentleman who examined the body of Annie Chapman, the last victim of the Whitechapel murderers, and Inspector Roots of the Criminal Investigation Department, Scotland-yard, have arrived at Bartley, accompanied by Col. White, chief constable of the county of Durham, and Supt. Harrison. Dr. Phillips saw the body during the afternoon, and made a very searching examination of the wounds, to see if they bore any resemblance to the injuries inflicted on the Whitechapel Victims. The result of the examination and the effect it had upon the doctor's mind were, of course, not divulged, but it is reported now that the authorities have little faith in the theory that the murder has had any connection with the tragedies in London. The resemblance in the two cases, however, is striking in the common fact that the wounds were made in the same parts of the body, and in both instances a mere fraction of the mutilation that actually took place would have been sufficient to have accomplished the murderer's object if killing was his only desire. Ever since the murder was discovered the police have been endeavouring to discover the man William Waddle, who, it is said, kept company with the deceased. Waddle was a labourer at Bartley Ironworks, and lodged in Bartley. He has not been at his lodgings since Friday week, and there are rumours of his having been seen in the neighborhood of Ouston wagon way, where the murder was committed, on Saturday night. No reason can be assigned for his sudden disappearance, and from information the police have concerning his antecedents they associate his absconding with the murder. He was arrested in Scotland.

Source: *The Derby Mercury*

THE RIPPER REPORTS

THURSDAY 4 OCTOBER 1888

AN ALARMING STORY
ATTEMPT AT ANOTHER OUTRAGE

An alarming story was told to a detective on Tuesday, and it is understood that the Metropolitan police have for some time been cognisant of its details. If this statement be true, and there appears to be no reason to question it, then some time between the date of the Hanbury-street murder and last Sunday the bloodthirsty maniac who is now terrifying Whitechapel unsuccessfully attempted another outrage.

The woman who so narrowly escaped death is married, but she admits having entered into conversation with a strange man for an immoral purpose. She alleges that he tripped her up, so that she fell upon the pavement. He made an effort to cut her throat, but she shielded herself with her arm, and in so doing received a cut upon it. Alarmed by his failure, and fearing her shrieks, the would-be murderer ran off, and the woman, when discovered, was removed to the hospital.

She has since been discharged, and the wound up on the arm is still to be seen. The occurrence is alleged to have taken place ten days ago, in a bye-turning off Commercial-street. Unfortunately the woman was so much in liquor when she was assaulted that she cannot recollect the man and has been unable to give a description of him, which may account for the secrecy which has been maintained in regard to the attack.

Source: *Western Mail*

THE RIPPER REPORTS

FRIDAY 5 OCTOBER 1888

THE EAST-END MURDERS

Five days have now elapsed since the discovery of the murdered bodies of the women Stride and Eddowes, and the police are as far from a clue as ever. An inquest was opened on the last-named woman yesterday, the only feature of which was the confirmation by the doctor of the general impression that the case tallied with that of Chapman as regards the absence of certain organs. This almost puts it beyond doubt that the four murders are the work of one man, but the theory tentatively put forward by Mr. Wynn Baxter, the coroner, in summing up the evidence in Chapman's case, is not practically abandoned on all hands. On this point some remarks of the British Medical Journal may be reproduced. It observes that that theory - propounded by the coroner, not without justification on the information conveyed to him - that the work of the assassin was carried out under the impulse of pseudo-scientific mania, is exploded by the first attempt at serious investigation.

"It is true," says the journal, "that inquiries were made at one or two medical schools early last year by a foreign physician, who was spending some time in London, as to the possibility of securing certain parts of the body for the purpose of scientific investigation. No large sum, however, was offered. The person in question was a physician of the highest respectability and exceedingly well accredited to this country by the best authorities in his own, and he left London fully 18 months ago. There was never any real foundation for the hypothesis, and the information communicated - which was not at all of the nature which the public has been led to believe - was due to the erroneous interpretation by a minor official of a question which he had overheard, and to whit a negative reply was given. This theory may be at once dismissed, and is, we believe, no longer entertained even by its author."

There were the usual number of arrests during Wednesday night, followed by an equal number of releases yesterday morning. One man confessed to being the murderer, but when the gained sobriety disclaimed - and with justice, as inquiries proved - any connection whatever with the crime. The second man was being followed in Ratcliffe-highway but a crowd of excited females, and by a boy who said he believed the man was the assassin, because he had seen him changing his clothes on the morning of the murders. The person was arrested, proved to be intoxicated, and was discharged after a few hours' detention. The third man came out of the Three Nuns Hotel at Aldgate late on Wednesday night, followed by a woman, who charged him with having threatened her. She was joined by others, and the man, to escape their cries, hailed a cab, which was soon followed by a howling and excited crowd. The vehicle was stopped by a Constable, who ordered the driver to go to Leman-street Police-station. The woman who had been the cause of the disturbance also went to the station and repeated her charge; and as the man was in a sullen humour, and refused to give any account of himself, he was detained for the night. In the morning, however, he was more communicative, and as nothing of a suspicious nature could be discovered concerning him, he was, of course, liberated.

THE INQUEST

Yesterday morning, in the City Coroner's Court, Golden-lane, Mr. Langham opened an inquiry into the circumstances attending the death of Catherine Eddowes, as unmarried woman, also known as Kate Kelly, who was murdered and mutilated in the early morning of Sunday last in Mitre-square, Aldgate. The City police were represented by Colonel Sir J. Fraser, Major Smith, assistant-commissioner, Superintendent Foster, and Detective-inspector M'William. Mr. Crawford, the solicitor to the Corporation, represented the City police authorities.

Eliza Gold, 6, Thrawl-street, Spitalfields, a widow, was the first witness called. She said:- I recognise the body as that of my poor sister, Catherine Eddowes. She was a single woman, about 43 years of age. She had been living with John Kelly for some years. She got a living by hawking, and was a woman of sober habits. Before she went to live with Kelly she lived with a man named Conway for some years, and had two children by him. I do not know whether Conway is still living. He was an army pensioner and used to go out hawking things. I cannot say whether they parted on good or bad terms, or whether she has ever seen him since.

By Mr. Crawford - I have not seen Conway for seven or eight years, and then my sister was living with him on friendly terms. I saw the man Kelly and my sister together three or four weeks ago on amicable terms

John Kelly, 55, Flower and Dean-street, a labourer, had seen the body, and recognised it as that of Catherine Conway, with whom he had been living for seven years. She used to sell a few things about the streets. He was last in her company at two o'clock on Saturday afternoon in Houndsditch, when they parted on very good terms. The last words she said were to the effect that she was going over to try to find her daughter Annie who lived in Bermondsey. She promised to return by four o'clock, but did not do so. he heard later on that she had been locked up at Bishopsgate-street Police-station, but he made no inquiries, feeling sure that she would be out on Sunday morning. He was told she was taken in charge for having had "a drop of drink." He never knew her to go out for improper purposes. She was not in the habit of drinking to excess. When the witness left her she had no money, her object being to see her daughter, with a view to obtaining some, to prevent them walking the streets.

The Coroner - What do you mean by that?

- Well, sir, many a time we have not had the money to pay for shelter, and have had to tramp about. The witness knew no one with whom the woman was at variance. He had never seen Conway in his life, and did not know where he was living.

By the jury - Kate usually returned to the lodgings by eight or nine o'clock.

By Mr. Crawford - The witness did not know with whom she had been drinking on the Saturday afternoon. There had been no angry words about money before they parted. He had heard that the daughter lived in King-street, Bermondsey. On Friday night last, as she had no money, she slept in the casual ward in Mile-end, while he remained at the lodging-house. The whole of last week they did not live together in the house, as until Thursday last they had been hopping in Kent. On that night they went into the Shoe-lane casual ward. He only earned 6d. on the Friday, and she insisted upon going to the casual ward to allow him to pay for his own lodging. He arranged to see her the next morning, but was surprised to meet her accidentally as early as 8 a.m. The tea and sugar found in a tin were bought of the money he obtained by pawning a pair of boots on Saturday morning. For them he received 2s. 6d. which they spent in drink and food. When she left to find her daughter she was sober. His boots might have been pawned on the Friday. The "missus" took them in while he stood outside the door with his bare feet.

Frederick Wilkinson, the deputy of the lodging-house in Flower and Dean-street, deposed to having known the woman and Kelly for the last seven or eight years. They lived on very good terms, never having more than a few words, and then only when the woman was in drink. He believed she got her living by hawking about the streets and cleaning for the Jews. He had never seen her husband drunk, nor did she stay out late at night.

By Mr. Crawford - He saw her on Saturday morning, when he believed she was wearing an apron. The distance from the lodging house to Mitre-square was about half a mile. He did not remember any one taking a bed about two o'clock on Sunday morning. The further examination of the witness was postponed for the production of his book.

Police-constable Watkins, of the City Police Force, stated that on Saturday night he went on duty at a quarter to ten. The beat extended from the corner of Duke-street, Aldgate, into Leadenhall-street, then into Mitre-street, Mitre-square, and around it into Mitre-street again, along King-street and back to Duke-street. The whole could be traversed in 12 or 14 minutes. He had been continually patrolling that beat from 10 p.m. until 1 a.m., during which time no person excited his attention. Passing through Mitre-square at 1.30 a.m. with his lantern shining from his belt, he, according to practice, inspected passages and warehouses. He saw no one about, and no person could have been there without his having seen them. About 1.44 he again entered the square, turned to the right, and saw a woman lying on her back with her feet facing the square. Her clothes were disarranged. He saw her throat was cut and her stomach ripped up. She was lying in a pool of blood. He did not touch the body, but ran across the road to the warehouse of Messrs. Kearney and Tonge and called Morris, the watchman, who went for assistance. The witness remained in the square until the arrival of Police-Constable

Holland. There was no one else there. Dr. Sequeira followed the constable, and Inspector Collard and Dr. Gordon Brown, the police surgeon, arrived. When the witness first entered the square he heard no sound of a person running away. When he called the watchman he found him working inside.

Frederick William Foster, of the Chief Office, produced plans of Mitre-square, with the route from Berner-street to Mitre-street, a distance of three-quarters of a mile.

In examination by Mr. Crawford, he said the direct route from Mitre-square to Flower and Dean-street would be through Goulston-street.

Mr. Crawford said evidence would be given that a portion of the woman's apron was afterwards found in Goulston-street, and the jury would at once she the importance of the evidence just given.

Wilkinson, the lodging-house deputy, recalled, after referring to his book, said that Kelly slept in No. 52 room on Friday and Saturday.

Mr. Crawford - Does your book enable you to tell us whether any person came into your lodgings about two o'clock on Sunday morning?

The witness - I cannot exactly say about the time.

Can you give me any information about it? - Not as to the time they came in.

You have nothing whatever to refresh your memory as to anybody coming in about two o'clock in the morning? - No.

Does your book show you had any strangers in? -We had six strange men in on Saturday evening sleeping.

Can you tell me whether any of these men came in about two o'clock on Sunday morning? - I cannot tell.

Do you remember any strangers going out soon after twelve o'clock on Sunday morning? - At twelve o'clock I would be very busy in the kitchen or at the door. I cannot say whether or not any stranger went out. The police came about three o'clock. I saw nothing to excite my suspicion. The house is usually shut up at half-past two o'clock. Sometimes more than 100 persons slept in the house.

Inspector Edward Collard said at five minutes before two on Sunday morning last he received information at Bishopsgate Police-station that a woman had been murdered in Mitre-square. Information was telegraphed to head-quarters, and a constable was dispatched for a doctor. On proceeding himself to Mitre-square, he found there Dr. Sequeira, several police-officers, and the body lying in the south-west corner of the square. The body was not touched till the arrival of Dr. Brown, who came to the square shortly after the witness. The medial men examined the body, and Sergeant Jones picked up some small buttons and other articles, including a small mustard tin, which contained two pawn tickets. The body was conveyed to the mortuary. No money was found about it, but there was a portion of an apron corresponding to the piece found in Goulston-street. Search was immediately made in all directions for the murderer, and several men were stopped and searched in the street without any result. House to house inquiries were made in the vicinity of Mitre-square, but nothing could be found or heard that related to the murder. In the square there was no appearance of a struggle, and from what he saw he inferred that the body had not been there more than a quarter of an hour. He could find no trace of footsteps, although a search was made at the back of the empty house.

Dr. Gordon Brown, 17, Finsbury-circus, surgeon to the City of London Police, said - I was called shortly after two o'clock on Sunday morning, and reached Mitre-square about 2.18. My attention was called to the body of a woman lying in the position described by Police constable Watkins. The woman was lying on her back with her head turned to the left shoulder, with the arms lying at the sides of her body.

The fingers were slightly bent, and a thimble was lying the ground near the right hand. The bonnet was at the back of the head. There was a great disfigurement to the face and the throat was cut across, below the wound being a neckerchief. The upper part of the dress was pulled open. The intestines were drawn out to a large extent, and placed over the right shoulder, and a piece of them about two feet in length was placed between the left arm and the body, apparently by design. The lobe of the left ear was cut completely through. There was a quantity of clotted blood on the pavement near the left side of the neck. The body was quite warm, no death stiffening having set in, and death had certainly taken place within 30 or 40 minutes before I saw the body. We looked for superficial bruises, but found none.

By Mr. Crawford - There was no blood on the front of the clothes.

Continuing, the witness said - I sent for Dr. Phillips, as he had seen some of the recent cases. When the body arrived at the mortuary in Golden-lane the clothes were carefully removed, and the piece of the ear dropped from them. The post-mortem examination was made on Sunday afternoon, and on washing the left hand carefully I found a recent bruise the size of a sixpence on the back of the hand between the thumb and first finger. The hands and arms appeared sunburnt. There were no bruises on the scalp, the back of the body, or the elbows. The face was very much mutilated. There was a cut about quarter of an inch in length through the lower left eyelid, dividing the structures completely. The upper eyelid on that side was scratched near the angle of the nose. The right eyelid was cut through for about half an inch. There was a deep cut over the bridge of the nose, extending from the left border of the nasal bone, down nearly to the angle of the jaw on the right side. The knife had gone into the nasal bone, and divided all the structures of the cheek, except the mucous membrane of the mouth. The tip of the nose was quite detached by an oblique cut from the bottom of the nasal bones to where the wings of the nose or corners of the nostrils join on to the face. A cut from this divided the upper lip and extended through the substance of the gum, over the right upper lateral incisor tooth. About half an inch from the tip of the nose was another oblique cut, also one at the right angle of the mouth, as if made with the point of a knife, which penetrated the mucous membrane, and extended about an inch ana half parallel with the lower lip. There was on each cheek a cut, which peeled up the skin, forming a triangular flap. On the left cheek there were two abrasions on the outer skin, also two slight abrasions under the left ear. The throat was cut across to the extent of about seven inches. The larynx was severed below the vocal cords, and all the deep structures were severed to the bone, the knife marking the vertebral cartilage. The carotid artery had a pin-hole opening, the internal jugular vein being open to the extent of one inch and a half. The anterior fibres of the muscles which cross the front of the throat were severed. The wounds must have been inflicted by some very sharp instrument. The cause of death was hemorrhage from the left carotid artery. Death must have been immediate. Most of the injuries were inflicted after death. With regard to the injuries to the abdomen the front wall was laid open from the breast down-wards. There were two incisions into the liver, and the left lobe of the liver was slit right through for three or four inches by a vertical cut. The witness then explained in detail the other injuries inflicted, showing that the same organs had been removed as in former cases.

By Mr. Crawford - My opinion is that when the throat was cut the woman was lying on the ground.

Mr. Crawford - Would you consider the person who inflicted the wounds had great anatomical skill? - Well, a good deal of knowledge of the position of the abdominal organs and the way of removing them. It requires a great deal of knowledge to abstract the left kidney, which might easily be overlooked. That knowledge would likely to be possessed by one accustomed to cutting up animals. The organs taken away would be of no use to medical science.

Do you think the murderer was disturbed? - I think he had sufficient time; he would not have cut the lower eyelids if he had been in a great hurry. The wounds could not have been inflicted in less than five minutes. The ladder was in no way injured in the body; and I may mention that a man accustomed to remove the portions removed was asked by me to do so as quickly as possible. He accomplished the task in three minutes, but not without injuring the bladder. I should think no struggle took place between the parties. The fact that there were no cries heard is easily understood, as the through would be cut so suddenly as to allow of no time to make any noise. There was a piece of apron found in Goulston-street, with finger marks of blood upon it, which fits onto the piece left round the body. I think the face was mutilated simply to disfigure the corpse.

The inquest was then adjourned until Thursday next.

On the paper of business brought before the meeting of the Court of Common Council yesterday afternoon was a notice of motion by Mr. John Pound authorising the Corporation to offer a reward of £300 for the apprehension of the Aldgate murderer. Immediately after the reading of the minutes, however, the Lord Mayor rose and said:- The court is aware of the course I was advised, and thought it right to take, as to the prompt offer in the name of the Corporation of a substantial reward for the apprehension of the Mitre-square murderer, and I am glad to see that not only is public opinion satisfied, but, judging from the paper of business, the court is also satisfied. I have now only to ask the court to endorse that which I have done in its name, and I am sure we all join in the earnest hope that the perpetrator or perpetrators of these hideous crimes will be speedily detected.

- Mr. F. Green said he was sure the court desired to endorse the action which had been taken by his lordship. All England had for days past been horrified by particulars of the terrible crimes that had been committed, and they had but one object in view, and that was to leave no stone unturned in their endeavour to lead to the arrest of the murderer. He, therefore, moved a resolution endorsing the action of the Lord Mayor in offering the reward.

- Mr. Alderman Cowan seconded the motion, remarking that it would be unnecessary for him, in doing so, to offer a single observation in support of it.

- The resolution was adopted unanimously.

The man Pizer who was arrested on suspicion of being connected with the murder of Annie Chapman in Hanbury-street, and who after giving a satisfactory account of himself complained to Mr. Lushington at the Thames Police-court yesterday that since he was released from custody he had been subjected to great annoyance, and that morning a woman accosted him in the street, and after calling him "Old Leather Apron" and other insulting expressions, struck him three blows in the face. Mr. Lushington told Pizer he could have a summons against the person who had assaulted him.

A telegram from Armagh says that last night a tramp whose name is unknown, but who describes himself as "Leather Apron," was arrested by the police there on a charge of drunkenness and disorderly conduct. When taken into the police barrack, he violently assaulted a constable. In his possession were found a 1½ d., a knife covered with blood, and a letter, also stained with blood addressed to the Roman Catholic Primate.

At the close of the morning service in the City Temple yesterday, Dr. Parker referred at length to the East-end murders. Replying to the question, how far the pulpit was responsible for such crimes, the rev. gentleman said the pulpit had undertaken instrumentally to convert society, and the pulpit had signally failed. Always allowing for exceptions, the pulpit was the paid slave of respectable society. It loved respectability and had lost its hold on the tragic and impetuous life of the world.

The outcasts of society turned away from the preacher, as from a man who talked in an unknown tongue, and troubled himself about antiquities and metaphysics, for which the sad and maddened heart of the world cared nothing. What the Home Secretary was doing or thinking of doing passed his (Dr. Parker's) comprehension. If offering a reward for the discovery of the criminal did not detect the perpetrator of the crime what harm was done? But if offering a reward should end in the detection of the criminal great good was done.

The Bishop of Liverpool last night addressing the Curates' Society said he knew East London intimately, and clergymen in the district, and could quite understand such tragedies as had horrified the Christian world taking place. Men were there living little better than beasts and the state of that district illustrated the opinion of an old divine, that if man was left to himself he was half devil, half beast.

Whilst such tragedies aroused people, it brought them to a sense of what should be done for the neglected classes, so that no room and no house should be left unvisited by the late clergy.

Source: *The Morning Post*

THE RIPPER REPORTS

FRIDAY 5 OCTOBER 1888

SIMILAR TO MURDERS IN TEXAS - AN AMERICAN THEORY

Not a great many months ago, says the Daily News' New York correspondent, a series of remarkably brutal murders of women occurred in Texas. The matter caused great local excitement, but aroused less interest that would otherwise have been the case, because the victims were chiefly negro women. The crimes were characterised by the same brutal methods as those of the Whitechapel murders. The theory has been suggested that the perpetrator of the latter may be the Texas criminal, who was never discovered. The Atlanta Constitution, a leading southern newspaper, thus puts the argument:- "In our recent annals of crime there has been no other man capable of committing such deeds.

The mysterious crimes in Texas have ceased. They have just commenced in London. Is the man from Texas at the bottom of them all? If he is the monster or lunatic he may be expected to appear anywhere. The fact that he is no longer at work in Texas argues his presence somewhere else. His peculiar line of work was executed in precisely the same manner as is now going on in London. Why should he not be there? The more one thinks of it, the more irresistible becomes the conviction that it is the man from Texas.

In these days of steam and cheap travel distance is nothing. The man who could kill a dozen women in Texas would not mind the inconvenience of a trip across the water, and once there he would not have any scruples about killing more women." The Superintendent of the New York police admits the possibility of this theory being correct, but he does not think it probable. "There is," he says, "the same brutality and mutilation, the same suspicion that the criminal is a monster or lunatic who has declared war literally to the knife against all womankind, but I hardly believe it is the same individual."

A SURGICAL THEORY

A surgical theory which is advanced in Paris about the Whitechapel murder is that the murderer is a fanatical vivisectionist and disciple of Haeckel, the German naturalist, who followed in the steps of Darwin in studying the origin of the species, and who advanced some startling ideas that have not yet been established. A naturalist's arm in visible in the way in which the knife was applied to the two unfortunate beings in Whitechapel. Perhaps there was not time to operate in an exactly like manner in the second series of murders.

LIST OF EAST-END MURDERS

Six women have now been murdered in the East-end under mysterious circumstances, five of them within a period of eight weeks. The following are the dates of the crimes and names of the victims so far as known:-

1. - Last Christmas week - An unknown woman, found murdered near Osborne and Wentworth streets, Whitechapel.

2. - August 7. - Martha Turner, found stabbed in 39 places on a landing in [model] dwellings, known as George-yard-buildings, Commercial-street, Spitalfields.

3. - August 31. - Mrs Nicholls, murdered and mutilated in Buck's-row, Whitechapel.

4. - September 7. - Mrs Chapman, murdered and mutilated in Hanbury-street, Whitechapel.

5. - September 30. - Elizabeth Stride, found with her throat cut in Berner-street, Whitechapel.

6. - September 30. - Woman unknown, murdered and mutilated in Mitre-square, Aldgate.

Source: *Cambridge Independent Press*

FRIDAY 5 OCTOBER 1888

THE EQUIPMENT OF THE POLICE

A great post in connection with the East-end murders is (says the Echo) not made enough of. One great help to the assassin is the heavy policeman's boot, which can be heard at any distance almost, and which warns him of the constable's approach. In Leeds this is obviated by putting indiarubber pegs into the heels of the constable's foot gear, so that at night-time he can move as noiselessly along as a panther, and drop upon a malefactor before the latter is aware of his approach. If our policemen are to have a chance of catching such criminals as the Whitechapel assassin they must wear light boots.

THE PROPOSED EMPLOYMENT OF BLOODHOUNDS

THE RIPPER REPORTS

Professor J Wortley Axe, principal of the Royal Veterinary College, London, has favoured a representative of the Central News with his views upon the employment of bloodhounds in the detection of murderers. Professor Axe stated that no doubt a leash of bloodhounds might be a useful police auxiliary, but its successful employment would depend upon the efficient training of the dogs, and the promptitude with which they were put upon the track. All dogs had a natural instinct for blood odours, but this instinct required development by training; and in the case of the bloodhound it was necessary to make it an expert at the business. The dog must in the first place, be familiarised with the odour of blood.

The incriminating element of the murder, so far as the dog was concerned, would, of course, be the blood carried in the clothes or upon the boots of the murderer. It was, in fact, a condition precedent of the hunt that some of the blood of the victim should be upon the person of the fugitive. In the country, where the ground and atmosphere might remain undisturbed for a longer period, this system of pursuit would work fairly well; but, said Professor Axe, when you come to deal with the streets of large towns, the ground surface of which must necessarily be impregnated with a number of odours, I apprehend that this fact would materially operate against your success in tracking the murderer with bloodhounds.

The pavements of our own city, for instance, may possibly be stained with the blood of carcasses such as sheep in transit, as well, indeed, as with human blood, the result of natural deposit. This would tend to confuse the scent which you desired to follow up, unless it were very fresh and strong. Again, the air in large towns is always shifting, or may have been shifted by the ordinary traffic of the street; so that the odour left by the fugitive would not be suffered to abide long without obliteration. Hence it comes to this, if you resort to bloodhounds for the tracking of bloodstained fugitives, your dogs must be perfectly trained, must be experts at the business, and the condition of the ground must be favourable to the retention of the odour forming the clue. In large towns the last condition presents a serious difficulty.

Source: *Aberdeen Free Press*

SATURDAY 6 OCTOBER 1888
THE MURDERS AT THE EAST-END TELEGRAM AND LETTER FROM "JACK THE RIPPER"

The Press Association says the following postal telegram was received by the metropolitan police at 11.55 last night. It was handed in at an office in the eastern district at 8 PM. :-"Charles Warren, Head of the Police News, Central Office. Dear Boss, - If you are willing to catch me, I am now in City-road lodging, but number you will have to find out; and I mean to do another murder to-night in Whitechapel. - Yours JACK THE RIPPER."

A letter was also received at the Commercial-street police station by the first post this morning. It was addressed to the "Commercial-street Police Station" in black-lead pencil, and the contents were also written in pencil and couched in ridiculous language. The police believe the letter to be the work of a lunatic. It was signed "Jack the Ripper," and said he was going to work in Whitechapel last night. He added that he was going to commit another murder in the Goswell-road to-night, and spoke of having "several bottles of blood underground in Epping Forest," and frequently referred to "Jack the Ripper under the ground."

Detective-Inspector Abberline has been informed of the correspondence, and the police of the G Division have been communicated with.

We are requested to state that Sir Charles Warren has been making inquiries as to the practicability of employ trained bloodhounds for use in special cases in the streets of London; and having ascertained that dogs can be procured that have been accustomed to work in a town, he is making immediate arrangements for their use in London.

The police authorities of Whitehall have had reproduced in facsimile and published on the walls of London the letter and post-card sent to the Central News agency. The language of the card and letter is of a brutal character, and is full of Americanisms. The handwriting, which is clear and plain, and disguised in part, is that of a person accustomed to write a round hand like that employed by clerks in offices. The exact colour of the ink and the smears of blood are reproduced in the placard and information is asked in identification of the handwriting. The post-card bears a tolerably clear imprint of a bloody thumb or finger-mark.

The daughter of the woman who was murdered in Mitre-square has been found. Her age is nineteen, and she is married. She states that her father, Thomas Conway, with whom the deceased lived for some time before she met with Kelly is still living, but he has not yet been traced. It will be remembered that Kelly stated in the course of his evidence on Thursday, before the coroner, that when the deceased left him early last Saturday afternoon she told him she was going to try and find her daughter Annie. The latter, however, now states that she did not see her mother that day.

Source: *St James's Gazette*

SATURDAY 6 OCTOBER 1888

THE WHITECHAPEL MURDERS
SELF ACCUSED

At the Birmingham Police Court to-day Alfred Napier Blanchard as charged on his own confession with having committed the murders in Whitechapel. The prisoner entered a Birmingham public-house about noon yesterday, and sat drinking beer for some hours. He led the conversation of the company to the recent murders, and, announcing himself the murderer, explained his method of procedure with much circumstantiality of detail. The excited company at length gave him into custody. The prisoner now declared that he was innocent, and that he could bring witnesses to prove him a book-canvasser of perfect respectability, travelling for a London firm. He was labouring under great excitement when he made the extraordinary statement now put in evidence against him. He was remanded.

Source: *Clonmel Chronicle*

THE RIPPER REPORTS

SATURDAY 6 OCTOBER 1888

THE EAST-END MURDERS
THE REIGN OF TERROR IN WHITECHAPEL
MORE ARRESTS
EXCITING SCENE
A FALSE ALARM
THE ALDGATE VICTIM
INQUEST
IMPORTANT MEDICAL EVIDENCE
STARTLING REPORTS
SIR CHARLES WARREN'S REPLY TO THE WHITECHAPEL BOARD OF WORKS
ANOTHER LETTER FROM "JACK THE RIPPER"

At the time of going to press, on Thursday, our last telegram purported that there were no persons in custody in conviction with the East-End murders since then. The Press Association states that the reign of "terror which has prevailed in the East-end" since Sunday continues and that the popular excitement and indignation seem to be growing more intense. Late on Wednesday night the wildest rumours were afloat and the district east of Aldgate witnessed a series of extraordinary scenes. Again and again reports were put about that the murderer had been captured in this and that district.

Shortly before midnight a story was circulating in Fleet-street to the effect that the murderer had been surprised in the act of attempting one of his now too familiar outrages on a woman in Union-street. This story, it appears had its origin in the following circumstances:- Just at ten o'clock a well-dressed man rushed out of the Three Nuns public-house in Aldgate, followed by a woman who, in a loud voice, declared to the loungers and passers-by that he had molested and threatened her. While he was thus being denounced to the crowd, the stranger hailed a cab, jumped in, and proceeded to drive off.

A hue-and-cry was at once raised, and the vehicle was followed by an excited mob, which rapidly grew in numbers. It was the general belief, that the murderer who has been terrorizing the East-end was the occupant of the cab, and a hot pursuit was given. In a moment of two the cab was stopped, and a police constable got in, secured the man, and directed the cabman to drive to the Leman-street police station. Here the prisoner was formally charged on suspicion. The cab was followed to the station by the woman who had raised the outcry. She stated to the police in the most emphatic manner that the prisoner had first accosted and molested her in the street, and that when she refused to accede to his proposals he threatened physical violence.

While the woman was making her statement the prisoner was holding down his head and looking at the ground, and he never once attempted to make a remark. When, however, a man stepped forward to interrogate the girl's story, he looked up angrily and denied the truth of the allegations with considerable emphasis. The woman was then asked if she desired to make any charge, but she declined to do so, and shortly after left the station. It was, however, deemed prudent by the officer in charge to detail the man pending inquiries. When removed to the cell his attitude became impudent and defiant, and in the course of conversation which he carried on with a slightly American accent while pacing up and down his place of confinement, the frequency with which he used the word "Boss" was particularly noticed.

Between nine and ten o'clock the same evening another arrest was made in the Ratcliff-highway by Sergeant Adams, of the H Division. The officer in question, hearing a woman screaming for help in an adjoining court, proceeded in the direction of the cries, and met a man who was evidently a foreigner, leaving the place.

The sergeant took the man into custody, more especially as it occurred to him that he bore a striking resemblance to the published police description of the man who is said to have been seen with "Long Liz" on the Saturday night preceding her murder. The captive, who went quietly to the Leman-street police station, told the sergeant that he was sailing from this country for America to-day. At the police station the man told the inspector in charge that he was a Maltese, and willingly furnished his name and address. No weapons were found upon him. The inquiries that were instituted proving to be satisfactory, the man was released in the course of the morning.

A third arrest was made in Shadwell at a late hour on Wednesday night in the neighbourhood of Cable-street, and the man brought to Leman-street. Here the man was able to give a satisfactory explanation as to his identity and other particulars, and he was at once discharged.

A later report says:- The man who was detained at the Leman-street Police-station during the night, was charged at half-past nine o'clock on Thursday morning, diligent inquiries by the Police leading them to a conclusion that the prisoner was not the man wanted. But for the obstinacy he displayed after his arrest, it is probably that he would have been released long before. Matters stand now, so far as the murderer is concerned, just where they did on Sunday last, and it is safe to state that not the faintest evidence likely to lead the detection and arrest has been forthcoming as yet.

THE INQUEST

THE RIPPER REPORTS

The inquest on the body of Catherine Eddowes, alias Conway, alias Kelly, found murdered in Mitre-square, Aldgate, on Sunday morning last, was opened before Mr. S. F. Langham, the City coroner, at the City mortuary, Golden-lane, at 11 o'clock on Thursday morning. Major Smith, Assistant Police Commissioner, and Superintendent Foster represented the City Police Force. Mr, Crawford, the City solicitor, said he appeared for the police authorities, and if it was necessary he hoped the coroner would allow him to put questions during the inquiry. The coroner assented.

Eliza Gold, residing at 6, Thrawl-street, Spitalfields, a widow, identified the deceased as her sister. Her name was Catherine Eddowes. She was a single woman, about forty-three years of age, and had been living for some years with John Kelly. She last saw the deceased alive four or five weeks ago. The deceased used to get her living by hawking, and was of sober habits. Before she lived with Kelly she had lived with a man named Conway, and had had two children by him. Conway had been in the army and was a pensioner. He used to go out hawking things.

The corner: Did they part on good or bad terms? The witness could not say. She could not say whether the deceased ever saw Conway since she parted with him. She had no doubt that the deceased was her sister. She had not seen Conway for seven or eight years. When she last saw the deceased and Kelly together they were living on happy terms in Flower and Dean-street.

John Kelly, a labourer, said that he earned a living by being about the markets. He identified the deceased. He knew her as Catherine Conway, and had lived with her seven years. The deceased used to hawk things about the street. She lived with him at Cooney's lodging-house, 55, Flower and Dean-street. He was in her company at 2 o'clock on

Saturday afternoon in Houndsditch. They parted on very good terms, and she told him that she was going over to Bermondsey to see if she could find her daughter Annie, the daughter she had had by the man Conway. She promised him that she would return by 4 o'clock. She did not return. He did not know of any one with whom she was at variance, or who was likely to injure her. He had never seen Conway, nor did he know whether the deceased saw him after they parted, or if Conway was living.

By Mr. Crawford: He did not know which whom the deceased had been in company on Saturday afternoon, or who paid for her drink. She left him some months ago in consequence for a few hours. They had had no angry words on Saturday about money. He slept at the house on Friday night, but the deceased was not with him, as she had not the money for her lodgings. She slept at the casual ward, Mile-end. He did not sleep at the lodging-house during the rest of the week.

On Monday night he was in Kent hopping, and the deceased was with him. They came up to town on Thursday night and slept at the Shoe-lane casual ward. They were all together all Friday until the afternoon, when he earned sixpence. He wanted her to remain with him, but she insisted on his going to the lodging-house while she went to Mile-end. He was aware that some tea and coffee were found on her. She got them with part of the half-crown which he obtained through pawning a pair of boots. They spent the rest of the money for drink and food. She was quite sober when she left him. She had never brought money to him in the morning which she had earned at night.

Frederick William Wilkinson, tenant of the lodging-house 55, Flower and Dean-street, identified the deceased. He had known her and Kelly for six or seven years. They passed as man and wife, and were always on good terms. They quarrelled now and again, but not violently, when the deceased was in drink. He saw the deceased on the Friday before her death, and on the Saturday morning between ten and eleven o'clock. He had no knowledge of her walking the streets at night. The deceased was sober on Saturday morning when he saw her.

By Mr. Crawford: Kelly and the woman last slept together at the lodgings five or six weeks ago, before they went hop picking. He never knew of a quarrel between Kelly and another man as to the deceased. No stranger took a bed at his lodgings between one and two o'clock on Sunday morning.

Police-constable Watkin gave evidence as to the finding of the body. Frederick William Foster, 26, Old Jewry, produced a plan of the square. In examination by Mr. Crawford, the witness said that the direct route from Mitre-square to Flower and Dean-street would be through Goulstone-street. Mr. Crawford said that evidence would be given to the effect that a portion of the woman's apron was afterwards found in Goulstone-street, and the jury would at once see the importance of the evidence just given.

By Mr. Crawford: He did not touch the body, but Dr. Sequeira said it was warm. There was no appearance of a struggle. He thought the body had not been in the square more than a quarter of an hour. There were no traces of footsteps. A search was also made at the back of some empty houses.

THE MEDICAL EVIDENCE

Dr. Gordon Brown, surgeon to the City of London Police, described the results of his examination of the body. There was great disfigurement of the face. The throat was cut across, and below the cut was a neckerchief. The upper part of the dress at the chest has been pulled open. The witness then described the terrible injuries inflicted upon the deceased. The woman had been dead only a few minutes, certainly not more than thirty or forty. Dr. Phillips also saw the body on its arrival at the Golden-lane mortuary.

A post-mortem examination was made at half-past two on Sunday afternoon, the results of which the witness described at length. The throat was cut right across to the extended of six or seven inches, and the large vessels on each side of the neck were severed. The larynx was severed just below the vocal cords; all the deep structures were severed to the bone.

The cause of death was hemorrhage from the throat, and death must have been immediate. There were other mutilations after death. The injuries on the lower portions of the body must have been made after death, and there would not be much blood on the hands of the murderer. The cuts were made by some one probably kneeling on the right side and below the middle of the body. The left kidney had been carefully taken out of the body and carried away, and he came to the conclusion that some one who knew the position of the kidneys had done it. The uterus was cut through, with the exception of about three-quarters of an inch, and the rest, with some portions of the ligaments, had been removed. He believed the woman was lying on the ground when the injuries were inflicted.

The injuries must have been done with a sharp-pointed knife at least six inches long. The perpetrator must have had considerable knowledge of the position of particular organs in the body and the way or removing them. The parts removed could be of no use for a professional purpose. A person who was accustomed to cut up animals would have such a knowledge.

Mr. Crawford: Do you think the perpetrator was disturbed while he was at work? - I think he had sufficient time, or he would not have nicked the lower eyelids. It would have occupied at least five minutes.

Can you as a professional man assign any reason why these parts of the body should be taken away? - I cannot. I feel sure there was no struggle and am not surprised that the deceased made no noise. The witness further said that he did not think there would be much blood on the man's hands. He had examined a portion of an apron found on the deceased with blood spots upon it of recent origin. He had also seen another portion of the apron found in Goulstone-street, which had smears of blood upon it as if hands or a knife had been wiped upon it. The mutilation of the face he thought was simply to disfigure the corpse. There was no reason to believe that any drug had been administered.

The inquest was then adjourned until half-past ten o'clock on Thursday week.

A FALSE ALARM

The Press Association was informed, upon inquiry at the chief police-station for the district in which it was stated that a watchman had been killed on Thursday morning, that no information had been received by the police of the alleged murder, and that no arrest had been made.

STARTLING REPORT

It may be mentioned in connection with the Mitre-square murder that the foreman of the sewer hands who are engaged at Aldgate in sweeping the streets and clearing away the refuse, &c., in the early hours of the morning, has stated most positively that at the time when the murder is supposed to have been perpetrated he was standing not more than 20 yards away from the spot where the body was subsequently found by the constable and himself. He states emphatically that he never heard any woman's cries for help, nor did any sounds of a struggle reach his ear.

SIR CHARLES WARREN'S REPLY
A LARGE FORCE OF POLICE IN WHITECHAPEL

Sir Charles Warren, replying to a resolution passed at a meeting of the Whitechapel District Board of Works, writes as follows:-

"Sir, - In reply to a letter of the 2d inst. From the Clerk to the Board of Works for the Whitechapel District, transmitting a resolution of the Board with regard to the recent atrocious murders perpetrated in and about Whitechapel, I have to point out that the carrying out of your proposal as to regulating and strengthening the Police Force in your district cannot possibly do more than guard, or take precautions against, any repetition of such atrocities, so long as the victims actually, but unwittingly, connive at their own destruction. Statistics show that London, in comparison to its population, is the safest city in the world to live in.

The prevention of murder directly cannot be effected by any strength of the Police Force, but it is reduced and brought to a minimum by rendering it most difficult to escape detection. In the particular class of murders now confronting us, however the unfortunate victims appear to take the murderer to some retired spot, and place themselves in such a position that they can be slaughtered without a sound being heard. The murder, therefore, takes place without any clue to the criminal being left.

"I have to request and call upon your Board, as proper representatives, to do all in your power and dissuade the unfortunate women about Whitechapel from going into lonely places in the dark with any persons, whether acquaintances or strangers. I have also to point out that the purlieus about Whitechapel are most imperfectly lighted, and the darkness is an important assistant to crime.

I can assure you, for the information of your Board, that every nerve has been strained to detect the criminal or criminals, and to render more difficult further atrocities. You will agree with me that it is not desirable that I should enter into particulars as to what the police are doing in the matter. It is most important for good results that our proceedings should not be published, and the very fact that you may be unaware of what the Detective Department is doing is only the stranger proof that it is doing its work with secrecy and efficiency.

"A large force of police has been drafted into the Whitechapel district to assist those already there to the full extent necessary to meet the requirements, but I have to observe that the Metropolitan Police have not large reserves doing nothing and ready to meet emergencies, but every man has his duty assigned to him, and I can only strengthen the Whitechapel district by drawing men from duty in other parts of the Metropolis.

You will be aware that the whole of the police work of the Metropolis has to be done as usual while this extra work is going on, and that at such times as this extra precautions have to be taken to prevent the commission of other classes of crime being facilitated through the attention of the police being diverted to one special place and object.

"I trust that your Board will assist the police by persuading the inhabitants to give them every information in their power concerning any suspicious characters in the various dwellings, for which object ten thousand handbills, a copy of which I enclose, have been distributed.

"I have read the reported proceedings of your meeting, and I regret to see that the greatest misconception appears to have arisen in the public mind as to recent action in the administration of the police. I beg you will dismiss from minds as utterly fallacious the numerous

THE RIPPER REPORTS

anonymous statements as to the recent changes stated to have been made in the police force of a character not conducive to efficiency. It is stated that the Rev. Daniel Greatrex announced to you that one great cause of police inefficiency was a new system of police whereby constables were constantly changed from one district to another, keeping them ignorant of their beats. I have seen this statement made frequently in the newspapers lately, but it is entirely without foundation.

The system at present in use has existed for the last twenty years, and constables are seldom, or never, drafted from their districts except for promotion, or for some particular case. Notwithstanding the many good reasons why constables should be changed on their beats, I have considered the reasons on the other side to be more cogent, and have felt that they should be thoroughly acquainted with the districts in which they serve. With regard to the Detective Department, a department relative to which reticence is always most desirable, I may say that a short time ago I made arrangements which still further reduced the necessity for transferring officers from districts which they knew thoroughly.

"I have to call attention to the statement of one of your members that in consequence of the change in condition of Whitechapel in recent years, a thorough revision of the police arrangements is necessary, and I shall be very glad to ascertain from you what changes your Board consider advisable and I may assure you that your proposals will receive from me every consideration.

I am, Sir, your obedient servant
(Signed) CHARLES WARREN
Metropolitan Police, 4, Whitehall-place, S.W., October 3, 1888."

Source: *The Star*

THE RIPPER REPORTS

SATURDAY 6 OCTOBER 1888

THE EAST-END MURDERS

So far as getting any clue to the identity of the murderer of the two women whose bodies were found on Sunday goes, the police are as far off as ever. Arrests have been made on suspicion, confessions have again been made by drunken and excited persons, but all have come to nothing. The medical student, William Bull, who declared that he was the Mitre-square murderer, was brought up again at the Guildhall yesterday, and discharged with a severe reprimand, expressing repentance, and stating that since he had been locked up he had taken the pledge. The police are actively engaged in following up every likely and unlikely clue. They have posted facimile copies of the letter and postcard purporting to have been written by the murderer, and signed "Jack the Ripper;" they have arranged for a systematic examination of the unoccupied houses and premises within the area of the East-end districts; and they are about to supplement their resources by the use of bloodhounds.

On the latter point, Sir Charles Warren has been making inquiries within the last day or two, and having ascertained that dogs which have been accustomed to work in a town are procurable, he is making immediate arrangements for their use in London. Whether they could possibly be of any use in this case, after so considerable a lapse of time, is more than doubtful. An extraordinary story is told in a New York telegram to the Central News. An English sailor named Dodge, so the narrative runs, states that he arrived in London from China by the steamship Glenorchy on August 13, and that he met at a Poplar music-hall a Malay cook, named Alaska. The Malay said he had been robbed by women of bad character in Whitechapel and swore that unless he found the thief and recovered his money he would murder every Whitechapel woman he met. He showed Dodge a double-edged knife which he always carried with him. He was, says the sailor, about 5ft. 7in. in height, apparently 35 years of age, and, of course, very dark.

The excitement in the district of the murders is calming down, but the crimes are still the chief topic of discussion. On Thursday night about 50 volunteer patrols, working men for the most part, swelled the number of uniformed and plain clothes constables in the streets of Whitechapel. They had been got together by the Vigilance Committee, were under the orders of a couple of private detectives, carried police whistles and stout cudgels, and wore galoshes over their boots. Their zeal was commendable, but their assistance was not required, for the night passed without incident. The remains of Kate Eddowes, the Mitre-square victim, will be interred at Ilford on Monday.

Yesterday afternoon Mr. Wynne E. Baxter resumed the inquiry at the Vestry-hall, Cable-street, St. George's-in-the-East into the circumstances attending the death of Elizabeth Stride, who was found with her throat cut in a yard at No. 40, Berner-street, Commercial-road, on Sunday morning last.

Dr. Phillips was recalled and said he had examined more fully the roof of the mouth of the deceased, and found no injury to or absence of any part of either the hard or soft palate. He was sure the woman had not swallowed either the skin or substance of a grape within many hours of her death. The abrasion that he spoke about on the right side of the leg was only an apparent abrasion, for on washing it the stain was removed and the skin found to be entire.

He had also examined a knife given him by the police, and he found it to be such a knife as would be used in a chandler's shop, and was called a slicing knife. It had blood upon it, which had characteristics similar to those of a warm-blooded animal. It had been recently blunted, and its edge turned by being rubbed on a stone, such as a kerbstone, and it had been evidently a once sharp knife.

By the Coroner - Such a knife could have produced the incision and wounds on the neck, but he thought it improbable that this particular knife had been used by the murderer. Witness believed that the woman had been seized by the shoulder, placed on the ground, and that the perpetrator was on her right side when he inflicted the cut. The cut was made from the left to the right, and therefrom arose the unlikelihood of a long knife being used.

The Coroner: Can you form any opinion how it was that the right hand of the deceased had so much blood upon it?

Witness - I cannot. It is a mystery. It was smeared all over, and had several clots upon it. Of course, in giving that answer, I am taking it for granted that the hand had always remained in the position I found it in, resting across the body.

The Coroner - Had she been dead long?

Witness - She must certainly have been alive within an hour of the time I first saw the body.

The Coroner - Would the injuries take long to inflict, do you think?

Witness - Only a few seconds. It might have been done in two seconds. There seemed to be a knowledge by the murderer of how to cut a throat in order to bring about a fatal result. There was a great dissimilarity in this case and Chapman's. In the latter case the neck was severed down to the vertebral column, and there had been an attempt to detach the vertebrae. It was not necessary that much blood should have been on the hands of the person inflicting the injury, as the hands had evidently been away from the wound. There was no perceptible trace of any anaesthetic having been used.

The absence of noise is a difficult question, under the circumstances, to account for. It must not be taken for granted that there was no noise. If, however, there was no noise, it was quite impossible to account for it. Witness believed the woman was lying down on the ground when her throat was cut, on account of the absence of blood from the left side of the body, and between that and the wall.

Dr. Blackwall, recalled, said that he had seen many severe wounds and more so, which were suicidal, but agreed with Dr. Philips generally on that point, and the knife found, although it might have been inflicted in the injury, was a most unlikely weapon. There were pressure marks on the shoulder as if the victim had struggled - faint at first, but which had since become quite distinct.

Mr. Sven Ollsen was the next witness called, and said he was pastor of the Swedish Church in Princess-square, and had known the woman for 17 years. She was a Swede, and was born at Landarv, near Gottenberg, on November 27, 1843. Her maiden name was Elizabeth Gustofstoller and her married name Stride. He could not say of his own knowledge that she was married, but he produced a register of marriages copied from an old book by a previous pastor. He had seen the original entry, and there she had described herself as married to an Englishman named Thomas Stride, a carpenter. He identified the book produced as a Swedish hymn-book which he had given to her last winter. He believed she was married in 1869. He could not remember when the husband died, but she was very poor at the time, and he relieved her.

William Marshall, 64, Berner-street, a labourer in an indigo warehouse, had seen the body in the mortuary. He saw the woman in Berner-street about 11.45 p.m. on Saturday last, standing on the pavement between Christian-street and Boyd-street. She was then talking to a man. They were not quarrelling, but talking quietly. There was no street lamp near, but the witness could see that the man was wearing a short black coat and dark trousers. He seemed to be middle-aged, and was wearing a round cap with a small peak, something like what a sailor would wear. He was about 5ft. 6in. in height, rather stout, and appeared decently dressed. He did not look like a dock labourer, nor a butcher, but had more the appearance of a clerk.

The witness did not think the man had any whiskers, not had he anything in his hands. He did not notice anything in the hands of the woman. The witness was standing at his door, and his attention was attracted by seeing the man kissing her. He heard the man say to her, "You would say anything but your prayers." He was "mild speaking," and spoke as an educated man would. The witness did not hear the woman say anything; she only laughed. The witness heard nothing more, as they went away, walking in the middle of the road towards Ellen-street. The woman was wearing a black jacket and dress. Neither of them appeared the worse for drink.

The witness went indoors about twelve o'clock, and heard nothing more until the cry of "Murder" was raised, just after 1 a.m.

James Brown, 35, Fairclough-street, deposed to seeing the body in the mortuary, and recognising it as the woman he saw on Sunday morning about 12.45. The witness was going from his own house to procure some supper at a chandler's shop, at the corner of Berner-street and Fairclough-street. He was in the shop three or four minutes, and while returning saw a man and woman standing by the Board School in Fairclough-street. He passed them in the road, just by the kerb, and heard the woman say, "No, not to-night; some other night." The witness then turned round and looked at them. He was almost certain that Stride was the woman he saw.

The man was leaning with his hand on the wall. So far as the witness could see, the man had on a long dark coat, which reached nearly to his heels. He saw nothing light in colour about either of them. The witness did not stop when he heard them talking, but passed on. He had nearly finished his supper, when he heard screams of "Murder" and "Police." That was about a quarter of an hour after he reached home. The man looked about the same height as the witness (5ft. 7in), and was not stout. Neither of them appeared to be the worse for drink.

Police-constable William Smith, 452 H, stated that on Saturday night last he went on duty at ten o'clock. His beat extended along the Commercial-road, down Christian and Fairclough Streets, into Grove-street and far as Back-church-lane, thence into Commercial-road again. That walk included all the interior streets, including Berner-street, the whole beat occupying about 30 minutes. He was in Berner-street about 12.35, and subsequently arrived at No. 40 in his ordinary round about one o'clock, and then saw the crowd of people in the yard and two policemen.

He heard no cries of police, and was not called to the spot. When he came through Berner-street at 12.30 he saw a man and the woman talking together. She was standing on the pavement, a few yards up the street, on the opposite side to where she was found. The man who was talking to her had a parcel, covered with a newspaper, in his hand. He was about 5ft. 7in. in height, and wore a hard felt dark deerstalker hat, and dark clothes. He had on a kind of "cutaway" coat. The witness overheard no conversation. Both appeared to be sober. He did not see much of the man's face, but he had no whiskers. He looked about 28 years of age. The man was of respectable appearance.

Michael Kidney, the man with whom Stride lived, identified the Swedish hymn-book as having belonged to the deceased. She gave it to a

Mrs. Smith on the previous Tuesday, saying she was going away. She gave it to Mrs. Smith, not as a gift, but to take care of.

By Inspector Reid - When she and he lived together, the door was padlocked when they were out. He had a key, and she borrowed one to get in, or waited till he came. On the Wednesday before her death he found she had got into the room, and taken some things, although it was locked.

Philip Krantz, of 40, Berner-street, said he was editor of a Hebrew Socialist paper. He wrote in a room, part of which is printing-office, beneath the club. On Saturday night he was in his room from nine o'clock till he was called and told that there was a woman lying in the yard.

He had not heard any cry or scream or anything unusual. His window and door were closed. If a woman had screamed he should have heard it but for the singing upstairs, which was very loud at the time. When he went out he saw the woman on the stones surrounded by members of the club. He did not think it possible that any stranger could have escaped from the yard unobserved after he arrived. He might have done so before.

By a Juror - The weather was quite dry at the time.

After some formal evidence had been given to prove the plans of the locality of the murder, put in by the police, the inquiry was adjourned until 23d inst.

Source: *Morning Post*

SATURDAY 6 OCTOBER 1888

THE RIPPER REPORTS

FRESH MURDERS THREATENED LATEST MOVEMENTS AND RUMOURS

The fact that the previous murders have mostly been committed either on Friday or Saturday morning caused the police in Whitechapel district to be exceptionally vigilant during last night. Not only was Whitechapel under observation hither to perhaps, unprecedented, but the whole of the metropolis is under the keenest surveillance in order to trap the mysterious murderer who, it is feared, may spring up in some other part of London.

Our detective system has during the past week been increased to a remarkable extent by men drawn from the ranks, and who have been sent out in plain clothes to patrol the street. Between the hours of one and two this morning Aldgate and Whitechapel presented an almost deserted appearance, but in dark corners and down innumerable courts and alleys lounged detectives and members of the Vigilance Committee, all of them strictly on the alert. In the City, at Aldgate, and near Mitre-square, the officers were to be seen walking in couples.

The utter absence of plain clothes officers and detectives from the streets, or rather from view, was certainly surprising to one who knew they were about in large numbers. It is an undisputed point that the authorities have realised the necessity of catching the murderer in the act, therefore there is motive in concealing the detectives from view in the courts, alleys, and squares which about in the neighbourhood. It is a general belief among the police that should they catch the assassin he will endeavour to make "short work" of them. They believe him to be a very strong and powerful man. Only two arrests were reported up to this morning, and in both cases the prisoners gave satisfactory accounts of themselves, and were discharged from custody.

The story circulated about a woman being lifted insensible from a cab, and deposited in Hare-street, Bethnal Green, turns out to have had no foundation in fact. The police acknowledge that they have practically no clue, but they feel confidant that the murderer is still in the East-end and certain suspected neighbourhoods are under observation. It is pointed out that the murderer, after the commission of his last crime, undoubtedly proceeded from Mitre-square by way of Church-passage, Duke-street, Houndsditch, Gravel-lane, Stoney-lane, to Goulston-street, at which spot all clue appears to have been lost of him. In this neighbourhood he evidently entered one of the notorious houses which exist in the locality.

It would take about 10 minutes for a person to get from Mitre-square to the neighbourhood, so that the murderer was wall away from the scene, and perhaps safely under cover before Constable Watkin obtained even medical assistance after the discovery of the body. This is a point put forward by the police in favour of bloodhounds being employed, as it is suggested that had one of the hounds been brought on the scene immediately there would have been little, if any, chance, of the murderer evading justice. The prevailing opinion among the police now is either that the murderer will keep in hiding for some time until the excitement abates or the precautions are relaxed, or that he will find a new field for his operations in another part of London.

THE MAN WITH THE BLACK BAG

It is pointed out by the Daily Telegraph that search for an individual answering to the description of the man seen talking to the Berner-street victim shortly before she was murdered on Sunday morning last has been made by police in the Whitechapel ever since Saturday, September 1, the day following the Buck's row tragedy. Information was tendered at the King David's-lane Police-station, at about that time, by a dairyman who has a place of business in Little Turner-street, Commercial-road. It will be recollected that on Saturday, September 1, a desperate assault was reported to have been committed near to the music-hall in Cambridge-heath-road, a man having seized a woman by the throat and dragged her down a court, where he was joined by a gang, one of whom laid a knife across the woman's throat, remarking, "We will serve you as we did the others."

The particulars of this affair were subsequently stated to be untrue; but the milkman has reason to suppose that the outrage was actually perpetrated, and he suspects that the murderer of Mary Ann Nicholls in Buck's-row had something to do with it. At any rate, upon that Saturday night, at five minutes to eleven o'clock, a man, corresponding with the description given by Packer of the individual who purchased the grapes in Berner-street, called at the shop, which is on the left of a covered yard, usually occupied by barrows, which are let out on hire. He was in a hurry, and he asked for a pennyworth of milk, with which he was served, and he drank it down at a gulp.

Asking permission to go into the yard or shed, he went there, but the dairyman caught a glimpse of something white, and, having suspicions, he rejoined the man in the shed, and was surprised to observe that he had covered up his trousers with a pair of white over-alls, such as engineers wear. The man had a staring look, and appeared greatly agitated. He made a movement forward, and the brim of his hard felt hat struck the dairyman, who is, therefore, sure of the kind he was wearing.

In a hurried manner the man took out of a black shiny bag, which was on the ground, a white jacket and rapidly put it on, completely hiding his cutaway black coat, remarking meanwhile, "It's a dreadful murder, isn't it?" although the subject had not been previously mentioned. Without making a pause the suspicious person caught up his bag, which was still open, and rushed into the street, towards Shadwell, saying, "I think I've got a clue!" The matter was reported to the police, and although strict watch has been maintained for the reappearance of the man he has not been seen in the street since. He is said to have had a dark complexion, such as a seafaring man acquires. He had no marked American accept, and his general appearance was that of a clerk or student whose beard had been allowed three days' growth.

His hair was dark, and his eyes large and staring. The bag carried by the young man, whose age the dairyman places at 28, is stated to have been provided with a lock at the top, near the handle, and was made, as stated, of a black glistening material. In connection with the Whitechapel murders a black bag has been repeatedly mentioned.

A STUPID HOAX

At the Birmingham Police-court to-day, a respectably-dressed man, named Alfred Napier Blanchard, was charged on his own confession with being the Whitechapel murderer. He gave himself up to a detective last night, but this morning he stated that he had simply done it as a hoax. He was discharged with a caution.

Source: *Globe*

SATURDAY 6 OCTOBER 1888

MRS STRIDE'S ANTECEDENTS - THE WIFE OF A BATH GENTLEMAN

Mrs. Mary Malcolm, who was examined at the coroner's inquiry on Tuesday afternoon, in the evening mad an important statement to a representative of the Press. She stated that she had again seen the body and was confident it was that of her sister. She could not answer all the questions put to her by the coroner, because she was so upset that her memory has failed her, and she had reasons for not wishing to answer others. She now volunteered a statement, in the course of which she said her sister, when a young woman, entered the services of a Mr. Watts of Bath. Her young master became enamoured of her. He afterwards married her secretly, and subsequently introduced her to his family as his wife.

They at first recognised her, but she was fond of drink, and became intimate with another man. Her husband sent her home to her mother, where she remained till after the birth of a child. When she returned to her husband's house at Bath she found the home sold up, her husband having in the meantime been sent to America. The family discarded her, and in her poverty she became acquainted with a policeman, by who she had a child in Holloway Workhouse. After that she became acquainted with a man at Poplar. Mrs. Malcolm knew the man, but she had reasons for withholding his name. Stride was not the man.

When reminded that by not disclosing all the circumstances she knew she might be defeating the ends of justice, Mrs. Malcolm said she did not think she was doing so, but if she thought so she would tell all. When her sister had lived with the man he kept a coffee shop at Poplar. They quarrelled, and he afterwards shipped for New Zealand, but was wrecked off the island of St. Paul. He was one of the few who were saved, and eventually he succeeded in reaching New Zealand. She did not disclose those matters to the coroner, one reason being that the man was very respectably connected at Poplar, where he had relatives living.

Source: *Somerset Standard*

MONDAY 8 OCTOBER 1888

ALLEGED STARTLING DISCOVERY BY SPIRITUALISTS
EXTRAORDINARY STATEMENT OT THE CARDIFF POLICE

The centre of the interest which is attached to the terrible London tragedies of the past few weeks has been transferred from Whitechapel to Cardiff. To accomplish this remarkable state of affairs some occult agency was evidently required - unless, indeed, the murderer himself has turned up in our midst - and this motive power has been supplied by the believers in spiritualism. On Saturday afternoon a respectably dressed middle-aged woman entered the Cardiff Central Police station and addressed herself to the officer who happened to be in charge for the moment.

She informed him very seriously that she believed she had discovered the personality and whereabouts of the Whitechapel murderer, but to his skeptical mind the value of the information was considerably discounted by the fact that she avowed herself to be a Spiritualist, indicating that it was by this means that the momentous disclosure had been made. However, here is the pith of her story, which we give for what it is worth. The previous evening, at the witching hour of night, when churchyards yawn and graves give up their dead, the informant, together with five friends, assembled in a house in Godfrey-street, Newtown, and gathered round the mystic table.

They placed their twelve hands with the fingers outstretched on the table, each of the six persons joining his thumbs and completing the circuit by touching with his little fingers those of his neighbours on either side. In solemn silence they sat, and the leader of the party invoked the spirit of Elizabeth Stride, who was foully done to death in Whitechapel last Sunday morning. For a time there was no response. Pale with determination, yet feeling somewhat creepy in their spinal cords, the company persevered, waiting awe-stricken for they knew not what. At last the table gave evident signs of disturbance, and after a few violent jumps in erratic directions the magic wood gave forth the weird knocks which announced the presence of the dead among the living.

"Who art thou?" queried the spokesman of the spiritualists in mechanical, yet trembling tones.

Knock, knock, went the table, as it unerringly spelled out the words, "Elizabeth Stride!"

"By whom wert thou murdered?" was the next question.

Again did the table oscillate and rap out the necessary letters, "B-y a m-a-n n-a-m-e-d J-o-h-n-n-y D-o-n-n-e-l-l-e-y," and then warming vindictively to the congenial task of giving up to justice the foul slaughterer, "he lives at number thirteen Commercial-road," or "street" - which of the two thoroughfares it was the listeners in their excitement could not positively determine.

"Did he commit all the Whitechapel murders?"

"No," rapped the spirit. "He is one of a gang of twelve who have sworn to commit these crimes, and different members of the gang have done the various murders."

At this juncture the current of magnetism was suddenly broken, nor could it be restored. Elizabeth Stride had wandered off into the chilly night, and the party separated. The conversation above is a verbatim record of the occurrence which was tendered to the police in all seriousness. There the matter stands.

Source: *South Wales Daily News*

MONDAY 8 OCTOBER 1888

GRIM HOAXES

An evening paper has perpetrated a hideous hoax upon the London public. It told a circumstantial story of how the murderer at Whitechapel had been caught. He had inveigled a girl round a hoarding in the Shadwell High Street, had been followed and watched by a watchman, who raised an alarm and tried to arrest him, had killed the watchman, and finally been overpowered by the police.

It so happened that on Thursday at 1.30 p.m., I ("About Town" in the "London Echo") chanced to be lunching with a great City magnate - a man who commanded millions, and possesses many friends. At his hospital board sat an actor, an army captain, a Magistrate, two or three professional men, a stockbroker, and a financier or two, and as they enjoyed the liberality of the genial gentleman who sat at the head of the board, the talk turned upon the story of the murderer's arrest. "We heard it in the house, early this morning," said the stockbroker. "Yes," said the actor; "but the watchman is not dead, he is only badly wounded."

"I hear," remarked a financier, "that a policeman was badly stabbed too." "And it seems to be a fact," added the financier, "that they find it is the man they have been looking for." Yet, after all, no such incident had occurred. The story was a catchpenny one, and had been published because… but I leave my readers to fill in the reason. Hoaxes are not infrequent. I once managed a great daily paper in London. One night a man came in - a "penny a-liner," as they call themselves - and brought in "flimsy" containing the account of a horrible tragedy.

A body, or parts of a body, had been found near Waterloo Bridge, cut up in such a way as to leave no doubt that a horrible murder had been committed. Did we want the news? "Why, cert'nly," our sub-editor said. And in it went. The details of that dreadful murder appeared in every paper next day; and they went on day after day, for fresh pieces of flesh or blood stained rags were discovered, and the police danced hither and thither, and found nothing and nobody. Then the papers led the police a lesson. They saw it was time for Henderson to resign; they hinted the detectives were better fitted for taking in plain sewing or light washing than detecting crime, and they pointed out what an awful state London was in.

Time rolled on, and at length it transpired that the whole "tragedy" was a hoax, in which the reporter had lead no inconsiderable hand, the parts of the body having been got from a wild medical student who shared in the plunder. Hoaxes are sometimes unintentional. For some years London papers used to be supplied with reports of hangings by an execution penny-a-liner, who saw the malefactor turned off in good form, and then wrote the report which appeared in every paper. He got to be quite an adept at this work, and knew exactly when a criminal would be respited and when he would be hanged, and there, as certainly as the principal performer in the execution scene appeared on the drop, this reporter appeared in the jail yard ready to see him "off." At length a case arrived in which the country was greatly interested, but the penny-a-liner was ill and could not go to the execution. So he "satisfied" himself that that man would really be hanged, and then on the morning of the execution sent round a neat little account of his "taking off."

The newspapers published it. There was some little comment on the part of the man's being hanged; and then came official news of a respite - the man had been reprieved at the last moment - not hanging at all. Well, this upset the reporter a little, but he got over the scrape somehow and determined to be all right next time. A little while afterwards he was again so ill that he could not go to the execution however. The murderer was on the scaffold; the chaplain was droning out the last part of the service; the execution was strapping his legs - all was ready, when suddenly a telegraphic messenger burst into the yard with a dispatch. "Stop!" roared the Governor of the jail, "perhaps it is a reprieve."

The murderer for a moment brightened up, the executional scowled, for he feared losing his fee; the chaplain stopped at "Dust to dust," and listened, while the Governor tore the envelope open. Then he read the following: - "From B——, to the Governor of —— Goal. Please telegraph at once to me whether the prisoner —— has really been hanged this morning. Reply paid."

FUNERAL OF KATE EDDOWES

The funeral of Catherine Eddowes, the victim of the latest of the Whitechapel tragedies took place to-day at Illford. The funeral cortege started at 1.39 from the City Mortuary in Golden Lane, outside where a great crowd had congregated, traffic in the thoroughfare being almost stopped. The body was enclosed in an elm coffin, and was borne in a [glass] car drawn by a pair of horses, and was followed by a mourning coach, in which were four of the deceased's sisters - Mrs Eliza Gold, Mrs Elizabeth Fisher, Mrs Harriet Jones, and the man Kelly, with whom Eddowes lived. The mourning coaches had some difficulty in penetrating the large crowd outside, among whom threats against "Jack the Ripper" were loud and frequent.

CURIOUS COINCIDENCE

It is pointed out as a singular coincidence that all the murdered women have at one time or another lodged in the house in Flower and Dean Street, and from this it is thought likely that the murderer has known his victims personally before taking their lives.

Source: *Aberdeen Evening Express*

TUESDAY 9 OCTOBER 1888

ANOTHER STRANGE REPORT

The Central News says a startling fact has just come to light in connection with the recent Whitechapel murders. After killing Catherine Eddowes in Mitre-square, the murderer, it is now known, walked to Goulston-street, where he threw away the piece of the deceased woman's apron upon which he had wiped his hands and knife. Within a few feet of this spot he had written upon the wall, "The Jews shall not be blamed, for nothing."

Most unfortunately one of the police officers gave orders for this writing to be immediately sponged out probably with a view of stifling the morbid curiosity which it would certainly have aroused. But in so doing a very important link was destroyed, for had the writing been photographed a certain clue would have been in the hands of the authorities. The witnesses, who saw the writing, however, state that it was similar in character to the letters sent to the Central News, and signed "Jack the Ripper;" and though it would have been far better to have clearly demonstrated this by photograph, there is now every reason to believe that the writer of the letter and postcard sent to the Central News (fac similies of which are now to be seen outside every police-station) is the actual murderer.

The police, consequently, are very anxious that any citizen who can identify the handwriting should without delay communicate with the authorities. The Central News, since the original letter and post-card of "Jack the Ripper" was published, has received from 30 to 40 communications daily, signed "Jack the Ripper," evidently the concoction of silly notoriety-hunters. A third communication, however has been received from the writer of "the original" Jack the Ripper letter and post-card which, acting upon official advice, it has been deemed prudent to withhold for the present. It may be stated, however, that although the miscreant avows his intention of committing further crimes shortly, it is only against unfortunates that his threats are directed, his desire being to "respect and protect honest women."

Source: *The Star*

WEDNESDAY 10 OCTOBER 1888

THREATENING BRYANT AND MAY'S GIRLS

Intimation was also given to the City police on Sunday morning that Messrs Bryant and May had received a letter from a person signing himself J. Ripper, couched in the following term:- "I hearby notify that I am going to pay your girls a visit. I hear that they are beginning to say what they will do with me. I am going to see what a few of them have in the stomachs, and I will take it out of them, so that they can have no more to do on the quiet.
- (Signed) JOHN RIPPER
- P.S.
- I am in Poplar to-day.

Source: *Taunton Courier, and Western Advertiser*

WEDNESDAY 10 OCTOBER 1888

THE MITRE SQUARE CRIME

THE RIPPER REPORTS

With respect to the crime, which occurred in Mitre-square a short time after the discover in Berner-street, the victim being not only murdered but most horribly mutilated, the body has been recognised as that of a woman who was taken into custody for drunkenness on Saturday night, and only released at one o'clock on Sunday morning, less than an hour before her death. Her name is Catherine Eddowes, otherwise Conway or Kelly. Her sister, Eliza Gold, Kelly with whom she lived, and Frederick Wilkinson, the deputy of the lodging-houses at which she had lived for nearly ten years, have seen and identified the body at the mortuary in Golden-lane.

From their statement it would appear that Eddowes, though in the poorest circumstances, and living with a man to whom she was not married, bore a generally good character, and was not a member of the unhappy class from which the other victims have been selected. Kelly, Wilkinson and Mrs. Gold agree in saying that she worked hard, charing among the Jews in "the Lane" during four or five months in the winter, and throughout the greater part of the summer tramping the country - always with Kelly - hopping, fruit picking, or hay-making.

The inquest on Catherine Eddowes was resumed on Thursday. John Kelly, who lived with the deceased, said she used to hawk things about the street for a living. He was last in her company at two o'clock on Saturday afternoon. She then said that she was going to Bermondsey to find her daughter. She sometimes drank to excess. She usually returned to her lodgings early at night. They were on good terms.

Wilkinson, deputy at the lodging-house, said that Kelly and the deceased were old inmates, paid regularly, and were on very good terms. Deceased was not often intoxicated, was a very jolly woman, and fond of singing. Could not remember whether any stranger came to the house early on Sunday morning.

Police constable Watkin detailed the circumstances connected with the finding of the body.

The City Surveyor stated that the scene of the two murders were three-quarters of mile apart.

Wilkinson, recalled, produced a book, but was unable to give any information about those who went in and out on Saturday night.

Inspector Collard said nobody heard any cries, and there were no signs of a struggle.

Dr Gordon Brown described the wounds on the deceased. Her intestines had been drawn out, and the lobe of the right ear was cut obliquely. When the body was undressed at the mortuary the severed portion of the ear fell from the clothing. Death was instantaneous, and the mutilations were made after death. The kidneys had been taken away. The wounds were inflicted with a sharp knife, at least six inches long. The person who inflicted the wounds possessed a good deal of anatomical knowledge. The parts removed would be of no use for surgical purposes. Such knowledge as the murderer allowed would be possessed by one used to cutting up animals. He could assign no reason for the parts being taken away. The inquest was adjourned.

In describing the proceedings at the inquest the Daily News reporter says: Dr. Gordon Brown explained that the left kidney had been removed in a particular manner. "Do you," said the City Solicitor, "draw any conclusions from that?" and the answer evidently received the deepest attention. "I think that somebody who knew the position of the kidney and how to cut it out must have done it."

It had been manifest for some little time that the City Solicitor in his cross-examination of the witness had been leading up to what he knew would prove sensational, and the profoundest interest was displayed by all in court as the fact of the anatomical knowledge of the assassin became established by repeated answers of the surgical expert; and when at length in answer to explicit inquiry he stated that precisely the same organ, or a large portion of the same organ, as had been found missing from the body of the last victim was also missing in this case, the sensation in court was profound.

The possibility of this had of course been surmised, but all information on the results of the post mortem examination had been steadily refused, and this announcement came as a startling confirmation of what had before been only suspected. In proof of the anatomical and surgical skill of the assassin, Dr. Brown added that for the purpose of practically testing the time required for what had been done to this unfortunate woman, an expert practitioner had actually performed the operation, and found that it took three minutes and a half.

The witness was disposed to believe that the murder had not been hurried, and had probably done all he intended to do, or he would not have slashed and hacked the face about, which he had no doubt done merely for the sake of concealing the identity of the woman. "Would the parts removed be of any use for professional purposes?" asked Mr. Crawford. "Not the slightest" was the reply - "Would the knowledge necessary for these mutilations be likely to be possessed by one engaged in cutting up animals?" was another question put, and the answer was unhesitatingly, "Yes, sir."

The Central News says: - The surgical evidence given at the inquest on Thursday has caused a profound sensation. It has to be supposed that the murderer did not have time to do more than take his victim's life, and then roughly mutilate her body, but it now appears that he completed his horrible work with reckless deliberation, and removed certain organs. The additional mutilation of the face is believed to be due to fears on the murderer's part that he may have been seen in the woman's company by someone, and therefore determined to make her identification as difficult as possible.

The announcement of Dr. Brown of the disappearance of the uterus revived for a time the theory put forward by Mr. Wynne Baxter, the coroner in the Hanbury-street case. The British Medical Journal, however, states that the foreign physician who sought to purchase specimens was a gentleman of the highest respectability, that he did offer a large price, and that he left London 18 months ago.

The funeral of Catherine Eddowes, murdered in Mitre-square, took place at Ilford on Monday. Vast crowds witnessed the departure of the cortege from the Mortuary.

THE SECRETS OF THE SLUMS

There is a very general belief among the local detective force in the East-end that the murderer or murderers are lurking in some of the dangerous dens of the low slums, in close proximity to the scenes of the murders. Among other circumstances which support this theory is that some of the houses supposed to be bolted up for the night are found to have secret strings attached to the bolts, so that the house can be entered by persons who are acquainted with these secrets without delay or noise.

It has been ascertained by the detectives that the house in Hanbury-street where Annie Chapman was discovered murdered had a bolt with a secret string, and this fact is believed to have been known to the deceased woman. Even the cellars in some of the slums are stated to be occupied for sleeping purposes by strange characters who only appear in the streets at night. These dilapidated hovels are unfit for human habitation, and are known to the police to be the hiding places of the most dangerous and desperate characters. The police, it is stated, are contemplating a series of immediate and sudden raids upon these dreadful dens, both in the City and Whitechapel.

Source: *Derby Mercury*

FRIDAY 12 OCTOBER 1888

THE HANDWRITING ON THE WALL WHO ORDERED IT TO BE RUBBED OUT? SIR CHARLES WARREN HIMSELF!!

The strange, startling rumour which we printed yesterday as being current in the City was amply confirmed at the inquest. We reprint the following extracts from the evidence:-

Alfred Long, 254 A, Metropolitan police-constable, said: I was on duty in Goulston-street, Whitechapel, on the morning of Sept. 30. At five minutes to three o'clock I found a portion of a woman's apron, which I produce. There appeared to be recent blood stains upon it; one corner was wet. It was lying in the passage leading to the staircases of 108 to 119 of the model dwellings there. Above it on the wall, written in chalk,

"The Jews are the men that will not be blamed for nothing."

I at once searched the staircases and areas of the building, but found nothing else.

Daniel Halse, detective officer of the City police, said: I went on to Gouston-street, and the spot was pointed out to us where the apron was found, I saw some chalk writing on the wall, the surface of the bricks being black. I remained there; Hunt went away to Mr. McWilliam, with a view of having the writing photographed. Mr. McWilliam gave directions that it should be photographed; but before the messenger returned, some of the metropolitan police said the writing might cause a riot or outbreak against the Jews. The words were then rubbed out.

By Mr. Crawford: I suggested that the top line of the writing might be taken out, and a metropolitan policeman suggested the rubbing out of the word "Jews." Before the writing was rubbed out I took a note of it. There was a lantern showing on it. My copy is: "The Juwes are not the men that will be blamed for nothing." The writing appeared to have been recently done. It was written with white chalk on black fascia.

A juror: When was your note made?

Witness: At the time.

A juror: Why did you allow it to be wiped out?

Witness: I did not allow it.

Mr. Crawford: After that I am bound to put this question - Did you protest against it being wiped out?

Witness: Yes; I asked that it should be allowed to remain there till Major Smith had seen it.

By the jury: I concluded the writing was recent because it would have been rubbed out by some of the residents had it not been recent. The writing was nearly an inch high.

The Constable Long recalled, said: I returned to the building about five o'clock. The writing was not then rubbed out. It was rubbed out in my presence at half-past-five. I heard no one object to its being rubbed out. It was not quite daylight; it was half past five or thereabouts.

Here we have the following facts proved:-

1. That there was no chalk writing on the wall before the murder.

2. That the writing was discovered at about five minutes to three, about one hour after the murder.

3. That a missing portion of the murdered woman's apron dripping with blood was found below the handwriting.

4. That the City police ordered it to be photographed and remained on guard to prevent it being tampered with.

5. That between five and half-past-five o'clock some of the "metropolitan policemen" having said that the writing might cause a riot or outbreak against the Jews, the words were scrubbed out.

6. That the City detective protested against the words being rubbed out, and a metropolitan policeman suggested the rubbing out of one word, Jews.
These protests and suggestions were overruled, and the writing was rubbed out at half-past five.

The question, therefore, is, who was the infatuated person who thus, in defiance of the protests of the City detective and the sensible suggestion of the metropolitan police, persisted in rubbing it out?

It was none other than Sir Charles Warren himself!

This we state on the best authority. The fact would have been brought out at the inquest if the City coroner had not feared to see as if he were holding up Sir Charles Warren to contempt. Our information is indirectly confirmed by the following report of a Press Association reporter, who took the statement in yesterday's Pall Mall Gazette to Scotland-yard for the purpose of ascertaining if it were correct:-

The representative saw Sir Charles Warren's private secretary, who, on returning from the Chief Commissioner's room, stated that "Sir Charles Warren was in Goulston-street shortly after the murders, and if he had wished to make any communication to the press on the subject he would have done so then." In reply to a further question as to whether it was to be understood from this that Sir Charles preferred to say nothing about the allegation, our representative was informed that such was the case.

Considering how promptly Sir Charles Warren contradicts any statement that can possibly be contradicted with any semblance of truth, his silence is equivalent to admission of the fact.

Source: *Pall Mall Gazette*

SATURDAY 20 OCTOBER 1888

THE LONDON MURDERS

The Home Secretary has sent the following reply to Mr. Rusk, of Alderney-road, Mile End, in answer to a request that a free pardon might be offered to the accomplice or accomplices of the Whitechapel murderer :-

"October 12. Sir, - I am directed by the Secretary of State to thank you for the suggestions in your letter of the 7th inst. On the subject of the recent Whitechapel murders, and to say, in reply, that from the first the Secretary of State has had under consideration the question of granting a pardon to accomplices. It is obvious that not only must such a grant be lived to persons who have not been concerned in contriving or in actually committing the murders, but the expediency and propriety of making the offer must largely depend on the nature of the information received from day to day, which is being carefully watched with a view to determining that question. With regard to the offer of a reward, Mr.

Matthews has, under the existing circumstances nothing to add to his former letter."

The murder scare has spread to other parts of the metropolis, as an instance of which, about noon on Saturday, a sensation was occasioned in the locality of High Holborn. A gentleman was proceeding along Holborn, in the direction of the City, when he was suddenly pounced upon by a strange man of the labouring class, who exclaimed in an excited manner, "This is Jack the Ripper." A struggle ensued, and the two fell heavily to the ground. The scene soon attracted a very large crowd of people, who quickly collected, thinking that the Whitechapel murderer had been arrested. Much excitement prevailed, and the man was conveyed to the police station. Such incidents are traceable to the effect of the threatening letters which have been circulated purporting to have been written by "Jack the Ripper."

STARTLING STATEMENT

The Press Association learns that the Metropolitan police were on Sunday watching anxiously a house at the East-end of London, which is strongly suspected of having been the actual lodging, or a house made use of, by someone connected with the East-end murders. A statement made by the landlady and the neighbours show that a lodger at this house returned home early on the Sunday morning that the murders were committed. The landlady on getting up noticed he had changed some of his clothes. He told her he was going away for a little time, and asked her to wash the shirt for him.

After he had gone she found that the wristbands and part of the sleeves were completely saturated with wet blood. When she heard of the murders she gave information to the police, who took possession of the shirt. The man did not return again to the house, which is now occupied by a couple of policemen and two detectives. It is believed that information received of his former movements may ultimately lead to the man's arrest.

POLICE VIGILANCE AT LIVERPOOL

A sensation has been caused in Liverpool by the rumour that the London murderer has been seen in one of the parks, a woman having given information that she was attacked by a man with a knife. Several women recently arrested have been armed with knives, which they say are for protection against "the ripper." An extra force of detectives are watching the outward-going steamers.

"JACK THE RIPPER" IN PARIS - ATROCITIES THREATENED

M. Goron, head of the Paris detective department, has received a letter, which is evidently intended to be a grim joke, from a disciple of Jack the Ripper. The communication is dated from Brest, and in it the writer says that the Whitechapel murders were committed by his colleague and himself, and that they were intended to startle Paris with a series of similar atrocities. "We are looking for something in the human body which medical science has never found yet. Our first victim will be a woman between 20 and 30 years old. You can send all the policemen in Paris after us, but they will not be able to catch us. Operations to be begun three weeks hence, at least. - Signed, H. L. P. C." The letter is dated 9th inst. Its concocter initially mentions that he and the Ripper have murdered women in New York as well as London.

THE RIPPER REPORTS

A REVOLTING COMMUNICATION

An extraordinary communication has been made to the members of the Whitechapel Vigilance Committee. Mr. Lusk, builder, of Alderney Road, has received several letters purporting to be from the perpetrator of the Whitechapel murders, but believing them to be the product of some practical joker, he has regarded them as of no consequence. On Tuesday evening, however, he received the following letter in a cardboard box containing some fleshy substance :- "From Hell. Mr, Lusk, - Sir, - I send you half the kidney I took from one woman. I preserved it for you. The other piece I fried and ate. It was very nice. I may send you the bloody knife that took it out if you can only wait a while longer. - Signed, Catch Me When You Can."

On Thursday Mr. Read, assistant to Dr. Wiles, examined the contents of the box, and declared the substance to be half a human kidney, divided longitudinally. But in order to remove any reason for doubt he conveyed it to Dr. Openshaw, who is pathological curator to the London Hospital Museum. He examined it, and also pronounced it to be portion of a human kidney. He was further of opinion that it was the organ of a woman about 45 years of age, and it had been taken from the body within the last three weeks. It will be within the public recollection of the public that the left kidney was missing from the body of the woman Eddowes, who was murdered and mutilated in Mitre Square. The matter is considered to be of great importance, and the box and its contents were left in the care of the police pending further investigation.

Source: *Runcorn Examiner*

SATURDAY 20 OCTOBER 1888

"JACK THE RIPPER" AND THE LEICESTER POLICE

At least two persons in Leicester have assumed the sanguinary title of "Jack the Ripper," and both have communicated with the police. Mr. Dunn received the following :-

Look out for Blood on Saturday night. Blood, Blood, and Entrails.

JACK THE RIPPER

The note is addressed "- Dunns, Esq., Head Constable, Town Hall, Leicester," and bears the Leicester postmark, and the date Oct, 11. It is written in red ink, and there are sundry blots, while at the foot of the witting appears a rough drawing or something that would do for either a knife or a sward bayonet, and an even rougher representation of a coffin. The writing is like that of a female, and if it is the work of a male he has sought to disguise his hand.

The other communication is a postcard, written in a select boy's hand, as follows:-

Leicester, Oct. 11, 1888

Dear old Boss, - I have come to Leicester, and am going to do 5 here. I hope you'll have a good look out. Am in hurry.

- Yours, etc.,

JACK THE RIPPER

The postcard has had the face torn off at the top, evidently to obliterate the name of the firm from which it was obtained, but sufficient has been left to enable to police to trace whence it came if they thought it worth while. Of course the police regard the whole thing as a hoax.

ANOTHER ARREST

The Press Association says:- Much importance is attached by the police to an arrest made at King-street Police Station, Whitehall, on Tuesday morning. The man entered the above-named station about nine o'clock, and complained of having lost a black bag. While the officials were taking note of his case he commenced talking about the Whitechapel murders, and offered to cut off the sergeant's head, and other rambling nonsense. It will be remembered that several people have testified to seeing a man with a black bag in the region of the murder, and who has not since been traced. This fact was at once remembered by the police, and the man was further questioned. In answer to an enquiry as to his business he said he studied for some years for the medical profession, but gave it up for engineering, and that he had been stopping for some nights in coffee houses.

His manner then became so strange that Dr. Bond, Divisional Surgeon, as sent for to examine the man. The doctor subsequently gave it as his opinion that the man was a very dangerous lunatic of homicidal tendency, and as his appearance somewhat tallied with that published of the man who was seen with the murderer woman he was removed to Bow-street, but before being taken thither photos of his person were taken. He was also asked to write his name, and it is stated that the writing is somewhat similar to that of the letters received by the police and others. He gave his age as 67, but it is said he looks fully twenty years younger. The police are endeavouring to trace his antecedents and movements for the past few weeks.

Source: *Northampton Mercury*

SUNDAY 21 OCTOBER 1888

THE EAST END MURDERS

Sir Charles Warren's bloodhounds were out for practice at Tooting on Thursday morning, where a sheep had been stolen, and were lost. Telegrams were dispatched to all Metropolitan police stations, stating that if the dogs were seen anywhere information was to be sent to Scotland-yard.

At the Guildhall police-court, on Thursday, Benjamin Graham, a glass-blower, of Fletcher-row, Clerkenwell, was charged on his own confession with having committed the murders in Whitechapel. On Wednesday afternoon the prisoner, who was drunk, was taken into Snow-hill police-station by a man, who said that Graham had told him that he had murdered the women in Whitechapel. He repeated his statement at the station, adding, "and I shall have to suffer for it with a bit of rope." - He was remanded for inquiries.

MAD THROUGH THE MURDERS

At the Thames police-court, on Wednesday, the divisional surgeon of police and the relieving officer asked the magistrate to sign the necessary papers for the removal to an asylum for a woman whose mind appeared to have been affected by the recent murders. The doctor's certificate stated that the woman, whose name is Sarah Goody, aged 40, a needlewoman, living in Wild-street, Stepney, had told him (the doctor) that she was followed about by a man who watched her movements, and who intended to do her harm. She was in such a terrified condition that she could neither eat not sleep. The lunatic attendant stated that the woman declared that she was followed about by murderers, who intended catching her. On one occasion she asked her landlady to see if there was any writing on the shutters. Mr. Lushington signed the necessary papers.

Source: *Lloyd's Weekly Newspaper*

SUNDAY 28 OCTOBER 1888

THE EAST-END MURDERS
INQUEST ON THE BERNER-STREET VICTIM
SATISFACTORY IDENTIFICATION

The coroner's inquiry into the death of Elizabeth Stride, who was murdered at Berner-street, Whitechapel, early on Sunday morning, the 30th ult., was concluded on Tuesday at the Vestry Hall, Cable-street, before Mr. E. Wynne Baxter, coroner for East Middlesex, and a jury. At the previous sitting evidence was given by Mrs. Malcolm to the effect that deceased was her sister, and that she was married to Mr. Watts, son of a wine merchant of Bath, but had latterly led a dissipated life, and that she had regularly contributed to her support up to the week of the murder. She added that she had a presentiment of the crime, because while lying in bed at the hour of the occurrence when felt a peculiar pressure. On Tuesday Mrs. Watts herself appeared and flatly contradicted the statements of her sister. It was further shown that the murdered woman was the widow of a carpenter.

Mr. E. Reid, inspector of police, deposed: Since the last sitting I have made inquiries and examined the books of the Sick Asylum, Bromley, and find therein an entry of the death of John Thomas Stride, carpenter, or Poplar, on 24th October, 1884. The nephew of Stride is here to give evidence. I have also seen Elizabeth Watts, whose sister is now married and resides at Tottenham. She informed me that the whole of Mrs. Malcolm's statement is false, that she had not seen her sister for years, and believed her to be dead. It was not true that she saw her sister on the Monday before the murder. I have directed her to appear here as a witness to-day, and she promised to attend. - Police-constable Walter Stride: I recognise the photograph of the deceased as that of the person who was married to my uncle, J. T. Stride, in 1872 or 1873. He was a carpenter, and the last time we saw him he lived in East India Dock-road, Poplar.

THE REAL MRS. WATTS

- Elizabeth Stokes, 5, Charles-street Tottenham, wife of Joseph Stokes, brickmaker, said: I was formerly married to Mr. Watts, wine merchant, Bath.

- The Coroner: He is dead?

- Witness: I have a letter which I wish to show you. (Witness was much agitated, and said that the case had excited her greatly.) Mrs. Mary Malcolm, of Eagle-street, Red Lion-square, Holborn, is my sister.

- The coroner, having read the letter handed to him, said it purported to have been written by "W. Y. Z." on board ship, and stated that the woman's husband was alive. (To witness): Are you on friendly terms with your sister?

- I have not seen her for years. She has given me a dreadful character, and said I was the curse of the family. I have not received a penny from her.

- Her evidence is false?

- All false. I can tell you the names of all of use. There were Matilda, Thomas, James, Mary and Elizabeth. I am positively sure that Mrs. Malcolm is my sister, who has given these cruel statements.

- A Juror: That must have been a mistake. Instead of referring to you, she must have referred to some other person.

- Another Juror: She referred to a sister with a crippled foot, and this person has a crippled foot.

- Witness: It was I that kept a coffee shop and was a disgrace to the family. It is infamy and lies, and I am truly sorry to think I have a sister in my family that has given me such a terrible and dreadful character. I hope the country at large will clear my character.

- The Coroner: You have contradicted the statements.

- Witness: It has put me to dreadful trouble. I am only a poor woman, and my husband, who is a cripple, is now outside. Why should my sister be allowed to tell such terrible falsehoods? A Juror: We did not know at the time they were false hoods.

- Witness: You can see.

- Coroner: We can see now.

- Witness: I hope you will allow me my expenses.

- The Coroner: Is Mrs. Malcolm here?

- Officer: No, sir.

REMARKABLE COINCIDENCE

- The coroner, in summing up, remarked upon the coincidence between the habits of the murdered woman and those of the person described by Mrs. Malcolm. If her evidence was correct there were points of resemblance which almost reminded one of "The Comedy of Errors." Both had been courted by policemen; they bore the same Christian name, and were of the same age; both lived with sailors; both at one time kept coffee-houses at Poplar; both were nicknamed "Long Liz;" both were said to have children in charge of their husband's friends; both were given to drink; both lived in East-end common lodging-houses; both had been charged with drunkenness at the Thames Police Court; both had escaped punishment on the ground that they were subject to epileptic fits, although the friends of both are certain this was a fraud; both had lost their front teeth; and both were leading very questionable lives.

The murdered woman, it appeared, was born in Sweden in 1843, but having resided in England twenty-two years could speak English fluently with a little foreign accent. At the time of her death she could have but a few pence in her pocket. It was shown that the man with whom she was seen shortly before was about 5ft. 7in. in height, and wore dark clothes, including an overcoat which reached nearly to his heels. There was no one among her associates to whom any suspicion attached, and it was not shown that she recently had a quarrel with any one.

The ordinary motives of murder - revenge jealousy, theft, and passion - appeared to be absent from this case, while it was clear from the accounts of all who saw her that night, as well as from the post mortem examination, that she was not otherwise than sober. In conclusion, the coroner, while expressing regret that the time and care bestowed on the inquiry had not eventuated in a result which would be a perceptible relief to the metropolis - the detection of the criminal - was bound to acknowledge the great attention which Inspector Reid and the police had given to the case.

The jury found a verdict of wilful murder against some person or persons unknown, and that the murdered woman was the widow of John Stride, carpenter.

A DRUNKEN CONFESSION

A man named Graham was charged, on remand, at the Mansion House on Thursday, with committing the murders in Whitechapel. The prisoner had given himself up on his self-accusation; he had been remanded that the state of his mind might be inquired into, and it was now stated that he had suffered from excessive drinking, but there was no trace of insanity.

Mr Alderman Benals discharged him, regretting that there was no means of punishing him.

Source: *The People*

SATURDAY 3 NOVEMBER 1888

SAD SEQUEL TO A PRACTICAL JOKE

THE RIPPER REPORTS

A terrible tragic ending has followed a practical joke, in which a man declared he was "Jack the Ripper." A young lady named Milligan, twenty-one years of age, has died at Kilkeel, county Down, under the following circumstances:- A fortnight since Miss Milligan was out walking with two lady visitors, and all three were startled by the sudden appearance of a man, who, personating the Whitechapel monster, brandished a knife, exclaiming, "I'm Jack the Ripper."
During the evening Miss Milligan became hysterical, and the next day fever set in, which, notwithstanding the efforts of Dr. Wilson, terminated fatally. The sad event has caused much sympathy with the relatives of the deceased, and the police are on the look-out for the man.

Source: *Illustrated Police News*

SATURDAY 3 NOVEMBER 1888

ANOTHER "JACK THE RIPPER" FOOL

At Clerkenwell Police-court on Monday, Frederick Dunbar, aged forty-eight, a hairdresser, of King-street, was charged with drunkenness and disorderly conduct in Reyham-street, Camden-town, the previous night. Police-constable 493 Y said the prisoner, who was surrounded by a crowd of people, was drunk, and he loudly shouted several times, "I am Jack the Ripper!" He was taken to the police station, and about a thousand persons gathered around. Dunbar, in defense, said he was sorry for what had occurred. He had taken too much drink. Mr Broe:

THE RIPPER REPORTS

You have made a fool of yourself, and I will send you to prison for twenty-one days with hard labour.

Source: *Illustrated Police News*

SATURDAY 3 NOVEMBER 1888

THE ATTACK ON DISGUISED DETECTIVES

At Middlesex Sessions, on Tuesday, Jas. Phillips and William Jarvis were indicted for maliciously wounding Detective-sergeant Robinson, and also for maliciously wounding Henry Doncaster. Prisoners pleaded "Not guilty."

Sergeant Robinson was on duty on the 9th October with Detective Mather and Doncaster in Phoenix-place, Clerkenwell, Robinson was watching a man supposed to be "Jack the Ripper," and had disguised himself in female attire. He concealed himself behind a cab in the yard, when the prisoners, who were in the employ of Mr. Kite, cab proprietor, came up, and commenced an altercation. Robinson told him he was a police officer. Conflicting evidence was given as to whether Jarvis or the officer, struck the first blow. Robinson was stabbed in the forehead, and Doncaster was also assaulted. Both prisoners bore good characters. Phillips was acquitted. Jarvis was convicted, but recommended to mercy. He was sentenced to six weeks imprisonment.

Source: *Manchester Courier and Lancashire General Advertiser*

TUESDAY 6 NOVEMBER 1888

THE MURDERS IN LONDON AN ARREST AT BELFAST

John Foster, who was arrested at Belfast on suspicion of being concerned in the Whitechapel murders, was brought up at the Belfast Police Court. The prisoner arrived in Belfast on Oct. 7 from Greenock, where he had spent two days; but he could not say where he stopped. Previous to that he was in Glasgow for four days, and before that in Edinburgh; but he did not know how long he was there, nor did he know any one living there. He was a watch-maker, but he did nothing at the trade as he had an income of his own, which he got from his father, who lived in London. He said his father was a brewer, but could not give the address. A silver watch and chain and locket (produced) were found in his pockets. He said the watch was his own. It bore the monogram "A.M.R." The prisoner was remanded for a week.

In connection with this arrest, it may be mentioned that a letter, of which the following is a copy, has reached the office of one of the Belfast evening papers: - "Dear Boss, - I have arrived in your city, as London is two warm for me just now, so that Belfast - had better look out, for I intend to commence operations on Sunday night (Oct. 14). I have spotted some nice fat ones, who will cut up well. I am longing to begin for I love my work. - Yours, &c., JACK THE RIPPER." The communication, which is written in red ink, and bears several blotches, evidently made in imitation of blood, is stamped with the Belfast postmark.

Source: *Times of India*

TUESDAY 6 NOVEMBER 1888

THE EAST-END MURDERS

At a late hour on Saturday night the following notice was read out to the police, as printed in the informations, at Whitechapel: - "To-day a piece of paper was picked up in Spitalfields on which was written :- Dear Boss, -In spite of all your police precautions, and in spite of all the efforts of the Vigilance Committee, I committed another murder last night, and have hid the body away in Osborne-street, headless, legless, armless and naked. Yours truly, Jack the Ripper." Though the matter is looked upon as a hoax, all constables were ordered to make every inquiry in the neighbourhood to see if anything had been found or whether any one was missing. There were, however, specially enjoined to use their utmost endeavours to try and trade the author of the writing. Special instructions were also ordered to be given to all the auxiliary detectives and officers who were on duty at midnight. - St. James's Gazette.

Source: *The Star*

MARY JANE KELLY

Died: 9 November 1888

FRIDAY 9 NOVEMBER 1888

ANOTHER WHITECHAPEL ATROCITY MURDER AND MUTILATION OF A WOMAN THIS MORNING SPECIAL DESCRIPTIVE ACCOUNT THE HEAD SEVERED FROM THE BODY GHASTLY SIGHT

(From our own Reporter)
The Whitechapel fiend has been at his ghastly work again, and though on this occasion the surrounding circumstances are different from those which have previously been found, the revolting treatment of the body of the victim leaves little doubt the same brutal hand has been at work. The victim in this case is a young woman named Mary Jane Kelly, who, so far as can be learned, is about 26 years of age. Like the previous victims she was an unfortunate. Little or nothing can be gained as yet about her previous history, but it seems that before she went to live in the neighbourhood of Whitechapel, or, to speak more correctly, Spitalfield, she was in a situation as a domestic servant.

She lost her situation, and a few months ago turned up in Spitalfields, and taking up with a man named Danny, who sells oranges in the adjacent market, went to live with him in furnished rooms, in M'Carthy's Court, Dorset-street, which runs westward out of Commercial-street, within a hundred yards of the Toynbee Hall. Dorset-street consists of a nest of courts, most of the houses in which are let off in furnished rooms, and in the off-streets are a number of registered lodging houses of the kind which are found in large numbers in Whitechapel.

Though the girl Kelly was living with a man she pursued immoral courses, and little notice would be taken of a man accompanying her to the small house where she lived. Last night she was in the streets, as usual, and twice this morning she was seen by neighbours. She is described as a tall woman, not bad looking, of dark complexion, and she generally wore an old black velvet jacket. She was wearing this jacket this morning, when at about quarter past eight she went down the court with a jug in her hand, and returned shortly afterwards with some milk for breakfast. She was next seen about ten o'clock, when she went to a small beerhouse at the corner of the street, and stayed drinking for nearly half an hour. This is the last that was seen of her alive, and what followed is a matter of conjecture.

Her mutilated body was discovered about eleven o'clock. At that hour a young fellow named McCarthy, the son of the woman to whom the furnished room belonged, went into the court to collect the rents, and going into the room occupied by Kelly was horrified to find the woman's head lying on the floor. His face white with terror, he rushed into the court shouting an alarm, and whilst the police were sent for the neighbours rushed into the room, well knowing that after the arrival of the police they would not be able to feast their eyes on the ghastly scene of blood.

The woman lay on the bed almost naked, whilst her severed head lay on the floor behind the bed. The body was hacked about in the most fearful manner, but the horrible nature of the scene was too much for the spectators, and they left the room without getting any detailed idea as to the injuries that had been inflicted. One statement which had its origin with the police is to the effect that the body was literally dissected by having been cut into no fewer than 42 pieces. This is, however, unofficial, as also are wild statements to the effect that her arms and legs had been cut off.

So far as we can learn the actual injuries inflicted besides the severing of the head are that large slices are cut off the thighs and placed on the table; that the breasts were cut off, and the cheeks were slit and lapped over the face. The district was at once up in arms. Dorset-street was so crowded as to be impassable, and it was with the greatest of difficulty that the police were able to clear the streets, and close it against traffic. In the meantime speculation was rife as to the manner in which the murder had been committed. The general impression seemed to be that after leaving the beerhouse the woman met her murderer in the street, and induced him to accompany her home.

If murder were his object, this, of course, would just suit his purpose. No man was seen with her, and indeed the woman was not seen after leaving the doors of the public-house. She left the house alone, and so far as is known did not speak whilst in the public-house to any one who was a stranger in the neighbourhood. No stranger had been noticed in the house, and it is believed that she met him almost immediately after leaving the house. The supposition is that she went straight home with her companion, and that as soon as they entered the room the horrible deed was committed. At present it is impossible to say how death was caused, but most probably the woman's throat was cut as she lay on the bed.

The police having arrived, information was at once sent to Scotland Yard, and in a very short time Mr. Anderson, the Assistant Commissioner of the Metropolitan police, was on the spot. In the meantime Dr. Duke and Dr. Phillips were summoned, and saw the body, but did not, of course, make a detailed examination. Inquiries were at once instituted by the police as to what strange characters had been seen about, but no information of this kind could be gleaned. The populace were in a state of the wildest excitement, and it was with great difficulty any coherent information could be got from them. They were too terrified to speak, and only asked if he had been caught.

There were numerous references to "Jack the Ripper," and the man would have had an exceedingly bad time of it had he fallen into the hands of the infuriated crowd. Many of the people in the street knew her well, but the descriptions they gave were confused. Some said that she was dark, others that she was fair, but all agreed that she was a tall woman, somewhat well favoured, and that she was a well developed and well-nourished woman. Few of them, however knew anything about her, and from what can be learned she seems to have had no friends in the neighbourhood. Mrs. M'Carthy, the woman to whom the furnished house belongs, keeps a small glass and china shop in Dorset-street at the entrance to the courts, but she declined to make any statement whatever. Her son had not got over his fright, and was still in the hands of the police, who keep him as much away from the public as they can.

Other people are more communicative, but they have little to say that bears on the actual tragedy, and none of them appear to be acquainted with the woman's history. Almost as soon as the discovery was made inquiries were made of the police whether the bloodhounds were to be fetched, and frequent demands were made that a man should be sent off immediately. Whether this was done or not we are at present unable to say, but in all probability the hounds were sent for. It will be remembered that after the last murder several trials with bloodhounds were made by the police, and Sir Charles Warren himself watched one of these trials, which was made in Hyde Park. After this a general order was given that in case of another tragedy instant communication was to be made to a certain address in the south-western district where the bloodhounds were kept ready for action and that until they arrived the body was not to be disturbed. With this object, it is believed, the doctors refrained from touching the body, or from doing anything which would be likely to throw the dogs off or put them on a wrong scent.

The police, as we have said, promptly closed the streets, and a large number of constables were placed at each end of the street, and also at one point in the centre where a narrow passage leads from Dorset-street to the market. At both ends of the street was a dense crowd, and the narrow passage in the centre was crowded with people, who mostly lived in the immediate neighbourhood. None but residents and a few press men were admitted to the street, where the excitement was at a painful tension. The fact that the terrible deed had been committed in broad daylight seemed to add to the horror of the crime. All the other murders have been committed during the night time or in the morning, and they caused a feeling of insecurity at night time.

Many people shut themselves up in their houses after dusk, and nothing would induce them to leave their doors after nightfall. Amongst the unfortunate class the wildest horror prevailed, and it was only the direct necessity which kept them out in the streets after the closing of the public-houses. Since the Berner-street and Mitre Square murders the police and the Vigilance Committees have kept up a ceaseless watch during the small hours and nearly the whole district was covered by police and voluntary watchers.

Many loose women were shadowed every night, and the fiend, who has now found seven victims, could not conduct his ghastly operations except at the almost certain hazard of discovery. Since Mitre Square tragedy the police have on several occasions found chalk writing on the walls in the neighbourhood, stating that "Jack the Ripper" would be at work again shortly. In many of these cases doubtless the writer was an innocent man, of that very silly class of practical jokers who find opportunities for the display of their idiotcy on occasions of this kind, but in one case the police though they recognised a similarity between the writing and the penmanship of the two letters which had been received by the Central News.

Still they could not attach much importance to it, but it is now important to remember that the writer threatened to "cut the head off the next time," and in this latest atrocity this is precisely what has been done. As we have said, the effect of the previous tragedies was to induce the women of the district to keep indoors at night. This morning the almost unanimous declaration of the terrified women was that they were not now safe in broad daylight. It will of course be said that the murderer has confined his attention to loose women, but in a population of the class that is found at the East end of London there are a terribly large number of women whose virtue is not above suspicion. Their poverty compels them to live under conditions of freedom and license in which virtue finds little part, and it is to be feared that many of them are often compelled to seek on the streets the bread which they have no other means of obtaining.

There are thousands of people who are unable to obtain work, and the dense population is every day receiving additions in people whom ill fortune has cast from a respectable life. Under these circumstances the general terror of the women is more easily understood. In the present case there were none of the bitter complaints which have previously been hurled against the police. It seems to be recognised that the police are doing what they can, and though there may have been one or two instances of official stupidity, yet, on the whole, the police have done as much as could have been expected of them. They have done their best, and were not to be blamed for the faults of organisation which have weakened the detective department. It is felt that they have had to deal with no ordinary criminal.

Many theories have been advanced as to who the fiend may be, but it is beyond doubt that his devilish cunning is beyond what might be expected from an ordinary man. The probability is that the man is a lunatic who has periods of homicidal passion. This theory was put forward some time ago by Dr. Forbes Winslow, the well-known authority on mental diseases, and he said that if the criminal were a lunatic of the kind he imagined the crimes might cease for a time, but would inevitably break out again. In this connection it is worth noticing that about five weeks have elapsed since the last murders were committed, and that the previous tragedy was about three weeks prior to that time.

ANOTHER ACCOUNT

Another account says:- The body was found in a second floor front room in what is termed M'Carthy's Court, Dorset-street, by the son of the landlord, M'Carthy, who collects the rents of the rooms from the "unfortunates" every morning. The deceased went by the name of Mary Jane Kelly. She is about 25 years of age and an Irishwoman. She was spoken to last evening by several persons who say she was of a very reticent disposition. She had been cohabiting with a fishmonger, but the connection was broken off recently through a quarrel. The head is stated to have been cut off, and placed under one of the arms and the entrails were cut out. The police are unusually reticent, but a rumour is prevalent that bloodhounds have been sent. This, however, requires confirmation.

The Central News says: Present indications go to show that the woman fell a victim to the man who has already made himself a terror to the East end of London. On this occasion, however, the fiend has departed from his usual method, inasmuch as the crime was committed, not in the open streets, but in a room in a lodging house. This should afford a more definite clue in tracing the murderer than has been given in any of the previous cases, though whether any one was seen to have accompanied the woman to her home or was known to have visited her is a point which has not yet been cleared up.

Sir Charles Warren, on receiving information of the crime, proceeded directly to the spot, arriving there shortly before two o'clock, and the large staff of detectives still kept in the neighbourhood, were told off for various duties. The body has been photographed this afternoon for the use of the police. Up to 2.30 there was no sign of bloodhounds being employed by the police.

A representative of the Central News, writing at 2.30, says:- The scene of the murder is Miller Court, Dorset-street, Commercial-street, within a quarter of a mile of Mitre Square, Hanbury-street, Buck's Row, and Berners-street. The entrance to Miller Court is not more than three feet wide, and the court itself is only about 30 feet by 10. The murdered woman, whose name has not yet been ascertained, is a tall, fair female, about thirty years of age, and she was like the former victims. She has for some time past hired the furnished room, in which her mutilated body was found about ten o'clock this morning.

Late last night she was heard coming in with a companion, and the couple retired immediately to the woman's room. Nothing more was heard of the man, and for all the people in the place know he may have left any time between one and five without fear of attracting attention. Shortly before ten o'clock a man who keeps a general shop at the corner of the court, went to the room, and not hearing the woman stirring, knocked at the door. He received no answer and, becoming suspicious, pushed open the door and then rushed shouting from the house. The body lay partly on the bed, the throat cut, and the breasts and other parts of the body hacked about in a fearful manner.

The police arrived on the spot by a quarter past ten, and at once drew a cordon at each end of the street. Superintendent Arnold and

Inspector Abberline taking charge. Several surgeons were soon in attendance, and proceeded to examine the remains. Meantime the whole of the houses and approaches were minutely examined, but without finding traces of the murderer. A photographer was sent for, but did not arrive till half-past one. He has taken several photos of the remains, but the light is very bad for such work. Sir C. Warren arrived at a quarter to two in a hansom cab.

TRIAL OF BLOODHOUNDS

A man who lives in Dorset-street, opposite Miller's Court, states that soon after eleven o'clock three bloodhounds were brought in a hansom cab by a private individual and were put on the scent, but they did not appear to be of any use, not having been properly trained.

LATEST PARTICULARS
REMOVAL OF THE BODY

The body of the unfortunate woman was removed at four o'clock, and up to that time there were no signs of the bloodhounds, though the police declared to our reporter that they had been sent for. This morning, at a quarter past one the woman, it is said, was seen in her room alone, the worse for liquor. She was singing at that time. The door of the room was locked, and the key was gone. The police have not discovered that the woman was seen to-day. The latest statement by the police is to the effect that the woman's ears have not been cut off.

THE IDENTITY OF THE MURDERER

A woman of doubtful reputation says that she saw the deceased going home about half-past five this morning in company with a woman. Other neighbours state that they heard an altercation going on within the house in Miller's Court, between the deceased and a man. It appears that Fisher let herself and her companion into the house with a latchkey, and it may be that nobody saw them enter nor, probably, would recognition of the man be possible, as their entrance most likely attracted no attention. It is, however stated by the gossips of the street that early this morning a man with a black moustache, wearing a tall hat, and carrying a black bag, was seen in the neighbourhood or the spot where the crime was committed.

Morris Lewis, a tailor, states that he was playing pitch and toss in the court at nine o'clock this morning, and an hour before that he had seen the woman leave the house and return with some milk. There is no evidence as to who was in the house with her.

A MEDICAL OPINION

Dr. Gabe, who resides in the locality, was called in to view the remains. In an interview with one of our London reporters he stated that the body was dreadfully mutilated. The ears and nose were cut off, the liver was lying between the legs, and the head was hanging by a thread. A certain organ, he added, is missing. Detective-inspector Ticke stated that both breasts were cut off, and were lying on the table.

Source: *Manchester Evening News*

THE RIPPER REPORTS

SATURDAY 10 NOVEMBER 1888
ANOTHER WHITECHAPEL HORROR

Whitechapel has on horror's head horrors accumulated. Another woman has been murdered and mangled, within a stone's throw of the places were women were murdered and mangled on 7th of August, the 31st of August, the 8th of September, and not far from the scene of either of the murders and mutilations of September the 30th. This latest murder far surpasses in hideous brutality any of the crimes which went before it. The mutilations are more wild and wanton and ghastly.

The murderer, whoever he may be, would seem to have taken a positive delight in cutting and carving at the body of his victim. But although there was more hewing and hacking that in any of the former murders, yet it is almost indisputably evident that this latest crime belongs to the same class as the crimes which went before it. The same kind of mutilation which put the trade mark of the assassin on other corpses is shown in the body of the young woman who was murdered yesterday.

Of course we do not suggest that this is any conclusive evidence that this murder was done by the hand which may have committed some or all of the other crimes. There is a ghastly imitativeness in the crime, a horrible "fashion" which may be set going in murder, and which reveals itself with the mechanical servility of any other imitativeness and any other fashion. A brutal man getting into a furious quarrel with a woman in some wretched slum of the East-end might have been content a few months ago with kicking her to death, or cutting her throat.

Now, however, when such a man has quarreled with a woman and killed her, it is quite possible that he will not be satisfied until he has followed the new Whitechapel mode, and gashed and disembowelled her. There for it is not to be hastily assumed that all the murders were done by the one hand, or that the last murder was the work of the same criminal as any of the former. What we are fairly warranted in believing is that it is a crime which comes of the same impulse; which would not have been committed in such a way if the preceding crimes had not given it inspiration.

The natural inclination of everybody would be to hope that the murders and mutilations are the work of some solitary wretch with a positive mania for women's blood. It would be better that such were the explanation than to believe that one murderer hacked a woman to pieces, and that several other murderers followed and improved upon his example. Nothing certainly in the history of crime has ever happened in this country which could be compared in horror and hideousness with the succession of Whitechapel slaughters.

It is well to trace back this recent history of crime in the East-end. It began last Christmas week, when a woman was found bleeding and mangled in one of the poorest streets of Whitechapel. She was barbarously wounded, and in a matter somewhat like that which has characterised all the subsequent murders. She lived, if we are not mistaken, long enough to say that the crime was the work of several men. No trace of any criminal was found. The murder did not attract much attention at the time. The very hideousness prevented the publication of full details, and the ordinary reader of newspapers learned little more than the fact that a woman had been killed somewhere down Whitechapel way.

Unhappily such an event as that is not so uncommon as to startle London from its propriety; and although, if the whole story had been told, the public might have been stirred up to serious alarm at the condition of things in the East-end, yet as the whole story was not told it was not generally supposed that any novelty in crime had been started. About Easter time another murder was committed in the same region which appeared to below to the newly-invented order of assassination. Early in August a woman was found dead on the landing of some model dwellings known as George-yard Buildings, Spitalfields. This poor creature was found to have been pierced with no less than thirty-nine wounds, most of which were in and about the abdomen.

There were in this case evidences of deliberation very much like in some respects to those which presented themselves in more recent instances. Then came the murder of August 31; the murder of September 7th, a mere duplicate of the preceding crime; and the followed quickly the two slaughter deeds of September 30. One of the victims of September 30 had been dealt with by the murderer after the fashion of the earlier sufferers. In the case of the other woman the work of mutilation had been begun, but not finished. In the murder of yesterday the mutilating business was carried farther, and to all appearances done more deliberately, than in any former instance.

In most, in nearly all, of these crimes we see certain common features. The woman is killed in the first instance by the cutting of her throat. She has no time to resist or even to scream. Then the assassin has her, to use a famous phrase employed for quite a different purpose, like a "corpse on the dissecting table," and he gashes her body at his deliberate pleasure.

The first of the crimes we have mentioned would appear from the woman's own account to have been the work of several men. With regard to all the others, such evidence as can be collected, or the fact that little or no evidence of any kind can be got at, would seem to show that in each case not more than one criminal could probably have been engaged.

Five of the murders, including that of yesterday, may be generally described as belonging to just the same order; the same way of killing first; the same sort of deliberate mutilation afterwards; only that in yesterday's crime, as we have said, the hideous completeness of the work surpassed all preceding attempts. We have, then, the grim fact to face that within eight weeks five women have been murdered in the same way, and mangled in the same way, within a small area of the East-end of London. The attention of the police authorities has been directed to that limited area for weeks and weeks back. The whole neighbourhood has been thrown into alarm and consternation.

Every man and woman in the entire region must have been aroused to watchfulness and to activity. Yet the murders have been going on just the same - and we do not hear of any clue to the perpetrator of the latest any more that to the perpetrator of the earliest. If we are to accept what is certainly the general opinion, that the last five murders at least are the work of one hand then the wonder becomes all the greater that one man can keep on doing such things, deed after deed, without being discovered. That such a man should again and again succeed in entrapping a woman into some lonely place and there slaughter her and yet never be seen, never be noticed, never be suspected by anyone one because of blood marks on his hands or his clothes, would certainly seem to border on the miraculous.

Of course there is the other possibility to which we have already drawn attention, that some at least of the later crimes may have been the mere outcome of man's perverted imitativeness. The newspapers have been full of cases of men who threatened their wives, or their sweethearts, or women who were neither their wives or sweethearts that they would treat them in the Whitechapel way. Only yesterday or the day before there was reported the case of a man who declared that he was willing to give ten shillings to anyone who would rid him of his wife by the Whitechapel process. Practical jokers in the East-end have frightened women almost out of their senses by brandishing knives and proclaiming themselves to be "Jack the Ripper."

One such frolic actually caused a poor nervous woman to lose her life. While a mania of this kind is in the air we may expect to find mimicry take the form of earnest as well as of jest. But however the crimes are wrought, whether by one man or by many, the fact remains that while the police and the public, terribly forewarned, are on the look out for one particular sort of crime in one particular locality the crime goes on all the same, and the criminal withdraws himself from all eyes as securely as though he possessed the charm which could make him invisible at will.

Source: *London Daily News*

MONDAY 12 NOVEMBER 1888

THE WHITECHAPEL MURDER

The scene of the last murder in Dorset-street attracted a numberless crowd of people throughout Saturday, and again yesterday, who manifested great curiosity as to the exact site of the deed, and talked loudly and incessantly of the murderer and his victim. By closing both ends of the street with cordons of police as soon as the murder was discovered the excitement was greatly repressed, and the several editions of the afternoon press appeared to satisfy the natural anxiety which prevailed to become acquainted with the details of the tragedy. The consequence was that when the police were withdrawn, soon after the removal of the body on Friday afternoon, very little difficulty was experienced in keeping order.

Two constables were placed at the narrow entrance to Miller's court, or, as is better known in the locality, McCarthy's-court, to prevent any one not living in the wretched houses forming the court from entering, and the same precaution was continued throughout the night and the whole of yesterday. This was to prevent the possibility of the scene of the murder being made into a show place. On Saturday afternoon and evening a crowd blocked up the narrow street opposite Miller's-court, and the remainder of the street was filled with an excited and thoughtless lot of people, the public-houses being densely thronged until closing time.

Dorset-street runs from Crispin-street to Commercial-street, and is about two hundred yards in length, and there are three public-houses in it - the Home of Plenty, the Bluecoat Boy, and the Britannia; and constantly on Saturday evening the voices of women singing songs could be heard proceeding from the Bluecoat Boy; and drunken women rolled about the streets shouting and jesting in shameless fashion. There are also six common lodging-houses in the street, accommodating from a hundred to three and four hundred men and women; and the patrons of these houses contributed largely to the crowded character of the street. The police say that there are occasions when these lodgers turn out armed with sticks and pokers, and it requires the strenuous exertions of six men to restore order.

Yesterday people flocked from all parts of the Metropolis to the place, and the street hawkers plied a brisk trade with drinks, nuts and oranges, while strong-lunged men offered for sale the history of all the murders in a red paper back. McCarthy's shop, in which he sells cheap provisions, was thronged through-out the day, people being greatly attracted, no doubt, but the fact that he, his son, and his man knew more about the murder than any one else, and were not at all reticent on the subject. The key of the murdered woman's door has been found, so that her murderer did not carry it away with him, as was at first supposed.

It has been ascertained that a very big fire must have been kept burning all Friday morning in the room in which the body of Kelly was found, as a kettle on the fire was very much burned, the spout having entirely disappeared. The police through it likely that the murderer had burned something before leaving the room after the crime, and accordingly the ashes and other matter in the grate were carefully preserved. Yesterday afternoon Mr. Phillips and Dr. Macdonald, the Coroner for the district, visited Miller's-court, and after the refuse had been passed through a sieve, it was subjected to the closest scrutiny by the medical gentlemen.

Nothing, however, was found which is likely to afford any clue to the police. The doctors were engaged for some hours yesterday morning at the mortuary in Shoreditch Churchyard, making a post-mortem examination. Every portion of the body was accounted for, and at the conclusion of the investigation the various pieces were sewn together and placed in a coffin. One of the surgeons had stated his opinion that the woman had been dead some hours when first discovered, and that in all probability the crime was committed between two and three o'clock in the morning. During yesterday a large number of persons called at the mortuary and asked permission to look at the remains. All such requests were, of course, refused.

The man known as Jack, who recently lived with the deceased, and whose name is Joseph Barnett, tells the following story:- "I first met the deceased last Easter twelvemonth, and lived with her from that time until last Tuesday week. I was in decent work in Billingsgate Market when I first met her, and we lived quite comfortably. She was then twenty-two years of age, fresh-looking and well-behaved, though she had been leading an irregular life for some three years previously. She told me that her maiden name was Marie Jeannette Kelly, and that she was born in Limerick. Her parents, who were fairly well off, removed when she was a child to Wales, and they lived in Carmarthenshire. When she was but little over sixteen years of age she married a collier, but I do not remember his name. He was killed in an explosion in the mine, and then Marie went to Cardiff with her cousin. Thence she went to France, but remained only a short time.

Afterwards she lived in a fashionable house in the West-end of London; but drifted from the West-end to the East-end, where she took lodgings in Pennington-street. Her father came from Wales, and tried to find her there; but, hearing from her companions that he was looking for her, Marie kept out of the way. A brother in the Second Battalion Scots Guards came to see her once, but beyond that she saw none of her relations, nor did she correspond with them. When she was in Pennington-street a man named Morganstone lived with her, and subsequently a man named Joseph Fleming passed as her husband. She lived with me first of all in George-street, then in Paternoster-court, Dorset-street; but we were ejected from our lodgings there because we went on 'a drunk' and did not pay our rent. We took lodgings afterwards in Brick-lane, and, finally, about four months ago, in Miller's-court, were the murder occurred.

We lived comfortably until Marie allowed a girl named Julia to sleep in the same room. I objected, and as Mrs. Harvey afterwards came and stayed there, I left her, and went and took lodgings elsewhere. I told her I would come back if she would go and live somewhere else. I used to call there nearly every day, and if I had any money I used to give her some. I last saw her alive at 7.30 on Thursday night. I stopped about a quarter of an hour, and told her I had no money. Next day I heard there had been a murder in Miller's-court, and on my way there I met my sister's brother-in-law, and he told me it was Marie. I went to the court, and there saw the police-inspector, and told him who I was, and where I had been the previous night.

They kept me about four hours, examined my clothes for blood-stains, and finally, finding the account of myself to be correct, let me go free. Marie would never have gone wrong again, and I should never have left her, if it had not been for the girls stopping in the house. She only let them in the house because she was good-hearted, and did not like to refuse them shelter on a cold bitter night."

The young woman Harvey, who had slept with the deceased on several occasions, added further to her statement yesterday, to the effect that Kelly was a woman of superior education to that of most persons in her sphere of life. There are doubts as to whether the boy spoken of on Saturday was really a son of the murdered woman. But several people declare that a boy belonging to some one else was frequently in the room of the deceased. Mrs. Harvey changed her lodgings to New-court some days previously, but was on friendly terms with the deceased.

The last she saw of her was on Thursday night, about half-past seven o'clock, when the woman was perfectly sober. As regards the pilot coat found int he murdered woman's room, that has been found to belong to the husband of Mrs Harvey.

Harry Bowyer, the man engaged in Mr. M'Carthy's shop, at the corner of Miller's-court, who discovered the crime, states that on Wednesday night he saw a man speaking to Kelly who resembled the description given by the fruiterer of the supposed Berner-street murderer. He was about eight-and-twenty, had a dark moustache and somewhat peculiar eyes. In appearance he was rather smart, and attention was drawn to him by his white cuffs and collar. He carried no black bag.

A gentleman engaged in business in the vicinity of the murder stated yesterday that the was walking through Mitre-square at about ten minutes past ten on Friday morning, when a tall, well-dressed man, carrying a parcel under his arm, and rushing along in a very excited manner, ran into him. The man's face was covered with blood splashes, and his collar and shirt were also blood-stained. The gentleman did not at the time know anything of the murder.

A woman named Kennedy, who was, on the night of the murder, staying with her parents at a house situated in the court immediately opposite the room in which the body of Mary Kelly was found, states that about three o'clock on Friday morning she entered Dorset-street on her way home. She noticed three persons at the corner of the street near the Britannia public-house. There was a man - a young man, respectably dressed, and with a dark moustache - talking to a woman whom she did not know, and also a female poorly clad, and without any head gear. The man and woman appeared to be the worse for liquor, and she heard the man say, "Are you coming?" whereupon the woman, who appeared to be obstinate, turned in an opposite direction to which the man apparently wished her to go. Mrs. Kennedy went on her way, and nothing unusual occurred until about half an hour later.

She did not retire to rest immediately she reached home, but sat up, and between half-past three and a quarter to four she heard a cry of "Murder" in a woman's voice proceed from the direction in which Mary Kelly's room was situated. As the cry was not repeated, she took no further notice of the circumstances until the morning, when she found the police in possession of the place, preventing all egress to the occupants of the small houses in this court. When questioned by the police, she made a statement to the above effect. She has since supplemented that statement by the following:- "On Wednesday evening, about eight o'clock, I and my sister were in the neighbourhood of Bethnal-green-road, when we were accosted by a very suspicious-looking man about 40 years of age. He was about five feet seven inches high, wore a short jacket over which he had a long top-coat. He had a black moustache, and wore a billycock hat.

He invited us to accompany him into a lonely spot, as he was known about there, and there was a policeman looking at him." She asserts that no policeman was in sight. He made several strange remarks, and appeared to be agitated. He was very white in the face, and made every endeavour to prevent them looking him straight in the face. He carried a black bag. He avoided walking with them, and led the way into a very dark thoroughfare, at the back of the workhouse, inviting them to follow, which they did. He then pushed open a small door in a pair of large gates, and requested one of them to follow him, remarking, "I only want one of you," whereupon the women became suspicious. He acted in a very strange and suspicious manner, and refused to leave his bag in possession of one of the women.

They became alarmed at his actions, and escaped, at the same time raising an alarm of "Jack the Ripper." A gentleman who was passing intercepted the man, while the women made their escape. Mrs. Kennedy asserts that the man whom she saw on Friday morning with the woman at the corner of Dorset-street resembled very closely the individual who caused such alarm on Wednesday night, and that she would recognise him again if confronted with him.

Last evening a young man - who did not wish his name to be published - made the following statement to the Inspector in charge of Commercial-street Station: - "I reside in Lambeth with my wife and family, but my work lies in an opposite direction - namely, at Limehouse.

By trade I am a 'colour blender,' and am in the habit of travelling by the workmen's tramcar from my place of business to Houndsditch morning and night. In accordance with my usual practice, I alighted at the last-named terminus about half-past seven o'clock on Wednesday evening last, in company with a fellow workman.

On reaching Mitre-street, close to the scene of the murder of Catherine Eddowes, we noticed a strange-looking person dressed in a light grey overcoat and wearing a large round felt hat, his general appearance betokening American origin. He was about 5ft. 10in. in height, of dark complexion, with a rather heavy moustache. Remarking his suspicious movements, we made up our minds to follow him, when suddenly he stopped, looked sharply round, and addressed a young woman who was gazing in a shop window. The girl took little or no notice, but walked on a few yards, the fellow following by her side.

On reaching a gateway he made an attempt to seize her hand, at the same time pushing her towards the gate. She, however, released herself, when he used a blasphemous expression to her. We still followed, and got close up - close enough to hear what was said. By this time a constable came in sight, and we requested the girl to give her assailant into custody. She demurred, however, on the ground that she was not hurt, and the police to whom we appealed refused to make an arrest unless at the woman's suggestion.

By this time, the man has crossed to the opposite side, and was seen from a distance speaking to two other women, who, in their turn refused to have anything to do with him. One of the men remarked the strange manner in which he held one hand as if wishing to conceal something. Again urging the police to arrest him on suspicion, the constable referred to a sergeant whom they met, and the reply was, "Oh, we can't arrest him in that way; he's been about here all day, and belongs to one of the cattle boats." Almost at this moment a strange lad came up, observing,

"I say, policeman, did you see that man? He is a strange-looking fellow," but no further notice was taken, and the man was soon lost to view."

Some men were drinking yesterday at a beerhouse in Fish-street-hill, when one of them began conversing about the Whitechapel murder. A man named Brown, who lives at 9, Dorset-street, through he detected a blood mark on the stranger's coat. On the latter's attention being called to it, he said the mark was merely paint, but Brown took out a pocket-knife, and rubbing the dried stain with the blade, pronounced it to be blood. The coat being loose, similar stains were seen on the man's shirt, and then he admitted that they were bloodstains. As he left the house at once, Brown followed, and when the stranger had got opposite Bishopsgate Police-station, Brown gave him into the custody of an officer on duty there.

The Prisoner gave the name of George Compton. On being brought before the Inspector on duty he excitedly protested against being arrested in the public street on the ground that, in the present state of public feeling, he might have been lynched. He had been arrested at Shadwell on Saturday by a police-constable, who considered his behaviour suspicious; but he had been discharged, and had come to London. It transpired that before he left the Fish-street-hill beerhouse he had, so Brown alleged, made contradictory statements respecting his place of residence, and the locality in which he worked.

Compton does not bear any personal resemblance to the published descriptions of the man who is supposed to be the murderer. Another arrest was effected early yesterday morning through the exertions of two young men living in the neighbourhood of Dorset-street. Like many other in the district, they appear to have constituted themselves amateur detectives, and have been perambulating the streets on the look out for suspicious persons. About three o'clock yesterday morning they had their attention drawn to two men in Dorset-street who were loitering about. The two men separated, and one of them was followed by the two youths into Houndsditch.

They carefully observed his appearance, which was that of a foreigner. He was about 5ft. 8in. in height, had a long pointed moustache, was dressed in a long black overcoat, and wore also a cloth deerstalker hat. When near Bishopsgate-street the young men spoke to a policeman, who stopped the stranger and took him to Bishopsgate-street Police-station. Here he was searched, and it was found that he was carrying a pocket medical chest, containing several small bottles of chloroform.

In rather imperfect English he explained that he lived in Pimlico, where he was well known. After this preliminary examination he was taken to Commercial-street Police-station, in which district the murder was committed. He was detailed on suspicion, but subsequently was taken to Marlborough-street for the purpose of facilitating his identification. Another man was detained at Commercial-street Station on account of his suspicious movements. A man named Peter Maguire says that about eleven o'clock on Saturday night he was drinking at the public house kept by Mrs. Fiddymont, in Brushfield-street, which is known as the Clean House, when he noticed a man talking very earnestly to a young woman.

He asked her to accompany him up to a neighbouring court, but she refused, and afterwards left the bar. Maguire followed the man, who, noticing this, commenced running. He ran into Spitalfields Market, Maguire following all the while. The man then stopped, went up a court, took off a pair of gloves he was wearing and put on another pair. By a roundabout route he proceeded into Shoreditch, and got into an omnibus, which Maguire still followed. A policeman was asked by Maguire to stop this vehicle, but he refused, and Maguire continued his pursuit until he met another constable, who stopped the omnibus. The man was inside huddled up in a corner. Maguire explain his suspicions, and the man was taken to Commercial-street Station, where he was detained pending inquiries. These three men, however, gave the police satisfactory accounts of their movements, and were released.

Shortly before ten o'clock last night a man with a blackened face, who publicly proclaimed himself to be "Jack the Ripper," was arrested at the corner of Wentworth-street, Commercial-street, near the scene of the latest crime. Two young men, one a discharged soldier, immediately seized him, and the crowds which always on Sunday night parade this neighbourhood raised a cry of "Lynch him." Sticks were raised, and the man was furiously attacked, and but for the timely arrival of the police he would have been seriously injured. The police took him to Leman-street Station.

He refused to give any name, but asserted that he was a doctor at St. George's Hospital. His age is about 35 years, height 5ft. 7in., complexion dark, and dark moustache, and he was wearing spectacles. He wore no waistcoat, but had an ordinary jersey vest beneath his coat. In this pocket he had a double-peaked light check cap, and at the time of his arrest was bareheaded. It took four constables and four civilians to take him to the station, and protect him from the infuriated crowd. He is detained in custody.

On Friday night there was found in a pillar box at the corner of Northumberland-street and Marylebone-road a letter directed to the police, and its contents were as follow:- "Dear Boss, -I shall be busy tomorrow night in Marylebone. I have two booked for blood and ——. Yours, JACK THE RIPPER. Look out about ten o'clock Marylebone-road."

During Friday evening, Mr. G. B. Phillips, the Divisional Surgeon, visited the House of Commons, where he had a conference with the Under Secretary of the Home Office, Mr. Stuart-Wortley.

The fallowing notice was posted in Dorset-street, and at all the police-stations in the Metropolis on Saturday:-

"MURDER. - PARDON

"Whereas, on Nov. 8th or 9th, in Miller's-court, Dorset-street, Spitalfields, Mary Janet Kelly was murdered by some person or persons unknown, the Secretary of State will advise the grant of her Majesty's gracious Pardon to any accomplice, not being a person who contrived or actually committed the Murder, who shall give such information and evidence as shall lead to the discovery and conviction of the person or persons who committed the Murder.

(Signed) "CHARLES WARREN,

"The Commissioner of Police of the Metropolis.

"Metropolitan Police Office, 4, Whitehall-place, Nov. 10th, 1888."

The inquest will be opened at the Shoreditch Town Hall, before Dr. Macdonald, this morning.

Source: *London Evening Standard*

MONDAY 12 NOVEMBER 1888

THE EAST-END HORRORS. INQUEST ON KELLY TO-DAY

The inquest on the body of Mary Jeanette Kelly, who was murdered in Miller's-court, Dorset-street, was opened at the Shoreditch Town Hall, before Dr. Macdonald, coroner, this morning. The room in which the inquest was held was exceptionally small, and very few of the general public were admitted.

At the opening of the proceedings, a juror, addressing the coroner, said the jurymen were not on the Whitechapel jury list; the murder happened in Whitechapel.

The Coroner: It happened it our district.

A Juror: No; it is in Mr. Baxter's district.

The Coroner: The jurisdiction lies where the body lies, and not where it is found.

The jury were then sworn in, selected their foreman, and proceeded to view the body at the Shoreditch Mortuary, and also to inspect the house where the murder was committed.

The inquiry is proceeding.

Source: *Globe*

MONDAY 12 NOVEMBER 1888

RESIGNATION OF SIR C. WARREN

The Globe states that Sir C. Warren has resigned his office as Chief of the Metropolitan Police.

The Press Association is informed that Sir Charles Warren sent in his resignation on Saturday, after the statement by Mr. Matthews in the House of Commons on Thursday last, regarding the article in Murray's Magazine, that Sir Charles Warren has been requested to observe the rule of the Home Office as to the publication of works on matters relating to the service. Sir Charles took counsel with his friends on Saturday, and the result was that on the same evening he sent in his resignation, couched in the briefest language, to the Home Secretary, stating as his grounds for doing so that he could not accept the reproof administered to him. This morning all his books and papers were removed from the Chief Commissioner's office at Scotland Yard, and this was the first intimation at Scotland Yard that he had relinquished his position.

Source: *Manchester Evening News*

TUESDAY 13 NOVEMBER 1888

THE WHITECHAPEL MURDER THE INQUEST AND VERDICT

Dorset-street was comparatively deserted last evening, owing to the rain. Two policemen still guarded the entrance to Miller's-court, and no strangers were allowed to pass. The door of the room in which the murder took place remained padlocked, and the two windows are boarded up. Nothing definite has yet been settled with regard to the funeral of the murdered woman.

Inquiries made at the London Hospital by the police have established the fact that the man arrested in George-yard is a surgeon, who has been acting as an amateur detective. In order to facilitate his self-imposed task he had besmeared his face and put on a jersey. He has been set at liberty.

Mrs. M'Carthy, the wife of the landlord of the house where the murder occurred, received yesterday a post-card, bearing the Folkestone postmark, and signed, "Jack Sheridan, the Ripper." In bad spelling, and equally bad calligraphy, the writer said:- "Don't be alarmed. I am going to do another, but this time will be a mother and daughter." The postcard was handed over to the detectives. The writing was compared with the other similar letters, and found to be of a different character.

A man, apparently of the labouring class, with a military appearance, who knew the deceased, last evening gave the police a detailed statement of an incident which attracted his attention on Friday. He states that, on the morning of the 9th instant, he saw the deceased woman in Commercial-street, Spitalfields, in company with a man of respectable appearance. The man was about five feet six inches in height, and 34 or 35 years of age, with dark complexion and dark moustache, curled up at the ends. He was wearing a long, dark coat, trimmed with astrachan, a white collar with black necktie, in which was affixed a horse-shoe pin. He wore a pair of dark gaiters with light buttons, over button boots, and displayed from his waistcoat a massive gold chain. The highly-respectable appearance of this individual was in such great contrast to that of the woman, that few people could have failed to remark them at that hour of the morning. The police attach some importance to this information, which is much fuller in detail that that hitherto received by them.

The detective police, who were despatched to inquire into the movements of the various employees on board the several cattle-carrying boats then in the port of London, completed their inquiries by six o'clock on Saturday afternoon, when the last of their reports were received at Scotland-yard. These reports show that no person employed on any of the cattle boats can have had anything to do with the murder, as the times of nearly all have been accounted for, and those not accounted for are practically beyond suspicion.

The rumour that the bloodhounds which were recently tested by Sir Charles Warren had been lost proves to be untrue. The hounds are the property of Mr. Brough, of Scarborough; and when that gentleman, after bringing them to London, had to return home, he left the dogs in the charge of Mr. Taunton, of Doughty-street. Negotiations were opened for the purchase of the animals by the police; but, as Sir C. Warren delayed giving any definite assurance on this point, Mr. Brough insisted on resuming possession of his dogs, and they were sent back to Scarborough some days since.

The inquest upon the body of Mary Janet Kelly, who was found with her throat cut and horribly mutilated in Miller's-court, Dorset-street, on Friday morning, was opened yesterday, in the Shoreditch Town Hall, before Dr. Macdonald and a Jury of 15.

On the names of the Jury being called, the officer asked the Jury to name their foreman. One was named but he objected, on the ground that the crime was not committed in Shoreditch but in Whitechapel.

The Coroner. - I am not going to discuss the matter of jurisdiction with the Jury at all. The body lies in my jurisdiction; that is all I know, and all I have to say. Jurisdiction arises where the body lies.

The Officer repeated his request several times; and one or two who were named refused to act as foreman; but at length one consented. He was accordingly sworn, and then the Jury went to view the body, and the Coroner directed that they should afterwards be taken to see the place where the body was found.

Upon the return of the Jury at noon, the following evidence was taken:-

Joseph Barnett said - I was originally a fish porter, but now I am a labourer. I work at the river side, and carry fish. I lived up to Saturday last at 24, New-street, Bishopsgate. Before that I was staying at my sister's, who lives at 21 Portpool-lane, Leather-lane. I lived with the Deceased for a year and eight months. Her name was Marie Jeannette. Kelly was her maiden name. I have seen the body of the deceased, and I identify it by the hair and eyes. I am positive that the deceased was the woman with whom I lived, and that her name was Maria.

How long have you lived with her at 13 Room, Miller's-court? - About eight months; but the landlord says it is more.

When did you cease to live with her? - Last Tuesday week, the 30th ult.

Why did you leave her? - Because she took in an immoral woman out of compassion. I objected to that. My being out of work had nothing to do with it.

When did you see her last alive? - About half-past seven on Thursday evening. I remained there about a quarter of an hour, from half-past seven to a quarter to eight. I went to call upon her to see her for her welfare.

Were you and she on friendly terms? - Yes, very friendly. We were always good friends.

Did you have a drink together? -No, sir.

Was she quite sober? - She was.

Was she, generally speaking, of sober habits? - As long as she was with me and had my hard-earned wages, she was sober.

Did she get drunk occasionally? - Occasionally, yes; in my eyesight once or twice.

Did she tell you where she was born? - Yes, hundreds of times. She said she was born in Limerick, and went to Wales when quite young. Then she told me her father was named John Kelly, and was a "gaffer" at some ironworks. I don't know whether she said Carnarvonshire or Carmarthenshire.

Did she tell you anything about her other relatives, sisters, or others? - Yes, she told me about her sister, who was respectable, and lived with her aunt, following her occupation. That was going from place to place selling things. But I never saw any of her relatives. [Witness spoke with a stutter, and evidently laboured under great emotion.] She said there were six of them at home and one was in the Army. I have never seen or spoken to them.

Did she say she had been married? - Yes; but she was very young at the time. The marriage took place in Wales. She told me that she was married to a collier in Wales, and his name was Davis or Davies.

Did she tell you how long she lived with him? - Until he met his death in an explosion. She did not tell me the exact time she lived with him, but it might have been a year or two. She said she married Davies at the age of 16.

She told you that she came to London about four years ago? - Yes, she did.

Was that directly after the husband's death? - After her husband's death she went to Cardiff with a cousin.

Did she live long in Cardiff? - Yes, from two to eight months, and she was in the infirmary there.

What was she doing in Cardiff? - She was carrying on with her cousin in a bad life. As I told her, it was her downfall.

When did she come to London? About four years ago.

What did she do when she came to London? - She lived in a house in the West-end - a gay house - with a madam.

How long did she live there? - As far as she described it to me, a few weeks. Then some gentleman asked her to go to France, and she went, but, as she described it to me, she didn't like it, and came back in about a week or two's time.

Did she tell you the name of the place in France? - She told me, but she did not remain long, as she did not like it.

When she returned from France where did she tell you she lived? - In the Ratcliff-highway.

Do you know how long she lived there? - She must have lived there for some time.

After that, where did she live? - Near the Commercial Gasworks, with a man named Morganstone. I have never seen him. I don't know how long she lived there. When she left the neighbourhood of the Gasworks she went to live, I think as far as I can remember, at Pennington-street. She lived with another man named Joseph Fleming, but why she left him I don't know. She described him to me as a mason's plasterer.

Did she tell you where Fleming lived? - Somewhere in the Bethnal-green-road.

Was that all that you knew of her history until you came to live with her? - She told me her history while I was living with her.

Who lived with her before you? - I cannot answer whether it was Morganstone or Fleming.

Where did you first pick up with her? - In the parish of Spitalfields or Whitechapel.

Did you go to live with her the first time you saw her? - We had a drink together, and then we made arrangements to meet on the Saturday.

What did you arrange on the Saturday? - On Saturday we agreed to come together, to keep with one another.

Did you take a house then at once? - No; but we took lodgings.

Have you lived with her ever since? - Yes, ever since, until we parted quite friendly before her murder.

Did she have any fear about any one? - No, not particularly; but she used to ask me to read about the murders, and I used to bring them all home and read them. If I did not bring one she would get it herself, and ask me whether the murderer was caught. I used to tell her everything of what was in the paper.

Did she go in fear of any particular individual? - No, sir. Only with me now and again, and that was always shortly over; one moment rowing, and for days and weeks always friendly. Often I bought her things coming home, and whatever it was she always liked it. She was always glad of my fetching her such articles - such as meat and other things, as my hard earnings would allow.

The Coroner told the Witness not to leave the precincts of the Court, and said he had given his evidence very well.

Thomas Bowyer said, - I live at 37, Dorset-street, Spitalfields. I am a servant to M'Carthy, the owner of a chandler's shop. I serve in the shop. The shop is situated at 27, Dorset-street.

The Coroner - Will you tell the Jury, quietly and slowly, what occurred on Friday morning?

Witness, - About a quarter to eleven on Friday morning I was ordered by M'Carthy to go to Mary Jane's room (No. 13). I did not know her by any other name.

What were you going to do there? - I went for the rent. I knocked at the door, and I received no answer. I knocked again, but got no answer. I went round the corner by the gutter-spout, where there is a small pane of glass broken in the large window.

Inspector Ledger, G division, produced a plan of the premises. [Before the examination of the Witness was continued the plan was shown to him, and he pointed to the window referred to in his examination.]

Examination of Bowyer continued. - There was a curtain before the window, which covered both windows. I pulled the curtain aside and looked in.

What did you see? - I saw too lumps of flesh lying on the table.

Where was this table? - In front of the bed and close against it. The second time I looked in I saw the body of somebody lying on the bed, and blood on the floor. I at once went quietly back to my master and I told him what I had seen. "Good God," he said, "do you mean to say that, Harry?" We both went down to the Police-station. No, first my master went and looked. At the station we told the police what we had seen. No one in the neighbourhood knew what had occurred. Nobody was in the shop. Master came back with the inspector. I have seen the deceased under the influence of drink once.

By a Juror. - I saw the deceased last alive on Wednesday afternoon, in the court. Mr. M'Carthy's shop is at the corner of the court. I spoke to her on Wednesday afternoon.

John M'Carthy, said. - I am a grocer and lodging house keeper. My shop is No.27, Dorset-street. On Friday morning about 10.30 I sent Bowyer to No. 13 to call for rent. He went there and he came back. The court is called Miller's-court. The man came back in five minutes. He said, "Governor, I knocked at the door, and couldn't make anyone answer. I looked through the window, and saw a lot of blood." I went out with him, looked through the window and saw the woman and everything. I couldn't speak at first, but at last I said, "Harry, don't tell any one; go for the police." I knew the deceased as Mary Jane Kelly. I have seen her alive and dead and have no doubt about her identity. I recovered myself, and went with Bowyer to the Commercial-street Police-station. I saw Inspector Beck, and told him what I had seen. He came to the house with me at once.

How long has the deceased lived in this room? - About ten months.

With this man Joe? - Yes: I did not concern myself. I did not know whether they were married or not. They had a row some time ago and broke two panes of glass. The bed, tables, and chairs in the room belonged to me, and the bed-clothes and everything. She paid 4s. 6d. a week for the room. The deceased was 29s. in arrear of rent. The rent was paid weekly. I often saw the deceased the worse for drink. She was not reeling about; but she was noisy when under the influence of drink. She was not helpless, and was able to walk about. She was an exceptionally quiet woman, but when in drink she was noisy, and I could tell that she had been drinking.

Mary Ann Cox said - I live at the last house at the top of Miller's court. I am a widow, and get my living on the streets. On Thursday night, at 11.45, I last saw the deceased. She was very intoxicated. There was a short, stout man, shabbily dressed, with her who had a pot of ale in his hand. He had a round black billy-cock hat on. He had a blotchy face, and a full carrotty moustache. The chin was bare. I followed them up into the court, and said, "Good night, Mary." She never turned round, and he banged the door. He had nothing but a quart can of beer in his hand. She said "Good-night, I'm going to have a song." Then the door was shut, and she sang, "The violet I plucked from my mother's grave when a boy." I remained a quarter of an hour in my room. She was singing all the time. I went out, and returned about one o'clock, and she was singing then. I went into my room to warm my hands a bit. It was raining hard; then I went out again and returned at 3.10 a.m. Then the light was out, and there was no noise. I went in, but I could not sleep, and did not go to bed. I can't sleep when I owe anything. When the murder was discovered I had not had a wink of sleep. I had no sleep at all that day. There are men who go to work in Spitalfields Market and who leave early. One such man lives in the court now. I heard a man go out at 6.15. He might have gone out and come back again for all I know.

It might have been a policeman. The man I saw with Kelly was short and stout. All his clothes were dark. He appeared to be between 35 and 36. I did not notice the colour of his trousers. All his clothes were dark. The man looked very shabby, but his boots made no noise whatever in going up the court. The deceased had no hat on, and a red pelerine, and a dark shabby skirt. I did not notice that the deceased was the worse for drink until I said "Good night" to her. She scarcely had time to say "Good night," as the man shut the door.

By a Juror. - There was a light in the room, but I could not see anything as the blind was down.

The Foreman. - Should you know the man again if you saw him?

Witness. - Oh, yes, I should.

By the Coroner. - I feel certain that if there had been a cry of "Murder" in the Deceased's room after three o'clock in the morning, I should have heard it. There was not the least noise whatever. I have often seen the deceased the worse for drink.

Elizabeth Prater, wife of William Prater, who deserted her five years ago, said - I live at No. 20, in Miller's-court. On Thursday I went out of the court about five o'clock, and I returned close upon one o'clock on Friday morning. I stood at the corner of the court waiting for a young man. No one came up to me. I never saw my young man. I went into my room and lay down. I went into M'Carthy's shop.

The Coroner. - Was it open at 1 a.m.?

Witness. - Yes, sir; and sometimes later. I told him to say to my young man that I had gone to my room. From where I was I could see if a light was on in the room of the deceased. I have only spoken to her once or twice. I lay down on the bed at 1.30, in my clothes. I fell asleep directly, because I had been having something to drink, and slept soundly. I had a little black kitten, which used to come on to my neck. It woke me from 3.30 to 4.00, by coming on to my face, and I gave it a blow and knocked it off. The lights were out in the lodging house. The cat went on to the floor, and that moment I heard "Oh, murder." I was then turning round on my bed. The voice was "a faintish" one, as though some one had woke up with a nightmare. Such a cry is not unusual, and I did not take any particular notice. I did not hear the cry a second time. I did not hear any bed or table being pulled out. I went to sleep, and awoke again about five o'clock. I was not awakened by any noise. I went downstairs, and saw some men harnessing their horses. I walked out and went into the Ten Bells public-house, where I had some rum. The last Witness could have come down the court and gone out, but I did not see her. I saw no one particular at the Ten Bells. I was there at a quarter to six, and shortly afterwards I returned home again, went to bed and slept till eleven o'clock on Friday morning. When I went home first, at half-past one, there was no singing going on in the deceased's room. If there had been I should have heard it.

Caroline Maxwell, of 14, Dorset-street, wife of Henry Maxwell, said - My husband is a lodging-house deputy. I have known the deceased for about four months. I also knew Joe Barnett. The deceased was a young woman who never associated with anyone much, beyond bowing, "Good morning." I saw her at the corner of Miller's-court on Friday morning at eight o'clock, because my husband had not left off, and he leaves off at half-past eight. My husband had a man to call at seven a.m. That was his last call. I had never seen the deceased about at that time in the morning. I spoke to her - "What, Mary, what brings you out so early?" and she said, "Oh, Carrie, I do feel so bad." Although I had only spoken to her twice previously, I knew her name and she knew mine. I asked her if she would have a drink. She said, "I have just had half a pint of ale, and I have brought it up." The beer she had thrown up was about three yards away from her on the pavement. She did not see where she had the beer, but by the motion she made with her head I should imagine that she had it at the Britannia beerhouse, at the corner of the street. I left the deceased then, saying I could pity her feelings. I went to Spitalfields Market to get my husband's breakfast, and on my return I saw her outside the Britannia public-house, talking to a man. That would be about a quarter to nine.

The Coroner. - What description could you give of this man?

Witness. - I could not give any. I did not pass them, but I saw them from the distance. I was between 20 and 25 yards away from them. I am sure it was the deceased that I saw outside the public-house. The man I saw was not tall. He was short, and a little taller than I am. (The Witness was a woman of medium height.) The man had a plaid coat on. I did not notice his hat. The deceased was wearing a dark skirt, velvet bodice, and a maroon shawl. She had no hat on. I have seen the deceased in drink, but she was not a habitual drunkard. She was a quiet girl as far as I saw of her. She was never about with anybody that I saw.

A Juror. - If the man that you saw the deceased with had worn a silk hat should you have noticed it?

Witness. - I don't know that I should have done so. I am accustomed to see all classes of people, but I don't take any notice of them.

But would you have noticed his hat if it had been a silk one? - If he had worn a silk hat I might have noticed it.

Sarah Lewis, living at 24, Great Pearl-street, Spitalfields, a laundress, said - I knew Mrs. Keyler, in Miller's-court and saw her on Friday morning, about 2.30 a.m. - this I noticed by Spitalfields Church clock. In Dorset-street I saw a man with a wideawake on, stopping on the opposite side of the pavement. The man was alone, and was not talking to anyone. He was tall, and "a stout-looking man." He had dark clothes on. A young man went along with a young woman who was drunk. The man, I noticed, was looking up at the court, as though he was waiting for some one. I stopped at Kelyer's flat that night. I had had a few words at home. The court was quiet. I sat in a chair and fell asleep. I woke up at 3.30 as the clock went. I sat awake until nearly five. A little before four I heard a female shouting "Murder," once. It was loud, and there was only one shout. The cry was from where the shop is. There was no repetition. It was not a young woman's voice. I took no notice. I was not alarmed. I left the house at half-past five in the afternoon. I could not get out sooner, because the police would not let us leave. On Wednesday night I was going with a friend along the Bethnal-green road, at eight o'clock in the evening, when a gentleman passed us, and he followed us back again. He wanted us to follow him; he said he didn't mind which of us. He went away, and came back to us, and said if we went along a certain entry he would treat us. He put down his bag, a black shiny bag, and said to my friend, "Are you frightened I've got something in my bag?" Then he began feeling about his clothes, and we ran away. He was a short, pale-faced man, with a black moustache. The man appeared to be about 40. His bag was not very large, about six to nine inches long. The hat he wore was a round hat, rather high - a stiff felt hat. He had a long overcoat on, and short black one underneath. His trousers were dark pepper and salt. On the night of the murder I saw him again in the Commercial-street. I cannot tell you where he went when we left him. We did not look behind us. On Friday morning about half-past two, on my way to Miller's-court, I met the same man, who was accompanied by a woman. They were in Commercial-street, near the Britannia public house. He was wearing the same clothes with the exception of the overcoat. He had the black bag with him. They were standing talking together. I passed on, but looked back at him. I went on my way. I did not tell a policeman, as I did not pass one on my way. I saw the man talking to the woman at the corner of Dorset-street, and left them there.

 The Coroner. - Should you know the man if you saw him again?

Witness. - I should.

Mr. G. B. Philips, M.R.C.S, said - I am surgeon to the H Division of the Metropolitan Police, and reside at 2, Spital-square. On Friday morning I was called by the police, about eleven o'clock, and proceeded to Miller's-court, which I entered at 11.15. I found a room numbered 13, having two windows. (A photograph of the premises was produced.) There were two windows looking into the court. Two of the panes in the smaller window nearest to the passage were broken, and finding the door locked I looked through the lower broken pane, and satisfied myself that the mutilated corpse lying on the bed was not in need of any immediate attention from me. I also came to the conclusion that there was nobody else upon the bed or within view to whom I could render any professional assistance. Having ascertained that it was probably advisable that no entry should be made into the room at the time, I remained until about 1.30, when the door was broken open leading into the room. The door was broken open by Mr. M'Carthy. The direction was given by Superintendent Arnold. The police before that prevented Mr. M'Carthy from breaking the door open. The yard was in charge of Inspector Beck. On the door being opened, it knocked against a table, which was close to the left hand side of the bed, and the bedstead was close up against the wooden partition. The mutilated remains of a woman were lying two-thirds over towards the edge of the bedstead nearest the door of entry. She had only her chaise upon her or some under-linen garment, and on my subsequent examination I am sure the body had been removed subsequent to the injury which caused her death from the side of the bedstead which was nearest to the wooden partition before named. The large quantity of blood under the bedstead, the saturated condition of the palliasse, pillow, and sheet, at the top corner of the bed-stead nearest the partition, leads me to the conclusion that the severance of the right carotid artery was the immediate cause of her death, and was inflicted while the deceased was lying at the right side of the bedstead, and her head and neck in the top right hand corner before alluded to.

Julia Van Turney said - I occupy a room in Miller's-court, and the man I am now living with is named Harry Owen. I knew the deceased. It was some time before I became acquainted with her; but when I knew her she told me that her name was Kelly, and she was a married woman. I know the young man Joe Barnett with whom the deceased lived. They lived happily together. He objected to her frequenting the streets. I have frequently seen the deceased the worse for drink; but when she was cross Joe Barnett would go out and leave her to quarrel alone. She told me that she was fond of another man, that she could not bear the man Joe she was living with, although he was very good to her. Strangely enough, the other man, she said, was named Joe. Witness went to bed on Thursday night in Miller's-court about eight p.m. She did not sleep, she could not tell why; but she did not sleep at all; perhaps she dozed a bit. She heard a strange sound with some door, which was not like the way in which the deceased used to shut the door. There was no noise in the court that night, and she heard no singing. If there had been any singing she must have heard it. The deceased used to sing Irish songs.

Maria Harvey, of New-court, Dorset-street, said - I knew the deceased. On Monday and Tuesday she slept with the deceased. She saw the deceased on the Thursday night about seven o'clock. Joe came in while she was there. Witness left some clothes to be washed, including a man's two shirts, petticoats belonging to a child, and a black overcoat.

Inspector Walter Beck, of the H Division, stationed at Commercial-street, said information was brought to the station at five minutes to eleven on Friday morning. He went at once, and gave directions to prevent any one leaving the court, and he directed other constables to make a search.

THE RIPPER REPORTS

Inspector G. Abberline, of Scotland-yard, said he was in charge of the case on behalf of the police. He reached the court about 11.30 on Friday. When he reached the place he was informed by Inspector Beech that the bloodhounds had been sent for and were on their way; and Mr. Phillips said it would be better not to force the door until the dogs arrived. At 1.30 Superintendent Arnold arrived, and stated that the order for the dogs had been countermanded, and gave directions for the door to be forced. I looked through the window and saw how matters really were before we entered. I subsequently took an inventory of the things in the room. There were traces of a large fire having been kept in the great, and the spout of the kettle had been melted off. We have since examined the ashes of the grate and found portions of the brim of a hat and portions of a shirt. I consider that the articles were burned to enable to murderer to see what he was about. There was a small piece of candle standing in a broken wine glass. The key of the lock had been missing for some time, and the door could be opened by pushing the latch back. A man's clay pipe was found in the room which belonged to Barnett.

The Coroner said that was all the evidence the police were prepared to lay before the Jury that day. It was for them to say whether they were satisfied with it, or whether they would adjourn and bear the further evidence on a future occasion. If the Jury came to the conclusion as to the cause of death, that was all they had to do. The police would take charge of the case if it was for the Jury to say whether they had heard sufficient evidence to enable them to come to a conclusion as to the cause of death of Mary Jane Kelly. If that was the case, there was no occasion for a further adjournment, but the matter was one entirely for the Jury.

The Foreman said the Jury considered that they had heard enough evidence to justify them in coming to a verdict.

The Coroner. - Then, gentlemen, what is your verdict?

THE RIPPER REPORTS

The Foreman. - Wilful Murder against some person or persons unknown.

The Coroner. - You are satisfied as to their identity of the deceased?

The Foreman. - We are, sir, perfectly satisfied.

This closed the inquiry.

Source: *London Evening Standard*

WEDNESDAY 14 NOVEMBER 1888

THE INQUEST AND VERDICT

Dr. Macdonald, M.P., Coroner for the North-east Middlesex, opened the inquest at Shoreditch Town Hall, on Monday, on the body of Mary Jeanette Kelly, murdered in Miller's-court, Dorset-street, Spitalfields, during Thursday night or Friday morning last. The jury having been sworn, proceeded to view the body, and afterwards visited the scene of the murder. On their return, evidence was taken. The crowd in the adjoining streets were much smaller than at the inquest on the previous victims.

Mr. Vander Hunt represented the Whitechapel Vigilance Committee, and Inspector Abberline was present on behalf of the police.

The Coroner complained of the unfounded statements in the Press as to alleged communication between himself and Mr. Wynn Baxter with regard to jurisdiction.

Joseph Barnett, labourer, deposed: I identify the body of the deceased as that of a young woman with whom I have lived for eight months. I separated from her on the 30th of last month. I left her because she brought a prostitute to live in our room. I saw deceased last between half-past seven and a quarter to eight on Thursday night. We were on friendly terms. Before leaving I said I had no money. Deceased was sober. Deceased told me her father's name was John Kelly, gaffer of ironworks in Carnarvonshire. She was born in Limerick, and was married in Wales to a man named Davis, who was killed in a colliery explosion. After leading an immoral life in Cardiff, deceased came to a house in the East End of London. A gentleman induced her to go to France. She returned, lived at Radcliffe Highway, then at Pennington-street. Witness first met her in Commercial-street, and arranged to live with her. At deceased's request, he read to her the newspaper reports of the previous Whitechapel murders. He did not hear her express fear of any person.

The jury expressed the wish that Dr. Phillips, police surgeon, not present, should attend, so that some medical evidence might be taken.

Thomas Bowyer, Dorset street, Spitalfields, said: On Friday morning, I went to the house of the deceased to collect rent for Mr. McCarthy. I knocked but got no answer. I found a window broken. I put the curtain aside. Looking in I saw two lumps of flesh on the table. Looking a second time, I saw a body on the bed, and a pool of blood on the floor. I reported the discovery to the police.

John McCarthy, grocer, lodging-house keeper, Dorset-street, deposed: I sent the last witness to Miller's-court for the rent. Within five minutes he came back, saying he had seen blood in No.13 room of Miller's-court. I went and saw the body. I could say nothing for a little time, but when I recovered I accompanied my man to the police. An Inspector came with me to the house. I do not know that Barnett and deceased had any serious quarrel. I let the room at 4s. 6d. A week.

Deceased was 29s. In arrears. I often saw deceased the worse for drink. When drunk she became noisy and sang.

Mary Ann Cox deposed: I lived at 5, Miller's-court opposite deceased. About midnight on Thursday I saw deceased in Dorset-street. She was very much the worse for drink. I saw her go up the court with a short stout man, shabbily dressed. He carried a pot of ale. He wore a black coat and hat, had a clean shaved chin, sandy wiskers and moustache. Deceased wished me good night and went into her room. I heard her singing the song, "A violet I plucked from mother's grave." I afterwards went out of my room. Coming back at one o'clock she was still singing. I again went out. Coming back I saw the light in the deceased's room had been put out. All was silent. I heard footsteps in the court about six o'clock. I did not sleep after going to bed. If there had been a cry of murder during the night I must have heard it.

Elizabeth Prater, Miller's Court, said I live in the same house, I went into my own room at one o'clock on Friday morning. I then saw no glimmer in deceased's room. I woke about four and heard a suppressed cry of "Murder," appearing to come from the Court. I did not take particular notice, as I frequently hear such cries.

Caroline Maxwell, wife of the lodging house deputy in Dorset Street, was next sworn.

The Coroner cautioned her to be careful, as her evidence differed from the other statements made.

Mrs. Maxwell then deposed: I saw deceased at the corner of Miller's Court shortly after eight o'clock on Friday morning. Deceased told me she felt ill, and vomited. On my return, I saw deceased speaking with a man outside the Britannia public-house. I cannot give a particular description of the man. He wore dark clothes, and a sort of plaid coat. Deceased wore a dark skirt, with velvet body and shawl, and no hat. The man was short and stout.

Sarah Lewis, Great Powell Street, stated:- I visited my friend at Miller's Court on Friday morning at half-past two o'clock. I saw a man standing on the pavement. He was short, stout, and wore a wideawake hat. I stopped with my friend Mrs. Keyler. I fell asleep in a chair, and woke at half-past three. I sat awake till a little before four. I heard a female voice scream "Murder" loudly. I thought the sound came from the direction of deceased's house. I did not take much notice. Such cries are often heard. At eight o'clock on Wednesday night when with a female friend, I was accosted in Bethnal Green-road by a gentleman who carried a bag. He invited one of us to accompany him. Disliking his appearance we left him, the bag was about nine inches long. The man had a pale face, dark moustache, wore dark clothes, an overcoat, and a high felt hat. On Friday morning when coming to Miller's-court about half-past two, I met that man with a female in Commercial-street. As I went into Miller's Court they stood at the corner of Dorset-street.

Dr. George Baxter Phillips deposed: I am surgeon to the H Division of the Metropolitan police. I cannot give the whole of my evidence to-day. On Friday morning, about 11 o'clock, I proceeded to Miller's Court. In a room there found the mutilated remains of a woman lying two-thirds over toward the edge of the bed nearest the door. Subsequent to the injury which caused death the body had been removed from the opposite side of the bed, which was nearest the wooden partition. The presence of a quantity of blood on and under the bed leads me to the conclusion that the severance of the carotid artery, which was the immediate cause of death, was inflicted while the deceased was lying at the right side of the bedstead, and her head and neck in the right hand corner. That is as far as I propose to carry my evidence to-day.

The coroner said he proposed to continue taking evidence for another hour.

The jury expressed a wish to adjourn for some time.

THE RIPPER REPORTS

The Coroner said he would resume in a quarter of an hour.

On resuming, Julia Venturney said: I am a char-woman, and live at Miller's Court. Deceased told me she liked another man other than Joe Barnett, and he often came to see her. I was at home during Thursday night. Had there been any noises I should have heard them.

Maria Harvey, laundress, said: I have slept with deceased on several occasions, and never heard her express any fear of anyone.

Inspector Beck, H Division, said: I accompanied Dr. Philips to the house. I do not know that deceased was known to the police.

Inspector Abberline, Scotland Yard, deposed: I went to Miller's Court at 11.30 a.m. on Friday. When there I received an intimation that the bloodhounds were on the way. I waited till 1.30, when Supt. Arnold arrived and said the order for the bloodhounds had been countermanded. The door was then forced. In the grate were traces of woman's clothing having been burnt. My opinion is they were burnt to give sufficient light for the murderer to do his work.

The Coroner said this concluded the evidence offered to-day. The question was whether the jury had not already heard sufficient testimony to enable them to determine the cause of death. His own opinion was they might conclude, and leave the case to the police.

The jury, after a moment's consultation, returned a verdict of "Wilful murder against some person or persons unknown."

Source: *Derbyshire Times and Chesterfield Herald*

WEDNESDAY 14 NOVEMBER 1888

THE WHITECHAPEL MURDER

Last evening a man, named George Hutchinson, a groom, who is now working as a labourer, made the following statement to the reporter of a news agency:-

"On Thursday I had been to Romford, in Essex, and I returned from there about two o'clock on Friday morning, having walked all the way. I came down Whitechapel-road into Commercial-street. As I passed Thrawl-street I passed a man standing at the corner of the street, and as I went towards Flower and Dean-Street, I met the woman Kelly, whom I knew very well, having been in her company a number of times. She said, 'Mr. Hutchinson, can you lend me sixpence.' I said, 'I cannot, as I am spent out, going down to Romford.' She then walked on towards Thrawl-street, saying, 'I must go and look for some money.' The man who was standing at the corner of Thrawl-street then came towards her, put his hand on her shoulder, and said something to her which I did not hear; they both burst out laughing. He put his hand again on her shoulder, and they both walked slowly towards me.

I walked on to the corner of Fashion-street, near the public-house. As they came by me his arm was still on her shoulder. He had a soft felt hat on, and this was drawn down somewhat over his eyes. I put down my head to look him in the face and he turned and looked at me very sternly. They walked across the road to Dorset-street. I followed them across, and stood at the corner of Dorset-street. They stood at the corner of Miller's-court for about three minutes. Kelly spoke to the man in a loud voice, saying, 'I have lost my handkerchief.' He pulled a red handkerchief out of his pocket, and gave it to Kelly, and they went up the court together. I went to look up the court to see if I could see them, but could not. I stood there for three-quarters of an hour to see if they came down again, but they did not, and so I went away. My suspicions were aroused by seeing the man so well dressed, but I had no suspicion that he was the murderer.

The man was about 5ft. 6in. in height, and about 34 or 35 years of age, with dark complexion, and dark moustache turned up at the ends. He was wearing a long, dark coat trimmed with Astrakhan, a white collar with black necktie, in which was affixed a horse-shoe pin. He wore a pair of dark "spats," with light buttons over button boots, and displayed from his waistcoat a massive gold chain. His watch chain had a big seal with a red stone hanging from it. He had a heavy moustache, curled up, dark eyes, and bushy eyebrows. He had no side whiskers, and his chin was clean shaven. He looked like a foreigner.

I went up the court, and stayed there a couple of minutes, but did not see any light in the house, or hear any noise. I was out on Monday night until three o'clock looking for him. I could swear to the man anywhere. I told one policeman on Sunday morning what I had seen, but did not go to the police-station. I told one of the lodgers here about it on Monday, and he advised me to go to the police-station, which I did, at night. The man I saw did not look as though he would attack another one. He carried a small parcel in his hand about eight inches long, and it had a strap round it. He had it tightly grasped in his left hand. It looked as though it was covered with dark American cloth. He carried in his right hand, which he laid upon the woman's shoulder, a pair of brown kid gloves. One thing I noticed, and that was that he walked very softly.

I believe that he lives in the neighbourhood, and I fancied that I saw him in Petticoat-lane on Sunday morning, but I was not certain. I have been to the Shoreditch mortuary, and recognised the body as that of the woman Kelly, whom I saw at two o'clock on Friday morning. Kelly did not seem to me to be drunk, but was a little bit spreeish. I was quite sober, not having had anything to drink all day. After I left the court I walked about all night, as the place where I usually sleep was closed. I came in as soon as it opened in the morning. I am able to fix the time, as it was between ten and five minutes to two o'clock as I came by Whitechapel Church. When I left the corner of Miller's-court the clock struck three. One policeman went by the Commercial-street end of Dorset-street while I was standing there, but not one came down Dorset-street. I saw one man go into a lodging house in Dorset-street, and no one else. I have been looking for the man all day."

On Monday night the police made a thorough search of the casual wards in the East-end, but no discovery of importance was made. In the course of the night, however, a message was received from the Holborn Casual Ward that one of the temporary inmates was behaving suspiciously. Constables were sent to the place, and arrested a rough-looking fellow, who gave the name of Thomas Murphy. He was taken to the police-station at Frederick-street, King's-cross-road, where, on being searched, he was found to have in his possession a formidable-looking knife, with a blade about ten inches long.

He was detained in custody. No further arrests were made yesterday. Some of the best men in the detective force have been instructed to watch individuals upon whom suspicion rests, but not so seriously as to justify their immediate arrest. Inquiries are again being made at Lunatic Asylums and Workhouse Infirmaries, with the object of obtaining a list as complete as possible of men discharged as cured within the last few months, who had previously been afflicted with dangerous mania.

The police have received from Mr. Samuel Osborne, wire worker, 20, Garden-row, London-road, a statement to the effect that he was walking along St. Paul's Churchyard yesterday behind a respectably-dressed man, when a parcel, wrapped in newspaper, fell from the man's coat. Osborne told him that he had dropped something; but the man denied that the parcel belonged to him. Osborne picked up the parcel, and found that it contained a knife, having a peculiarly-shaped handle and a thick blade, six or seven inches long, with stains upon it resembling blood.

The parcel also contained a brown kid glove, smeared with similar stains on both sides. Osborne found a constable, and together they searched for the mysterious individual, but without success. The parcel was handed to the City Police authorities, who, however, attach no importance to the matter.

The funeral of the murdered woman will not take place until after the arrival from Wales of some of her relatives and friends, who are expected to reach London this evening. If they are unable to provide the necessary funeral expenses, Mr. H. Wilton, of 119, High-street, Shoreditch, has guaranteed that the unfortunate woman should not be buried in a pauper's grave. The remains will be interred either to-morrow or on Friday, at the New Chingford Cemetery. The plate on the coffin bears the inscription:- "Mary Jeannette Kelly, died Nov. 9, 1888, aged 25 years."

Source: *London Evening Standard*

THURSDAY 15 NOVEMBER 1888

THE EAST-END CRIMES
A STRANGE STORY

THE RIPPER REPORTS

Mr. Matthew Packer, of Berner-street, the fruiterer who sold some grapes to a man who, just before the Berner-street murder was in company with the murdered woman, vouches for the following extraordinary statement. He says:- On Tuesday evening two men came to my home and bought 12s. worth of rabbits off me.

They then asked me if I could give an exact description of the man to whom I sold the grapes, and who was supposed to have committed the Berner-street and Mitre-square murders as they were convinced they knew him, and where to find him. In reply to some questions by Packer, one of the men then said, "Well, I am sorry to say that I firmly believe it is my own cousin. He is an Englishman by birth, but some time ago he went to America, stayed there a few years and then came back to London about seven or eight months ago.

On his return he came to see me, and his first words were, "Well, boss, how are you?" He asked me to have some walks out with him, and I did round Commercial-street and Whitechapel. I found that he had very much altered on his return, for he was thoroughly harum-scarum. We met a lot of Whitechapel women, and when we passed them he used to say to me, "How do you think we used to serve them where I come from? Why, we used to cut their throats and rip them up. I could rip one of them and get her inside out in no time." He said, "We Jack Rippers killed lots of women over there. You will hear of some of it being done over here soon, for I am going to turn a London Jack Ripper."

The man then said I did not take much notice then of what he said, as he had had a drop of drink, and I thought it was only his swagger and bounce of what he had been doing in America, at some place which Packer says he mentioned, but he forgets the name. But, continued the man, "When I heard of the first woman being murdered and stabbed all over, I then began to be very uneasy, and to wonder whether he really was carrying out his threats. I did not, however, like to say anything about him, as he is my own cousin. Then, as one murder followed another, I felt that I could scarcely rest. He is a perfect monster towards women, especially when he has had a drop of drink. But, in addition to what he said to me about those murders in America, and what was going to be done here, I feel certain it is him, because of the way these Jack Ripper letters which have appeared in the papers begin.

They all begin "Dear Boss," and that is just the way he begins his letters. He calls everybody "Boss" when he speaks to them. I did not want to say anything about him if I could help it, so I wrote to him, but he did not answer my letter. Since this last murder I have felt that I could not remain silent any longer, for at least something ought to be done to place him under restraint. - Packer states he feels sure the men are speaking the truth, as they seemed very much concerned, and hardly knew what to do in the matter.

He says he knows where to find the men, one works at some ironworks and the other at the West India Docks, and the man they allude to lives somewhere in the neighbourhood of Whitechapel. The reporter to whom the above statement was made at once sent off a copy of it to the Home Secretary, and also Sir J. Fraser, the Chief Commissioner of the City Police. Sir J. Fraser immediately acted on the information, and sent Detective-sergeants White and Mitchell to investigate it. They read the letter to Packer, who said it was true, and then took the detective to the man's house. On being questioned by the police he stated where his own cousin was generally to be found.

On inquiry this afternoon our reporter was informed that nothing has, as yet, resulted from the above statement, to which, as a matter of fact, neither the City nor the Metropolitan Police attach much importance. Considerable excitement is still evident in Whitechapel, and this afternoon, in spite of the drizzling rain, numbers of persons loitered outside the court in Dorset-street, which is still guarded by two constables.

"JACK THE RIPPER'S" CORRESPONDENCE

This morning two tradesmen in the neighbourhood of the last murder each received a post-card bearing the Islington post mark, and signed "Jack the Ripper." They were written in red ink, and bore only the word "Beware." The agitation in regard to the alleged insufficient police protection is taking a definite form, and it is expected that within a few days the Home Secretary will be waited upon by a deputation representing the district.

AN EXCITING ARREST IN THE OLD KENT-ROAD

At the East-end police-stations this morning a reporter was informed that the night had been an usually quiet one. At Leman-street Station no one was in custody charged with complicity in the recent murders, some men who were arrested last night being discharged as soon as their identity was established. At Commercial-street two men were in custody, but it was stated that neither bore the least resemblance to the man upon whom the attentions of the police are now centred.

In one case the man's presence at the station was attributable to drink, while the other man was arrested for acting in a suspicious manner. Considerable excitement was caused in the Old Kent-road last night, it being freely reported that "Jack the Ripper" had been captured in the neighbourhood. The details which were spread about were of a highly sensational character, and it was said that not only had the murderer been taken, but that the knives with which he had been in the habit of carrying out his fiendish operations had also fallen into the hands of the police.

Inquiries showed that yesterday afternoon a man called at the Thomas A'Beckett public-house, in the Old Kent-road, and partook of refreshments. He was carrying a long, black shiny bag, and on leaving he asked the barmaid to look after it for him, and he would call for it later on. During the man's absence the barmaid's suspicions were aroused by the black bag, and she opened it, when to her astonishment she found it contained a dagger, a pair of scissors of very large pattern, a four-bladed pocket-knife, and a life preserver broken in two. She at once communicated the discovery to the proprietor of the establishment, Bassett, and he lost no time in letting the authorities at Rodney-road Police-station know of it.

A couple of detectives were despatched to the house, and being informed of the man's intention to return for the bag they concealed themselves in anticipation of his arrival. About six o'clock last evening the man walked into the public-house very much the worse for drink, and at his request the bag was handed over to him. Accompanied by another man, whom he picked up in the public-house, the supposed murderer made his way down the Old Kent-road in the direction of the Canal Bridge, and while he was in a pawnbroker's shop negotiating for the disposal of his watch, the two detectives, who had followed close behind, apprehended him. He acted in a disorderly manner, and appeared to be very drunk.

At the station he was charged with being drunk and disorderly. He said he was a hairdresser, and that he lived in Penethorne-road, Peckham. From information since obtained by the police it appears that he had been indulging in a drinking bout, and had left his home on

Tuesday. While in the cell he frequently shouted out, "I'm Jack the Ripper."

The prisoner, who gave the name of John Benjamin Perryman was charged at the Lambeth Police-court to-day with being drunk and disorderly. It was stated that he was known as the "Mad Barber of Peckham."

A sister of the prisoner said he had been intoxicated for a long time. She knew he had a dagger, but for what purpose he kept it she was not aware.

Mr. Partridge remanded the prisoner, remarking that if he was not right in his mind it would perhaps be necessary to send him to an asylum.

The authorities at the Midland Railway goods station in Lower Whitecross-street yesterday found on their premises a sleeveless smock, which evidently had been thrown by some persons from the footway to the spot where it was discovered. On its being examined it was found to be smeared with blood-stains, and being thought that it might have belonged to the Whitechapel murderer it was handed over to the City police. The police at Notting-hill last night received by post a letter purporting to have come from "Jack the Ripper," in which he stated his intention to commit another murder at Whitechapel in a day or two.

A suspicious looking character was seen near the railway station at Dover, and, as he answered the description given of the Whitechapel murderer he was taken into custody. He made a statement to the police, and two constables were sent in charge of the man to verify it. It proved accurate and he was released. The railways and Channel steamers are being watched by the police.

THE RIPPER REPORTS

SIR C. WARREN AND HIS SUBORDINATE OFFICERS

It having been represented to Sir. C. Warren that the officers of the Metropolitan Police, so recently acting under him, wanting an opportunity of expressing personally their deep regret at his leaving them, and their high esteem of him as a chief, and opportunity was given this afternoon at his residence, 44, St George's-road, S.W. Out of the 24 superintendents of the divisions in the Metropolis no less than 21 attended, viz., Superintendents Cutbush, Giles, Jones, Arnold, Brannan, Neylan, McHugo, Harris, Hunt, Saines, Lucas, Beard, Hurst, and Skeats. Two superintendents, Keating and Sherlock are out of town on leave, and Superintendent Shore, indisposed, wrote expressing his regret at inability to attend.

Sir C. Warren, on receiving them said that he too was anxious to meet his officers, as he was most anxious to express to his officers, and through them the men, his keen appreciation of the loyal manner in which he had been supported during his tenure in office. They had supported him in a thorough manner, and the successful result arrived at could not have been attained otherwise. Sir Charles then referred to the cause of his resignation, and briefly but generally attributed it to the interference of Home Office subordinates with what he considers the routine work of his department.

The absolute veto or control of the Home Secretary he had never disputed. Continuing, he referred to his two years' hard work from morn till night in putting the organisation on its proper footing. After such exertions he had hoped that now the internal administration had been perfected he could have devoted more time to divisional inspection. These benefits, however, he trusted, would be transmitted to his successor. He could fearlessly say that he had worked for the benefit and better protection and government of the metropolis, and the benefit of the force as a body, and, whatever the public may say, the police have been trying to do their duty, though some person, for political purposes, had been trying to find fault with them.

In conclusion, Sir C. Warren said he had made many friendships which he valued, but he had never tried to make himself popular. He had worked himself, and had expected others under him to do so. With regard to the police generally he had never come across a body of men who had better or more zealously and indefatigably done their duty and he tanked officers and men most heartily and sincerely.

Superintendent Draper, as the oldest member of the force, and who had been deputed to speak on behalf of his brother officers, in a few well-chosen words, said they could not fail to sensitively feel the resignation of their esteemed chief. From the first they had felt confidence in him as a leader, and he had reciprocated that confidence. They felt, too, that in all he had done he had had their interests at heart, and to render the service efficient. Whatever his (Sir C. Warren's) future career may be they should watch it with interest, and in his retirement he carried with him the respect and admiration of every man in the force. - Superintendent Fisher endorsed the opinions of the previous speaker, and the interview ended.

Source: *The Globe*

THURSDAY 15 NOVEMBER 1888

THE RIPPER REPORTS

ANOTHER WHITECHAPEL MURDER TERRIBLE MUTILATION OF A WOMAN IN SPITALFIELDS

On Friday forenoon the inhabitants of the East End of London were thrown into a state of consternation by the discover in their midst of another revolting crime, far worse in its barbarity than any of the previous five murders which have shocked London during the past five months. The victim is again a woman of the impure class, and the murderer committed the crime under her own roof in broad daylight and easily escaped. Dorset-street, Spitalfield, is filled with lodging houses, tenanted chiefly by the lowest classes, amongst them some of the most degraded thieves and immoral women.

It was here that Annie Chapman, who was murdered in Hanbury-street on the 8th of September, lived, and by a strange coincidence the scene of the present crime is a court directly opposite the house to which that unfortunate woman was in the habit of resorting. Close by is Mitre Square, the scene of one of the murders of September 30, and Hanbury-street is scarcely a stone's throw away. The victim of the crime of Friday is a young woman named Mary Jane Kelly, aged 26. She lived in Miller Court, Dorset-street, a turning out of Commercial-street, Spitalfields. There are eight or ten small houses in the court, which is entered by a low archway and a narrow passage from Dorset- street, and forms a cul-de-sac.

There is a small general shop in Dorset-street adjoining the entrance to the court, tenanted by Mrs. M'Carthy, who also owns the houses in the court. Kelly appears to have tenanted a room in one of Mrs. M'Carthy's houses. She had a little boy aged about six or seven years living with her, and latterly she had been in narrow straits, so that she is reported to have stated to a companion that she would make away with herself as she could not bear to see her boy starving. There are conflicting statements as to when the woman was last seen alive, but that upon which most reliance appears to be placed is that of a young woman, an associate of the deceased, who states that about half-past ten o'clock on Thursday night she met the murdered woman at the corner of Dorset-street.

Kelly told her that she had no money and if she could not get any she would never go out again, but would do away with herself. Soon after they parted, a man who is described as respectably dressed came up, and spoke to Kelly and offered her some money. The man then accompanied the woman home to her lodgings. A tailor named Lewis says he saw Kelly come out about eight o'clock on Friday morning, and go back. Another statement is to the effect that Kelly was in a public-house know as "Ringers," at the corner of Dorset-street and Commercial-street, about ten o'clock, and that she there met a man with whom she had been living. It seems clear that the woman was alive at eight o'clock on Friday morning, that she went out for something, and returned to the house.

The murder must have been committed between that hour and a quarter to eleven o'clock. At the latter hour Mrs. M'Carthy, with her son, went to pay her customary visit for the rent. Young M'Carthy sent a man named Bowyer to the house, which, though entered from the court, is really a part of No. 26, Dorset-street. Bowyer failed to obtain an answer to his knocking, and looking through the window he saw to his horror the woman lying on the bed horribly mutilated and naked. He called M'Carthy, who also looked through the window, and seeing that the body was cut up almost beyond recognition, he ran away with Bowyer, and ran to Commercial-street Police Station, where they informed the police.

THE RIPPER REPORTS

Inspector Beck and Sergeant Betham proceeded to the house. The news had spread so rapidly that over one thousand persons were gathered in the street. These were rapidly cleared away from the court and the side of Dorset-street, while the inspector entered the house. The dwelling in which the murder was committed is entered by two doors situated on the right hand side of a passage, and has several rooms. The first door up to the court from the street leads to the upper rooms; but the second door opens only into one room, which is situated on the ground floor. It was in this room that the murder was committed. The fireplace faces the door, and the bed stands behind the door.

A terrible sight presented itself to the police officers. "The body of the woman, in a state of nudity, was stretched out on the little bedstead, the clothing of which was saturated with blood. The unfortunate woman had been cut and mangled by the assassin's knife in a manner which was revolting beyond all description. The fiend was not content with taking the life of his victim by severing the head from the body, but he had subjected her remains to the most frightful barbarities.

The murder has aroused the greatest excitement in London, not only among the populace but in the ranks of the police. Several persons have been arrested and released, and there is apparently little prospect of the discovery of the murderer. A proclamation has been issued by the authorities offering a pardon to any accomplice who will give information that will lead to the conviction of the miscreant who has committed the crime. An extraordinary scene was witnessed at ten o'clock on Sunday night in Commercial street, not far from the scene of the murder.

A man with a blackened face, who styled himself "Jack the Ripper," was arrested. There was a cry of "Lynch him" and the man was beaten with sticks. He would have been seriously injured had not the police protected him. He refused to give his name but asserted that he was a medical man.

LIST OF THE EAST END MURDERS

Seven women have now been murdered in the East-end under mysterious circumstances, five of them within a period of eight weeks. The following are the dates of the crimes and the names of the victims as far as known:-

1. Last Christmas week. - An unknown woman found murdered near Osborne and Wentworth-streets, Whitechapel

2. August 7. - Martha Turner found stabbed in 39 places, on a landing in modal dwellings, known as George-yard Buildings, Commercial-street, Spitalfields.

3. August 31. - Mrs. Nicholls, murdered and mutilated in Bucks-row, Whitechapel.

4. September 7. - Mrs. Chapman, murdered and mutilated in Hanbury-street, Whitechapel.

5. September 30. - Elizabeth Stride, found with her throat cut in Berners-street, Whitechapel.

6. September 30. - Woman unknown murdered and mutilated in Mitre-square, Aldgate.

7. November 9. - Mary Jane Kelly, murdered and mutilated in a house in Miller-court, Dorset-street, Commercial-street, Spitalfields.

The inquest on the body of the woman Kelly, who was murdered in Whitechapel on Friday, was held on Monday. The evidence threw no additional light whatever on the crime, and the formal verdict of "wilful murder against some person unknown" was recorded. At a late hour on Monday night no person was under arrest in connection with the crime.

Source: *Souldby's Ulverston Advertiser and General Intelligencer*

SATURDAY 17 NOVEMBER 1888

RESIGNATION OF SIR CHARLES WARREN

In the House of Commons, on Monday afternoon, Mr Matthews announced that Sir Charles Warren resigned on Thursday last, and the resignation has been accepted.

In the House of Commons on Tuesday, Mr. Matthews stated that Sir Charles Warren had resigned because he would not submit to the instructions of the Home Secretary regarding articles relating to the department. The resignation had nothing whatever to do with the Whitechapel murders.

WHY BLOODHOUNDS WERE NOT USED

The explanation given of why the bloodhounds were not used is that they would be of no use whatever in the locality in which the murder took place. Had it occurred in an open, unfrequented part, the dogs might have had some chance of success.

There was very widespread disappointment that bloodhounds had not been at once employed in the effort to track the criminal. The belief had prevailed throughout the district that the dogs were ready to be let loose at the first notice of a murder having been committed, and the public had come to possess greater confidence in their wonderful canine instincts and sagacity than in all Sir Charles Warren's machinery of detection. They even attributed the fact that more than a month had passed since the last revolting outrage to the fear which it was thought had been inspired by the intimation that these detectives of nature would be employed. They were not absolutely forgotten, but apparently were not at hand, and the conclusion was come to that the trail must inevitably have been destroyed long before they could have come upon the scene by the constant stream of persons to and from the narrow street. The validity of this objection has been called in question by experts, and it would certainly have given satisfaction to the public mind if an experiment had been made. A better opportunity than the present instance afforded could hardly have occurred.

PREVIOUS UNDISCOVERED CRIMES IN WHITECHAPEL

April 3 - Emma Elizabeth Smith, forty-five, had a stake or iron instrument thrust through her body, near Osborn-street Whitechapel,

Aug 7 - Martha Tabram, thirty-five, stabbed in thirty-nine places, at George-yard-buildings, Commercial-street, Spitalfields.

Aug 31 - Mary Ann Nichols, forty-seven, her throat cut and body mutilated, in Hanbury-street, Spitalfields.

Sept 30. - A woman, supposed to be Elizabeth Stride, but not yet identified, discovered with her throat cut, in Berner-street, Whitechapel.

Sept 30 - A woman, unknown, found with her throat cut and body mutilated, in Mitre-square, Aldgate.

Nov 9. - Mary Jane Kelly (24), her throat cut and body terribly mutilated, in Miller's-court, Dorset-street.

Source: *Worcestershire Chronicle*

TUESDAY 20 NOVEMBER 1888

THE WHITECHAPEL MURDERS FUNERAL OF MARIE KELLY

The funeral of Marie Jeanette Kelly, the victim of the latest Whitechapel murder, took place yesterday at Leytonstone Cemetery in the presence of a large number of people. An hour before the Redmaine's left the mortuary many hundreds of persons assembled around Shoreditch Church, and watched in silence the funeral arrangements. The coffin, which was of elm and oak, with metal fittings, was placed on an open hearse drawn by two horses, and was followed by two mourning carriages, containing the man Joseph Barnett who lived with the deceased, and several of the unfortunate woman's associates who gave evidence at the inquest. The coffin bore the following inscription:- "Marie Jeanette Kelly, died November 9, 1888, aged 25 years" and on it were placed two crowns and a cross, made of heartsease and white flowers. The whole of the funeral expenses are defrayed by Mr. Wilton, who for 50 years has acted as sexton to St. Leonards's, Shoreditch, in the mortuary of which the body has been lying.

At half-past twelve, as the coffin was borne from the mortuary, the bell of the church was tolled, and the people outside, who now numbered several thousands, manifested the utmost sympathy, the crowd, for an East-end one, being extremely orderly. Vehicles of various descriptions took up positions outside the church railings, and traffic was completely blocked until the hearse moved off.

The funeral procession, which left Shoreditch Church at a quarter to one, made but slow progress through the crowds of people and vehicles. All along the route through Whitechapel and Cambridge Heath signs of sympathy were to be seen on every hand, and it was a very touching sight to witness many poor women of the class to which the deceased belonged greatly affected. The cortège reached St. Patrick's Roman Catholic Cemetery, Leyton, a few minutes before two o'clock. It was met by the Rev. Father Colombian, O.S.F., who led the way, preceded by two acolytes and a cross-bearer, to the north-east corner of the burial ground, where the internment took place. There was only a small attendance in the Cemetery.

MORE WRITING ON THE WALL

The Press Association is informed by Arthur Bachert, the young man who gave the police a description of a man seen in the neighbourhood of Berber-street at the time of the murder of Elizabeth Stride, that he was awakened at his home in Newnham-street yesterday by a policeman, who called his attention to some chalk-writing on the blank wall of the house, as follows:

"Dear Boss,

I am still about; look out.

Yours, Jack the Ripper."

It is stated by Bachert that the writing resembles that on the now famous postcard and letter published by the police, especially the B in "Boss" and the R in "Ripper." A crowd collected, and Mrs. Bachert partly removed the cause of their attraction by washing out the letters. Otherwise the police would have photographed the writing.

THE RIPPER REPORTS

SCARE AT WEST BROMWICH

A correspondent telegraphs that much excitement has been caused in West Bromwich by the visit of a man resembling much in appearance the published description of the Whitechapel murderer. About dusk on Sunday evening he went to a house in Tentany-lane, and asked the woman who answered his knock whether there were any houses of ill-fame in the neighbourhood, saying he had come down from London specially to destroy the frequenters of such dwellings. He added that he was determined they should no longer cumber the earth. On being told that there were no such houses anywhere near the man walked quickly away. The woman had not sufficient presence of mind to raise an alarm, and the man got away without molestation. The police have been communicated with, but no arrest has been made. The man is described as of medium height, about 35 years of age, with dark moustache, and of gentlemanly address.

Source: *The Globe*

WEDNESDAY 21 NOVEMBER 1888

THE SAME TUMBLETY
HIS ARREST IN LONDON NOT HIS FIRST EXPERIENCE IN THAT LINE.

THE RIPPER REPORTS

The New York Times says - The Dr. Tumblety who was arrested in London a few days ago on suspicion of complicity in the Whitechapel murders, and who when proved innocent of that charge was held for trial in the Central Criminal Court under the special law covering the offences disclosed in the late "Modern Babylon" scandal, will be remembered by any number of Brooklynites and New Yorkers as Dr. Blackburn, the Indian herb doctor. He is the fellow who in 1861 burst upon the people of Brooklyn as a sort of modern Count of Monte Cristo. He was of striking personal appearance, being considerably over six feet in height, of graceful and powerful build, with strongly marked features, beautifully clear complexion, a sweeping moustache and jet black hair.

He went dashing about the streets mounted on a handsome light chestnut horse, and dressed in the costliest and most elaborate riding costumes, and soon had a stream of customers at his office and laboratory on Fulton street, near the city hall. In these rides he was invariably accompanied by a valet as handsomely apparelled and horsed as himself, and a brace of superb English greyhounds. He boarded with a Mrs. Foster, at 93 Fulton street, then a fashionable quarter of the city, and cut a wide swath in the affections of the feminine lodgers.

After a few months he dropped out of sight as suddenly as he had appeared, and was next heard of as being implicated in the famous "fellow fever importation" and "black bag" plots that the rebel sympathisers tried to develop in New York during the civil war. It was at this time that his relation to the celebrated Blackburn family of Kentucky became known, and he thereafter went by his real name instead of his curious assumed name, Tumblety. His interest in the two previously-mentioned plots was, luckily for him, so slight that he was allowed to go unpunished, while several of his associates did not get off so easily. For several years after this he kept pretty well out of the public gaze, and then suddenly took up his herb-doctoring business with its attendant swagger again. He visited both this city and Brooklyn at about semi-yearly intervals, and became a member of several questionable clubs. He dropped out of sight some ten years ago, and the first that has been heard of him since is the new of his arrest and imprisonment in London.

Source: *Toronto Daily Mail*

SATURDAY 24 NOVEMBER 1888

FRESH EAST-END OUTRAGE

An outrage - at first magnified into a murder - was committed last Wednesday morning in Whitechapel. About four o'clock in the morning, a man, and a woman named Farmer, of the unfortunate class, engaged a bed at a common lodging-house in George-street, Spitalfields. The man suddenly made an attempt to cut his companion's throat. The woman, however, struggled with all her might, and screamed loudly for assistance. Her throat was only slightly wounded, so that she was able to exert all her strength in coping with her assailant.

He hastily fled from the house. Meanwhile the screaming had attracted a few persons to the locality. These gave chase to the fugitive, but only for a short distance, as the man disappeared somewhere, it is said, in the direction of Heneage-street. The woman was placed on an ambulance by the police and conveyed to Commercial-street station. The wound having been dressed, she gave detailed description of her assailant as follows:- Age about thirty, height 5ft. 5in., with a fair moustache, wearing a black diagonal coat and a hard felt hat. The woman who has so fortunately escaped is between forty and fifty years of age. Perhaps the most important point for the purposes of identification was that the man had an abscess under his jaw. The woman declares that the same man accosted her twelve months ago.

Source: *Penny Illustrated Paper*

SATURDAY 3 NOVEMBER 1888

A statement to which the police attach considerable importance has just been made by Matthew Packer, the keeper of the fruit shop next to the gateway where the Berner-street murder was committed. He reports that during the past few nights he has been greatly alarmed by having seen the man who bought the grapes from him for the unfortunate woman Elizabeth Stride a short time before the murder was committed. He alleges that he had often seen the man before the murder, as well as the woman who was murdered in Berner-street, but he had not since the night of the murder seen anyone resembling the man till he saw him again last Saturday night.

He (Packer) was then standing with his fruit-stall in the Commercial-road, when he caught sight of him staring him full in the face. He kept calm and collected for a little time, hoping that a policeman would come by; but in this he was disappointed. After passing and re-passing him several times the man came behind him in the Horse-road, and looked at him in a very evil and menacing manner. He was so terrified that he left his stall and ran to a shoeblack, who was near, and, pointing to the man, asked him to keep his eye on him and watch him. His great fear was that the man was going to stab him to prevent him from identifying him as the man who was in the company of the murdered woman immediately before her death.

No sooner, however, had he called the shoeblack's attention to him than the man ran away as fast as he could, and succeeded in getting on a passing tram. Packer would have followed the tram had he been able to run, or if he could have left his stall; but he could not, as there were several pounds worth of fruit on it. It may be added that during the past few days there have again been several complaints from women in the East-end of having been accosted after dark but a respectably-dressed man who answered to the description of the supposed murderer. One woman who was so accosted blew a whistle, and in a very short time about 20 policemen were on the scene, and the man was taken to Leman-street Police-station, but he was liberated on Saturday morning, as he succeeded in giving a satisfactory account of himself. The police force throughout the district is still augmented every night.

DR. FORBES WINSLOW'S OPINION

Dr. Forbes Winslow and other leading authorities on mental disorders are reported to be still of opinion that the murders in Whitechapel were committed by a homicidal lunatic, and Dr. Forbes Winslow believes that the murderer has been lately in a "lucid interval," in which conditions he would be comparatively rational and forgetful of what he had done. As soon as this passes off he will resume his terrible work.

ANOTHER THREATENING LETTER

By the last post on Tuesday night a letter, purporting to come from the East-end assassin, was received at the Poplar Police-station, in which the writer said he was going to commit three more murders. The following is said to be the wording:- "October 30th, 1888. - Dear Boss, - I am going to commit three more murders, two women and a child, and I shall take their hearts this time. - Yours truly (signed) JACK THE RIPPER." The letter was enclosed in an envelope which, in addition to the Poplar postmark, also bore the Ealing postmark, and was directed to the sergeant. A copy was sent to the Commissioner of Police. The information, with instructions, were at once telegraphed to the different stations, ordering every possible vigilance to be used in case of an attempted repetition of the crimes.

Source: *Weston Mercury*

WEDNESDAY 26 DECEMBER 1888

IS THIS THE WHITECHAPEL MURDERER? AN EXTRAORDINARY PERSONAGE

A man calling himself Dr Tumblety was arrested some time ago in London on suspicion of being concerned in the perpetration of the Whitechapel murders. The police, being unable to procure the necessary evidence against him in connection therewith, decided to hold him for trial for another offence against a statute which was passed shortly after the publication in the Pall Mall Gazette of "The Maiden Tribute," and as a direct consequence thereof Dr Tumblety was committed for trial and liberated on bail, two gentlemen coming forward to act as bondsmen in the amount of £300. The last seen of him was at Havre, and it is taken for granted that he as sailed for New York. The man is declared by U.S. papers to be well known for his eccentricities.

William P. Burr, of No 320 Broadway, speaking of the man, said:- "The English authorities, who are now telegraphing for samples of his writing from San Francisco, ought to get them in any city of Europe. I had a bit batch of letters sent by him to the young man Lyon, and they were the most amusing farago of illiterate nonsense. Here is one written from the West. He never failed to warn his correspondent against lewd women, and in doing it used the most shocking language. I did not know how he made his money. My own idea of the Whitechapel case is that it would be just such a thing as Tumblety would be concerned with; but he might get one of his victims to do the work, for once he had a young man under his control he seemed to be able to do anything with the victim."

Col. C.A. Dunham, a well known lawyer, who lives near Fairview, N.J., was intimately acquainted with Tumblety for many years, and in his own mind had long connected him with the Whitechapel horrors. "The man's real name," said the lawyer, "is Tumblety, with Francis for a Christian name. I have here a book published by him a number of years ago, describing some of his strange adventures and wonderful cures - all lies, of course - in which the name of 'Francis Tumblety, M.D.,' appears. When, to my knowledge of the man's history, his idiosyncrasies, his revolting practices, his antipathy to women (and especially to fallen women), his anatomical museum, containing many specimens like those carved from the Whitechapel victims - when, to my knowledge on these subjects, there is added the fact of his arrest on suspicion of being the murderer, there appears to me nothing improbable in the suggestion that Tumblety is the culprit. He is not a doctor. A more arrant charlatan and quack never fattened on the hopes and fears of afflicted humanity. I first made the fellow's acquaintance a few days after the first battle of Bull Run. The fellow was everywhere. I never saw anything so nearly approaching ubiquity. Go where you would, to any of the hotels, to the War Department, or the Navy Yard, you were sure to find the 'doctor.' He had no business in either place, but the went there to impress the officers whom he would meet. He professed to have had an extensive experience in European hospitals and armies, and claimed to have diplomas from the foremost medical colleges of the Old World and the New. At length it was whispered about that he was an adventurer.

"One day my Lieutenant Colonel and myself accepted the 'doctor's' invitation to a late dinner - symposium, he called it - at his rooms. He had very costly and tastefully furnished quarters in, I believe, H. Street. Some one asked why he had not invited some women to his dinner. His face instantly became as black as a thunder cloud. He had a pack of cards in his hand, but he laid them down and said, almost savagely - No, Colonel, I don't know any such cattle, and if I did I would, as your friend, sooner give you a dose of quick poison than take you into such danger. He then broke into a homily on the sin and folly of dissipation, fiercely denounced all women, and especially fallen women. Then he invited us into his office, were he illustrated his lecture, so to speak. One side of this room was entirely occupied with cases, outwardly resembling wardrobes.

"When the doors were opened quite a museum was revealed - tiers of shelves with glass jars and cases, some round and others square, filled with all sorts of anatomical specimens. The 'doctor' placed on the table a dozen or more jars containing, as he said, the matrices of every class of women. Nearly a half of one of these cases was occupied exclusively with these specimens. Not long after this the 'doctor' was in my room when my Lieutenant Colonel came in and commenced expatiating on the charms of a certain woman. In a moment almost the 'doctor' was lecturing him and denouncing women. When he asked why he hated women, he said that when quite a young man he fell desperately in love with a pretty girl, rather his senior, who promised to reciprocate his affection. After a brief courtship he married her. The honeymoon was not over when he noticed a disposition on the part of his wife to flirt with other men. He remonstrated, she kissed him, called him a dear jealous fool - and he believed her.

"Happening one day to pass in a cab through the worst part of town, he saw his wife and a man enter a gloomy-looking house. Then he learned that before her marriage his wife had been an inmate of that and many similar houses. Then he gave up all womankind. Shortly after telling this story the 'doctor's' real character became known, and he slipped away to St Louis, where he was arrested for wearing the uniform of an army surgeon.

"Tumblety would do almost anything under heaven for notoriety, and, although his notoriety in Washington was of a kind to turn people from him, it brought some to him."

Source: *Dundee Courier*

SATURDAY 29 DECEMBER 1888

HORRIBLE CRIME AT BRADFORD
A BOY MURDERED AND MUTILATED

A murder, similar in its most prominent and ghastly details to the recent series of crimes in Whitechapel, was discovered this morning at Bradford. The victim is a boy nine years of age, named John Gill, the son of a cabman, who lives in a thoroughfare known as Thorncliffe-road. The boy was last seen by his parents on Thursday night, when he was in the street playing with a number of his companions. Later he was seen talking with a milkman, but there was then nothing calculated to excite any suspicion. As the boy did not return home at night inquiries were made yesterday respecting him, but nothing of a satisfactory nature could be obtained by his friends.

At daybreak this morning the body of the poor lad, cut and mutilated in the most horrible manner, and in an entirely nude state, was found in an outhouse at the back of premises in Thorncliffe-road. The legs had been cut off near to the trunk, and were lying by the side of the body. Both ears had been sliced off, and the abdomen ripped open, and some of the internal organs, notably the heart, had been torn from the body, and placed near it upon the ground. There were also stabs in the chest, and other forms of mutilation too sickening to be described.

The boots had been taken off, and thrust ruthlessly into the body of the victim, and the whole appearances constituted a sickening spectacle. When the discovery was made the police were communicated with, and a large number of detectives were quickly on the spot, investigating the facts so far as they could be ascertained. They refused to supply any information to the Press, except to indicate a belief that they were in possession of a clue which was believed to be important. An examination of the building in which the body was found, showed that there was little or no blood near the corpse. This led to the assumption that the murder has been committed elsewhere, and the body conveyed to the outhouse either late last night or early this morning. The remains were wrapped in a coarse covering and might have been carried through the streets in this way. It is also said that the dismembered limbs were tied to the body by a piece of cord.

Owing, however, to the reticence of the police, it is extremely difficult to obtain reliable information. The affair has created tremendous excitement throughout the town and district. The police are said to have a man in custody on suspicion of being concerned in the perpetration of the crime.

ANOTHER REPORTED MURDER

The Press Association says:- A report from Keighley this morning states that a youth has been found murdered and mutilated at Kilwich, a village a few miles to the north-west of that place. Details will follow.

Source: *The Globe*

MONDAY 31 DECEMBER 1888

THE WHITECHAPEL MURDERER SEARCH IN AMERICA

THE RIPPER REPORTS

Inspector Andrews, of Scotland-yard (the Daily Telegraph's correspondent says) has arrived in New York, from Montreal. It is generally believed that he has received orders from England to commence his search in this city for the Whitechapel murderer. Mr. Andrews is reported to have said that there are half a dozen English detectives, two clerks, and one inspector employed in American in the same chase.

Ten days ago Andrews brought hither from England Roland Gideon Israel Barnet, charged with helping to wreck the Central Bank, Toronto; and since his arrival he has received orders which will keep him in American for some time.

The supposed inaction of the Whitechapel murderer for a considerable period, and the fact that a man suspected of knowing a good deal about this series of crimes left England for this side of the Atlantic three weeks ago, has produced the impression that Jack the Ripper is in America. Irish Nationalists pretend that the inspector is hunting up certain evidence to be given before the Parnell Commission.

Source: *St James's Gazette*

INDEX OF NAMES

Aarons, Mr 133

Abberline, Detective-inspector 75, 194, 259, 293, 294, 298

Abrahams, Mr 162

Adams, Sargeant 198

Alaska 208

Anderson, Dr 168

Anderson, Mr 253

Andrews, Inspector 329

Arnold, Superintendent 45, 258, 291, 293, 298, 308,

Bachert, Mr Albert 45, 317

Bachert, Mrs 317

Bailey, Mr 77, 87, 92, 93

Banks, Mr 6, 42

Barham, Mr 163

Barnett, Jack (see Mr Joseph Barnett)

Barnett, Mr Joseph (Joe) 267, 281, 288, 292, 293, 295, 298, 316,

Barrett, Constable T 3, 5, 9, 11, 13

Barrow, Mr Edward 118, 133

Bassett, Mr 306

Baxter, Mr Wynne E 1, 27, 38, 50, 92, 95, 96, 114, 124, 148, 155, 171, 177, 208, 230, 241, 277, 294, 297,

Bagster-Philips, Dr George (see Dr George Baxter-Philips)

Barnet, Mr Roland Gideon Israel 289

Baxter-Philips, Dr George (see Dr George Bagster-Philips) 75, 291,

Beard, Superintendent 308

Beatmoor, Jane 99, 175

Beck, Inspector Walter 285, 291, 292, 298, 312

Beech, Inspector 293
Benals, Mr Alderman 245
Bennett, Sir James Ridson 142
Berry, Superintendent 88
Betham, Sergeant 312
Bishop of Bedford, 144
Bishop of Liverpool, 188
Blackburn, Dr 319
Blackwall, Dr 210
Blackwell, Dr 128, 130
Blanchard, Mr Alfred Napier 195, 217,
Bond, Dr 239
Bousfield, Mrs Mary 15, 21,
Bowyer, Mr Harry 269,
Bowyer, Mr Thomas 284, 285, 295, 311,
Brannan, Superintendent 308,
Brough, Mr 280
Brown, Dr Gordon 104, 114, 115, 130, 163, 182, 183, 201, 228, 229, 230,
Brown, Mr James 211, 273
Bryan, Mary 15
Bull, Mr William 173, 174, 207
Burke, Mr 147
Burrell, Emily 116
Cadosh, Mr Albert 76
Cansby, Inspector 86
Caramelli, Mr 163
Catmur, Mr 161, 163
Caunter, Detective Sergeant 16, 17, 18
Cavendish, Lord L 147
Chandler, Inspector 65, 67, 75, 86,

Chappell, Mrs Mary 62
Chapman, Annie 57, 60, 62, 70, 75, 77, 79, 81, 83, 92, 94, 97, 98, 102, 130, 135, 143, 175, 177, 187, 191, 209, 230, 310, 313
Collard, Inspector Edward 104, 114, 182, 183, 228
Collier, Mr George 6, 10, 11, 12, 21, 42,
Colombian, Rev Father 317
Colwell, Mrs 32
Compton, Mr George 273
Connelly, Mary Ann 14, 16, 17, 18, 20, 22,
Conway, Kate 172
Conway, Mr Thomas 179, 180, 194, 200,
Conway, Catherine (see Catherine Eddowes)
Cooksley, Mr Charles 47
Cooksley, Eliza 54
Cowan, Mr Alderman 187
Cox, Mary Ann 286, 296
Crawford, Mr S.F. 179, 180, 181, 182, 184, 185, 199, 200, 201, 202, 229, 232
Cross, Mr Charles 43, 51
Crow, Mr Alfred George 8, 12
Cutbush, Superintendent 308
Dark Annie (see Annie Chapman)
Davies, Mr (see Davis)
Davis, Mr 58, 59, 282
Davis, Mr John 54, 55, 73, 74, 75, 77, 78, 92
Davis, Mrs 55
Diemschitz, Mr Lewis 149, 158,
Dodge 208
Doncaster, Mr Henry 247
Donnelley, Mr Johnny 220

Donovan, Mr Timothy 79, 80, 92
Draper, Superintendent 309
Dudman, Sergeant 153
Duke, Dr 253
Dunbar, Mr Frederick 246
Duncan, Mr J 165
Dunham, Col. C.A. 324
Dunn, Mr 238
Eagle, Mr Maurice 148, 157
Eddowes, Catherine 177, 179, 199, 208, 223, 224, 227, 230, 237, 272
Eddowes, Kate (see Catherine Eddowes)
Edmunds, Mr 39
Ellesdon, Inspector (see Inspector Ellison)
Ellison, Inspector 4, 5
Evans, Mr John 80, 92
Farmer, Amelia 80, 81, 82, 83
Farmer, Mrs 320
Fiddymont, Mrs 61, 62, 64, 82, 92, 274,
Fisal, Mr 45
Fish, Mr John 99
Fischer, Mrs Elizabeth 224
Fisher, Superintendent 309
Fleishmann, Herr Louis 7
Fleming, Mr Joseph 268, 283
Forbes Winslow, Dr 145, 167, 257, 322
Foster, Frederick William 160, 176, 182, 201,
Foster, Mr John 248,
Foster, Mrs 319
Foster, Superintendent 114, 172, 179, 199,
Fraser, Colonel Sir James 151, 179, 304

Gabe, Dr 260

Gaborian, M 94

Geary, Mr 6

Giles, Superintendent 308

Gill, John 327

Gilleman, Mr 148,

Gladding, Mr Robert 161

Gold, Mrs Eliza 179, 199, 224, 227

Goody, Sarah 241

Goron, Mr 236

Graham, Mr Benjamin 240, 245

Greatorex, Rev. Daniel 162, 206

Greatrex, Rev. Daniel (see Greatorex)

Green, Mrs 29, 30,

Green, Mr F 187

Gustofstoller, Elizabeth (see also Elizabeth Stride)

Halse, Mr Daniel 231

Harderman, Mr 55

Harriman, Mrs 74, 76a

Harris, Mr B 133,

Harris, Superintendent 308

Harrison, Superintendent 175

Harvey, Mrs Maria 268, 269, 292, 298,

Haslip, Mr George 2

Helson, Inspector 35, 37, 40, 43, 46, 50, 51, 94

Henderson, Mr 222

Henson, Detective Inspector 75

Hodden, Jane 52

Holland, Police constable 182

Hunt, Mr Vander 294,

Hunt, Superintedent 232, 308
Hurst, Superintendent 308
Hurtig, Mr 153
Hutchinson, Mr George 299
Isaacs, Mr 109, 149
Izzard, Inspector George 173,174
Jack the Ripper 131, 139, 165, 168, 169, 193, 194, 196, 207, 224, 225, 235, 236, 238, 246, 247, 248, 249, 254, 255, 265, 271, 275, 305, 307, 312, 317, 323, 329
Jarvis, Mr William 247
Jones, Mrs Harriet 224
Jones, Sargeant 183
Jones, Superintendent 308
Kaye, Dr 128
Keating, Superintendent 308
Keleene, Dr Timothy Robert 3, 5, 6, 9, 11, 13,
Keeling, Dr (see Dr Timothy Rober Keleene)
Kelly, Jane 116
Kelly, Kate 179
Kelly, Mary Jane 251, 252, 257, 267, 268, 269, 270, 276, 280, 281, 285, 287, 292, 293, 294, 295, 299, 300, 302, 310, 311, 313, 315, 316
Kelly, Mary Janet (see Mary Jane Kelly)
Kelly, Marie Jeanette (see Mary Jane Kelly)
Kelly, Mr John 170, 171, 172, 179, 181, 182, 184 194, 199, 201, 224, 227,
Kennedy, Mrs 270, 271
Keyler, Mrs 289, 297,
Kidney, Mr Michael 171, 212
Kirby, Sir Alfred 152
Kite, Mr 247
Kozebrodski, Mr 109

Krantz, Mr Philip 213

Langham, Dr 155, 179

Langham, Mr S.F. 199

Lawton, Mr 133

Leather Apron 66, 67, 68, 69, 84, 85, 91, 92, 131, 187

Ledger, Inspector 284

Lecoq, M 94

Leech, Inspector 18

Lewis, Sarah 289, 297,

Lewis, Mr Morris 260

Llewellyn, Dr 34, 50, 97, 98

Long Lizzie (see Elizabeth Stride)

Long, Mr Alfred 231, 232

Lucas, Superintendent 308

Lushington, Mr 187, 241

Lusk, Mr George 138, 237

Lyons, Ms 66

Macdonald, Dr 267, 276, 280, 294

Maguire, Mr Peter 274, 275

M'William, Detective Inspector (see Detective Inspector McWilliam)

Mahoney, Mrs Elizabeth 7, 12

Mahoney, Mr Joseph 7

Malcolm, Mrs Mary 168, 171, 218, 241, 242, 243, 244

Malcom, Mrs (see Malcolm)

Marks, Mr Harry H 141, 152

Marshall, Mr William 210

Mather, Detective 247

Matthews, The Right Hon. Henry, QC 118, 119, 141, 152, 168, 235, 277, 314

Maxwell, Mrs Caroline 288, 296

Maxwell, Mr Henry 288
M'Carthy, Mr (see McCarthy)
McCarthy, Mr John 252, 295, 269, 284, 285, 287, 291, 311
McCarthy, Mrs 254, 257, 279, 310, 311
McHugo, Superintendent 308
McWilliam, Detective inspector 104, 114, 179, 232
McWilliams, Inspector (see Detective Inspector McWilliam)
Mickeld Joe 69
Miles, Sargeant 172
Milligan, Miss 246
Mitchell, DS 304
Mogg (see Mary Ann Connelly)
Monk(s), Mary Anne 37, 52
Montagu, Mr Samuel, MP 152, 153
Morganstone, Mr 268, 283
Morris, Mr 181
Murphy, Mr Thomas 301
Myles, Sargeant 173
Nathan, Mr 84
Neale, Police Constable (see Constable John Neil)
Neil, Constable John 25, 30, 34, 41, 121
Neylan, Superintendent 308
Newall, Mrs 99
Nichols, Mary Ann 29, 42, 46, 47, 49, 54, 57, 67, 69, 72, 73, 74, 75, 76, 94, 96, 97, 98, 101, 135, 190, 216, 313, 315
Nicholson, Mr 162
Nicholls, Mary Ann (see Mary Ann Nichols)
Nicholls, Mr William 39, 49, 51
Norris, Mr George James 104
Ollsen, Mr Sven 210

O'Neill, Mr 121
Openshaw, Dr 237
Osborne, Mr Samuel 301, 302
Outram, Sargeant 116, 172
Owen, Mr Harry 292
Packer, Mr Matthew 303, 304, 321, 322
Parker, Dr 187, 188
Partridge, Mr 307
Pearce, Constable 103, 104
Pearly Poll (see Mary Ann Connelly)
Pemberton, Mr E Leigh 152
Perkins, Mr 30
Perryman, Mr John Benjamin 307
Phillips, Dr B.E (see Dr G.E Phillips)
Phillips, Dr G.E. 60, 97, 104, 109, 128, 130, 144, 175, 184, 202, 208, 253, 275
Phillips, Mr 74, 146, 151, 267, 293
Phillips, Mr Jas. 247
Pigott, Mr William Henry 87, 88, 91, 92
Pinnock, Police constable 75
Piser, Mr John 84, 85
Pound, Mr John 186
Prater, Elizabeth 287, 296
Prater, Mr William 287
Read, Mr 237
Reeves, Mrs Louisa 19
Reeves, Mr 19, 133
Reeves, Mr John Saunders 3, 5, 8, 9, 11, 12
Reid, Detective-Inspector E 4, 5, 6, 8, 10, 16, 18, 22, 161, 213, 242, 245
Richardson, Mr 54, 55

Richardson, Mr John 76
Richardson, Mrs 54, 55, 57, 59, 65, 78
Ripper, Mr John 226
Robinson, Sergeant 247
Roots, Inspector 175
Rusk, Mr 234
Russell, Mary 2
Ryan, Mr Thomas 163, 164, 165
Saines, Superintendent 308
Salisbury, Lord 119, 168
Saunders, Dr Sedgwick 130
Savage, Dr George H. 132
Seguira, Dr. (see Sequeira)
Selso, Mr Louis 130
Sequeira, Dr. 104, 114, 115, 130, 182, 183, 201
Sheridan, Mr Jack 279
Sherlock, Superintendent 271
Shore, Superindendent 308
Sieve, Annie (see Annie Champan)
Sieve, Mr Jack (see Mr Jack Sivvy)
Siffey, Annie (see Annie Chapman)
Simmons, Mr Frederick 60
Sivvy, Mr Jack 60, 70, 79
Sivvy, Annie (see Annie Chapman)
Skeats, Superintendent 308
Smith, Emma Elizabeth 1, 95, 135, 315
Smith, Mr William 153
Smith, Major Henry 104, 114, 172, 173, 179, 232
Smith, PC William 212
Smith, Mrs 213

Stonley, Mr Ted 81
Spratling, Inspector 42, 50
Stokes, Elizabeth (See Elizabeth Watts)
Stokes, Mr Joseph 242
Stone, Mr Alderman 173, 174
Stride, Elizabeth 110, 113, 123, 148, 150, 153, 154, 155, 171, 177, 191, 208, 210, 211, 212, 218, 220, 221, 241, 313, 315, 317, 321
Stride, Police Constable Walter 242
Stride, Mr J.T. 242
Stride, Mr John 245
Stride, Mr Thomas, 210, 218
Stuart-Wortley, Mr 275
Tabram, Ann (see Martha Tabram)
Tabram, Martha 21, 41, 95, 97, 135, 315
Tabran, Martha (see Martha Tabram)
Tabran, Mr Henry Samuel 21
Tanner, Elizabeth 171
Taunton, Mr 280
Taylor, Mr Joseph 62
Telfer, Mr 162
Thane, PC 34
Thompson, Mr Robert 55, 78, 79
Thomspon, Mrs 79
Ticke, Detective Inspector 260
Tomkin, Mr Henry 43, 51
Tomkins (see Mr Henry Tomkin)
Tumblety, Dr Francis 319, 323, 324, 325, 326
Turner, Mr Henry 21
Turner, Mrs Martha (see also Martha Tabram) 6, 12, 15, 16, 18, 21, 101, 190, 313

Van Turney, Julia 292, 298
Venturney, Julia (see Julia Van Turney)
Victoria, Queen 118, 120, 138
Violenia, Mr Emanuel Delbast 86
Waddle, Mr William 175
Walker, Mr Alfred 76
Walker, Mr Edward 38, 46
Warren, Sir Charles 118, 146, 163, 168, 169, 193, 194, 196, 204, 206, 207, 231, 233, 234, 240, 254, 258, 259, 276, 277, 280, 308, 309, 314, 315
Watkin, Police Constable (see Police Constable Watkins)
Watkins, Police Constable 103, 104, 114, 127, 181, 183, 201, 215, 238
Watts, Elizabeth 171, 242
Watts, Mr 218, 241, 242
West, Acting Superintendent 75,
West, Chief Inspector 2, 45,
West, Mr William 148, 155
White, Colonel 153
Wilkinson, Mr Frederick 170, 172, 181, 182, 200, 227, 228
Wilton, Mr H 302, 316
Winslow, Dr Forbes 322
Withers, Mrs 15
Wortley Axe, Professor J. 192

INDEX OF STREET NAMES

Albany Road 38
Albany Street 49
Alderney Road 236, 237
Aldgate 112, 114, 122, 125, 151, 173, 178, 179, 181, 186, 191, 196, 197, 199, 203, 214, 313, 315
Back Church Lane 212
Bakers Row 46, 49, 55
Berber Street 317
Berner Street 104, 105, 108, 110, 111, 112, 114, 117, 119, 122, 127, 130, 134, 136, 148, 153, 155, 157, 158, 162, 168, 170, 171, 182, 191, 208, 210, 211, 212, 215, 216, 227, 241, 255, 258, 269, 303, 313, 315
Bethnal Green 26, 51, 215
Bethnal Green Road 297
Billingsgate Market 268
Bishopsgate Street 62, 80, 110, 172, 180, 274
Blackfriars Bridge 134
Blackman Street 134
Bow Street 239
Boyd Street 210
Brady Street 31, 32, 37, 51
Brick Lane 4, 5, 9, 11, 13, 56, 62, 78, 88, 92
Broadway 324
Brown Lane 57
Brushfield Street 82, 274
Bucks Row 25, 27, 28, 29, 31, 32, 33, 34, 35, 37, 41, 42, 43, 46, 49, 50, 51, 57, 74, 75, 96, 101, 124, 190, 215, 216, 258, 313
Cambridge Heath Road 216
Cannon Street Road 140
Cavendish Square 142
Chapmans Court 46
Charles Street 242
Cheapside 15
Christian Street 210, 212
Church Lane 140
Church Passage 102, 127

Church Street 66
Coburg Road 49, 51
Commercial Road 12, 21, 67, 78, 83, 106, 109, 111, 112, 117, 122, 148, 154, 155, 157, 158, 208, 212, 216, 220
Commercial Street 4, 5, 21, 55, 57, 59, 63, 64, 65, 71, 75, 77, 81, 84, 91, 140, 154, 176, 190, 193, 251, 258, 266, 271, 274, 275, 279, 285, 290, 295, 299, 301, 203, 305, 310, 311, 312, 313, 315, 321
Coventry Street 51
Crispin Street 266
Dorset Street 22, 60, 61, 70, 77, 79, 83, 116, 171, 251, 253, 254, 255, 257, 258, 259, 265, 266, 268, 270, 271, 273, 276, 278, 280, 284, 285, 288, 289, 290, 292, 294, 295, 296, 297, 299, 305, 310, 311, 312, 313, 315
Doughty Street 280
Duke Street 125, 126, 136, 181, 215
Eagle Place 39,
Eagle Street 60, 242
East India Dock Road 242
Ellen Street 211
Epping Forest 194
Essex Wharf 42
Fairclough Street 157, 211, 212
Fashion Street 299
Fish Street Hill 273
Finsbury Circus 114, 130, 183
Fleet Street 196
Fletcher Row 240
Flower and Dean Street 66, 110, 113, 123 ,154, 171, 179, 181, 182, 199, 200, 201, 224, 299, 316
Frederick Street 301
Fulton Street 319
Garden Row 301
George Street 140
George Yard 3, 4, 5, 11, 15, 22, 41, 67, 159, 278
George Yard Buildings 3, 5, 7, 8, 9, 11, 12, 14, 18, 21, 97, 190, 263, 313, 315
Godfrey Street 220
Golden Lane 105, 115, 130, 154, 172, 179, 184, 199, 203, 223, 227
Goswell Road 193
Goulston Street (also Gouldson and Goulstone) 182, 183, 186, 201, 203,

215, 224, 231, 233
Gravel Lane 215
Great Garden Street 140
Great Pearl Street 289
Great Powell Street 297
Green Street 50
Grove Street 158, 159, 212
Hackney Road 42, 50
Halfmoon Street 62
Hanbury Street 46, 54, 55, 57, 58, 64, 67, 72, 74, 78, 83, 86, 91, 92, 93, 95, 102, 124, 176, 187, 191, 230, 258, 310, 313, 315
Hare Street 215
Heneage Street 320
High Holborn 206
High Street 235,
Holborn 69, 113, 118, 123, 235, 242, 301
Honey's Muse 31
Horse Road 322
Houndsditch 120, 179, 200, 215, 272, 274
Hyde Park 254
Jewry Street 101, 114
King Davids Lane 216
King Street 180, 181, 239
Kings Cross Road 301
Leadenhall Market 76
Leadenhall Street 21, 181
Leather Lane 69
Leman Street 40, 85, 86, 127, 140, 174, 178, 197, 198, 275, 305, 322
Little Turner Street 216
London Road 87, 301
Lower Whitecross Street 307
Maidwell Street 49
Marlborough Street 274
Marylebone Road 275
McCarthy (or M'Carthy) Court 251, 257, 266
Mile End Road 82, 133
Mile End Waste 118, 133
Millers (or Miller) Court 266, 267, 268, 269, 276, 278, 280, 281, 285, 287, 288, 289, 290, 291, 292, 295, 296, 297, 299, 301, 315

Mitre Square 112, 114, 117, 120, 127, 130, 134, 136, 137, 139, 143, 146, 151, 153, 154, 162, 170, 171, 172, 173, 174, 179, 181, 182, 183, 186, 191, 194, 199, 201, 203, 207, 208, 214, 215, 224, 227, 230, 270, 303, 313, 315,
Mitre Street
Mordwell Street 38
Mulberry Street 84, 85
New Court 269, 292
New Road 148, 157
New Street 281
Newnham Street 45, 317
Northumberland Street 275
Old Kent Road 49, 51, 305
Old Montague Street 46, 75
Osborne Street 2, 37, 190, 249, 301, 302, 313
Oxford Street 81
Paternoster Court 268
Penethorne Road 306
Pennington Street 268, 283, 295
Petticoat Lane 300
Phoenix Place 247
Pickering Place 163
Portpool Lane 281
Prince Street 87
Princess Square 210
Ratcliffe Highway 178
Red Lion Square 242
Reyham Street 246
River Terrace 21
Rodney Road 306
Shadwell High Street 221
Shoe Lane 180, 200
Snow Hill 240
Spital Square 75, 104
Spitalfields Market 59, 63, 73, 77
St. James's Place 102, 103
St. James's Street 125
Stannard Road 173
Stewart Street 62, 82
Star Place 12, 21,

THE RIPPER REPORTS

Star Street 21
Stoney Lane 215
Strand, The 118
Tentany Lane 318
Thornecliffe Road 327, 328
Thrawle Street 36, 50,
Tower of London, The 13, 14, 20
Union Street 133, 197
Victoria Park 118, 133
Wandsworth Common 37
Waterloo Bridge 222
Wellington Barracks 16, 18, 22
Wentworth Street 97, 190, 275, 313
Westow Hill Market 308
Whitechapel Road 1, 5, 21, 37, 46, 96, 299
Whitehall Place 206, 276
Whites Row 116
Wild Street 241
William Street 148
Winthorp Street 43, 51

Printed in Great Britain
by Amazon